On Being Human

An Operator's Manual

By

David V. White

Copyright © 2013 David V. White
All rights reserved.
ISBN-10: 0615770983
ISBN-13: 9780615770987
Library of Congress Control Number: 2013939850
Meaningful Life Books, Sevierville, TN

All Rights Reserved. No part of this book may be used or reproduced in any manner whatsoever without written permission, except in the case of brief quotations. For information, contact Meaningful Life Books.

Meaningful Life Books
P. O. Box 1988
Knoxville, Tennessee 37901

Web Site: ameaningfullife.org

Recommendations for *On Being Human*

When you read *On Being Human* you acquire a wise new friend who respects and cares for your well-being and is devoted to increasing your understanding of yourself and how to overcome life's complexities. To clarify how we can make the best decisions for living, David combines the rational, emotional and spiritual dimensions in considering what makes life worthwhile. In reading this book you will gain much insight and feel dignified by what you have come to know.

—Phillip Moffitt, past editor-in-chief of Esquire Magazine and author of *Dancing with Life* and *Emotional Chaos to Clarity*

We get thrown into life, and end up in the most frustrating places! Why don't they give us a road map for how to be a human being?" In my psychotherapy practice, this question arises often. In *On Being Human: An Operator's Manual* David White tackles this very problem. He takes the big questions about what it is to be a human being and renders them into a language for today. Questions about how to live a fully expressed, moral, and rational life have been the domain of philosophers, theologians, poets and psychologist since the beginning of time. Gently, with humor, intelligence, and understanding, he takes the big questions down from the "Ivory Towers" of the wisdom traditions and translates them into this useful and very readable book.

—Bonnie L. Damron, PhD, LCSW, Archetypal Pattern Analyst

I have followed David White's work for more than a decade, and have attended many of his lectures and participated in several discussion groups he has organized. What makes this book unique is that it presents a cohesive, wonderfully-crafted summary of more than thirty years of reading, introspection, and inner work. The book will be invaluable to those who are either beginning, or have already embarked on, a journey of self-discovery.

—Rafael C. Gonzalez, PhD, Distinguished Service Professor, Emeritus, Electrical Engineering and Computer Science Department, The University of Tennessee, Author of the best-selling textbook, *Digital Image Processing*

David shares here his vast, comprehensive knowledge of wisdom traditions along with his own thoughts and humor, making *An Operator's Manual* both a rich resource for living a meaningful life as well as a delight to read. When life throws you the hard, fast curve that makes you question why you are here and disrupts your game, *On Being Human* is the place to find a fix.

—Sue Painter, Blogger, Business Coach, and Founder of the Confident Marketer

If you've ever paused to ponder the meaning of your own life, this book is for you. From a rocking chair on his front porch, David White guides us on a romp across vast expanses of culture—philosophy, psychology, science, and the best that the wisdom traditions, both eastern and western, have to offer—always bringing it back home to this time...this place...this individual life.

—Ronda Redden Reitz, PhD, Clinical Psychologist, Past President of the Appalachian Psychoanalytic Society

A reflection on the currents that shape us, the decisions we make, and the guidance available in attempting to live a fulfilled human life.

CHAPTERS

	Introduction	1
1	It Starts with Questions	5
2	Do Stories Create the World?	11
3	10,000 Decisions Create a Life	27
4	Whim	43
5	Culture and Community	63
6	Are You Rational?	83
7	The Place of Intuition	109
8	What Is Reality?	125
9	Worldviews—Path or Prison?	151
10	Imagination, Intention, Attention	171
11	Whose Values—Yours, Mine, or Ours?	195
12	Wisdom from the Past	223
	Epilogue	241
	Acknowledgments	245
	Suggested Readings	247
	Endnotes	251

INTRODUCTION

Every human being must make decisions about what is important, how to spend one's time, how best to live. In the modern world this is especially difficult because the cultural and religious answers of old are being questioned and many of the young people who had been expected to carry them forward are unlikely to do so. Given the tenuous hold that cultural, religious, and political institutions have on our loyalty today, how do we go about making the best decisions about life? Where do we turn for guidance?

One frequent approach has been to divide what it means to be a human being into compartments—psychological, economic, sexual, emotional, cultural, spiritual, religious, scientific, artistic, political, rational, and sociological—and to study each separately. Problem is, lived life happens at the intersection where these currents meet, at the point where all the different aspects mix and mingle.

Put differently, everyone has motivations and expectations involving food, shelter, sex, pleasure, adventure, power, wealth, fame, achievement, relationship, spiritual fulfillment, and more. All these can be thought about separately, and it is valuable to do so. At the living edge, however, where we decide and act, these currents do not exist in individual boxes that can be examined one by one; rather, they form a continuing swirl of life and living. This means that to live a fulfilled life, we must attend to the point at which the currents converge, for worthwhile answers will only come from a place that encompasses the whole and harmonizes all.

The pioneering physicist Erwin Schrödinger was getting at this when he wrote: "Consciousness is never experienced in the plural, only in the singular."[1] Years earlier, William James, one of the foremost intellects in American history, noticed the importance of this living center, adding the thought that there is no line between this center and the numerous currents that surround it, nor with those that impact us from the unconscious.[2] In other words, the conscious self is the organizing center of each person's life, but swirling all around are numerous currents coming toward us from the world outside, while others constantly arise from unacknowledged desires and motivations within. In this swirl, how do we develop a coherent pattern for living?

To sort this out, an operator's manual might be helpful (in case you did not receive one or if the one you received seems outdated). Here, then, is a manual for operators of that marvelous and mysterious entity called a "human being." It explores ways to answer the deepest questions and discusses the tools available for creating a fulfilled life.

No one, of course, can be expert in all the areas with which we must contend in a human life. Living, however, does not offer the choice of avoiding any of them. Whether expert or not, each of us must come to terms with the full scope of human questions, emotions, and possibilities. As you face this daunting task (no matter what has befallen you to this point in life), here is a most worthwhile question: "In what direction shall I move—starting right here, right now?"

In search of an answer to this question, this book will explore the wisdom streams of history (put forward by philosophers, spiritual and religious leaders, artists, psychologists, and scientists). We will investigate the creation of a fulfilled life by considering a broad range of guidance from many traditions, the overlapping waters contained in this varying guidance, and finally, how the whole of oneself can be brought into harmony. My hope is that various ideas contained herein will be familiar to you (although approached perhaps in a new way), and that you will find others new to your reflection. My special hope is that all the currents will coalesce in a way that you experience as coherent and consistent, and that this unifying vision will aid your search for the best way to live the human life you have been given.

※※※

Life is complex, and the current volume is the beginning of a series of reflections. Look for these additional titles by the same author in the coming months:

Often Allies: Art, Science, Religion, and Spirituality—And Their Role as Guides to a Fulfilled Life

The Unseen Order

Consciousness, Identity, and Beyond

Perhaps it would be of value to list the people who have most influenced the thoughts, ideas, opinions, and feelings shared in this book. Below are those who have had the greatest impact on my understanding—through the written word or by the way a person's living presence directly impacted my life.*

Gautama Buddha	Ramana Maharshi	**Friends and Family**
Joseph Campbell	Nelson Mandela	Ralph Gonzalez
Confucius	Dennis Merzel	Ronda Redden Reitz
Ram Dass	Robert Moore	Phillip Moffitt
Emily Dickinson	Friedrich Nietzsche	Sandra Sundari Smith
Fyodor Dostoyevsky	St. Paul	John Berry
Albert Einstein	Jalal ad-Din Rumi	Sue Painter
T. S. Eliot	Jean-Paul Sartre	Shoray Kirk
Ralph Waldo Emerson	Indries Shah	Birney Hand
Francis of Assisi	William Shakespeare	Sandy Cartwright
Viktor Frankl	Rupert Sheldrake	Judith Ideker
Mahatma Gandhi	Huston Smith	Don & Glenda Henry
Stan Grof	Shunryu Suzuki	Anthony Durham
George Gurdjieff	Henry David Thoreau	Bonnie Damron
Martin Heidegger	J. R. R. Tolkien	LeRoy Graf
Herman Hesse	Lao Tzu	Kathryn Grskovich
Aldous Huxley	Evelyn Underhill	White
William James	Ken Wilber	Esther Viar White
Jesus	Colin Wilson	William R. White
Carl Jung		Jim & Natalie Haslam
Immanuel Kant		Lamar & Honey Alexander
Abraham Lincoln		Howard Baker
Helen Luke		

---

* Some of these people held core ideas I do not agree with, but the power of their presentations forced me to wrestle with what they had to say and to come to an answer strong enough to withstand their challenge.

CHAPTER 1

It Starts with Questions

I sit on my porch and look out at a mountain, a mountain that in spring is lush, radiant—a vibrant sea of green. Although it is very close, sometimes it drapes itself so fully in a cloak of clouds that I cannot see the faintest hint of its outline. Yet I believe it is still there. What other realities are out there that I cannot see, hidden behind clouds in the mind?

As I sit on my porch I ask myself, "What shall I do today?" And as I ask, I realize again that this is not an easy question. Good fortune has smiled on me in many ways. I have a beautiful home in the mountains, good health, close friends, a reasonable bank account.

In my younger days, I was filled with ambition: for power, for fame, for wealth, for experience, for knowledge, for passion. I felt a burning desire to save the world from pain, confusion, and suffering.

I have ambition still.

But I've also had enough achievement to know that one more success of the same variety, or a dozen more, will not quench my thirst. If there is a really thirst-quenching drink to be found, it must be mixed with a different set of ingredients.

I say this with some conviction, for all of my past accomplishments have not brought me peace, or happiness, or fulfillment. Oh, there have been many wonderful moments generated by accomplishments, victories, and success. But such moments have been amazingly short-lived. And when they are over, there is usually a crash, followed by the growing urge for another rush, another shot of the adrenaline of challenge and achievement.

And disconcertingly, the moments of elation following victory seem to shorten as the age beside my name continues to mount.

There is another problem. Each time I set out to accomplish something, feelings of failure usually come along for the ride. It happens like this: I set off in pursuit of some goal (often naively, in relation to the challenge, expecting a quick and easy victory), and the next thing that happens is a series of failures—at least in relation to *my* expectations. But if I am willing to: (a) persevere, (b) devote increasing amounts of time and energy to the task, (c) learn from my mistakes, and (d) modify the goals as I proceed, then sometimes success will come. However, by this time, weeks, months, even years have gone by. Who I am now is different from who I was when I began. Sometimes the "me" who committed to the goal is nowhere to be found when the delayed and modified goal is achieved. Is this victory?

Perhaps if I could say, "I want *this*" and it could be instantly fulfilled, I would experience the pleasure anticipated with the thought. But if time must flow between the wish and the fulfillment, who knows what the result will be? If the goal can be reached only in the future, I might no longer want the same fruit. Or the "me" who is present for the eating might even be repelled by the taste.

This is one of the most insidious problems of life, this problem of *time*. Even if I know clearly what I want right now, how do I know I will want the same thing at some point in the future? Most fulfillments do not come instantaneously; the inevitable pause between wish and fulfillment requires that moments of my life spent getting "this" cannot be spent getting "that." Yet how do I know, when the moment of fulfillment comes, that I would not have preferred "that" to "this"?

Well, maybe I'll get both, if I work hard enough.

Perhaps that's true for you. But my images and desires do not seem to be limited to two, or three, or ten. I seem to have an unlimited number, all of which will take time to achieve—usually a great deal more time than I anticipated at the beginning (if they can be achieved at all). And most, if achieved, will not provide the fulfillment

I imagined when I began. Yet I passed up the pursuit of "that" in order to achieve "this." Oh, no!

Consider this image: Our lives could be compared to a gambler in the casino of life. In this casino, the "chips" are the minutes of our lives, and the prizes are wealth, power, relationships, fame, wisdom, inner peace, love, joy—and anything else you wish to name. We each have a bag of chips but cannot look in the bag to see how many chips remain. We walk around the casino, observing each game in progress, trying to decide where to place our bets. Shall I enter this game? Will it last ten minutes—or ten years? What if I have a great hand and believe I am close to victory when another player ups the ante and I reach in my bag and discover that I'm out of chips?

Perhaps I should play several small games at once, trying to accumulate many small victories. But what if something crucial happens in one game while I'm concentrating on another? And gradually I notice that my bag of chips is getting lighter with each passing day, whether I enter a game or not.

As I look out at the mountain, a ruby-throated hummingbird, psychedelic neck glistening in the sun, perches on our feeder. Those who study such things say hummingbirds fly to the Yucatan Peninsula in the fall, crossing the Gulf of Mexico in one nonstop flight. I tend to believe them, since it is written in all the best scientific texts. (I also believe because I have a great deal of respect for hummingbirds.) Yet I have never seen one hummingbird make such a flight. Moreover, when I read the history of science, there are many facts contained therein that seem patently ridiculous today.[a]

---

[a] Like the belief in parts of Europe for several centuries that the earth was flat, in spite of earlier knowledge to the contrary. Or the belief that germs did not cause disease. (Louis Pasteur was greeted with a firestorm of derision when he sought to prove, little more than one hundred years ago, that disease was being spread by health practitioners.) Or the view that Newtonian physics

Is this the first age in the eons of human history that has gotten the facts right? Or are scientific facts accepted today that will seem ridiculous to those who come after? If history teaches that this is the most likely result, which facts shall I make the bedrock of my reality? On which facts shall I rely as I decide how to spend the remaining "chips," the remaining minutes of my days?

So I sit on my porch and ask, "What shall I do today?" There is no necessity for me to hunt for food, seek shelter, or protect myself or my loved ones from predators. (Except the occasional developer, who in these hills can, at times, be predatory; I know, I've been one myself.)

The blessings of my life are many. I live in a time and a place where it is not necessary for me to take up arms or build walls or moats to protect my dwelling. I am not called upon to fight in foreign wars (that burden being borne by those much younger than me).

Don't get me wrong. I have a number of urges still: for excitement, for wealth, for recognition, for fame. But these urges are not demandingly strong. Perhaps they are not strong enough, for although I feel such desires, they do not propel me off the porch into the thick of the battle with the numerous gladiators already signed up for the next fight. Having signed up many times in the past myself, the prizes today don't seem so alluring. And other prizes, some that might be incompatible with the old games, seem equally important. Or more so.

"Such as?" a defiant voice asks. Well, perhaps friendship, love, wisdom, joy, inner peace, wholeness, salvation, enlightenment. A connection to the source of things, an experience of the ground of being.

---

fully explained the world, or that giant meteors had not struck the earth. Or the ridicule directed toward a young, obscure Australian physician who, only twenty-five years ago, suggested that bacteria were a primary cause of ulcers (now accepted as true).

Not easily deterred, my inquisitor persists: "Well, perhaps wealth, power, and fame will bring you all these other goods—will bring them along in their wake."

Perhaps. Perhaps not. This is part of the wager we each must make. But the report of many of those who seem to have embodied wisdom, joy, peace, and love is that wealth, power, and fame can be hindrances in achieving these other aims. "Who said that?" the voice demands. Well, Christ and Socrates and Buddha and Henry David Thoreau. Gandhi, Moses, Lao Tzu, Rumi, and Hildegard of Bingen. Then there are Hillel, Dogen, Ramakrishna, and Immanuel Kant, as well as Shankara, Francis of Assisi, Theresa of Avila, and Tolstoy—and many, many more (but you get the point). Of course, I don't have to take their word for it. But their instruction does give me pause in rushing to a quick and easy decision.

※※※

I have now been sitting on the porch a long time, and there is a chill in the air. Perhaps I'll go inside and record some thoughts about this journey on which we are all embarked, drawing a map of the terrain as I see it—while realizing that this map may someday be as out-of-date as old maps found in musty shops that depict America as a turtle, or a part of China. Perhaps getting it all exactly right doesn't matter; perhaps, as T. S. Eliot said, "For us there is only the trying. The rest is not our business."[3]

Where to begin? Do I start with religion, or psychology, or philosophy, or mythology? Art, sociology, or economics? But then I realize that, in the end, "What shall I do today?" is a question about life. What it is. What it's about. The lived experience of life cannot be broken down into categories. In the living, the categories overlap endlessly in the woven tapestry that becomes a life.

What I sense is that this individual "me" can experience life only as an interconnected web of thoughts and feelings that intertwine, intermesh, and interact—forming one seamless bolt of cloth. This "whole cloth" of "me" is not separable into individual threads, for if the cloth were unwound into threads, there would be no "me."

Further, when I try to look outside, at whatever reality *really* is, at whatever is "out there," separate from "me," it can be dealt with, thought about, and experienced only through this nexus of "me." It is as if this organizing field of "me" is a magnet, and from this magnet, all the metal filings of my reality align themselves into patterns flowing out from the center—patterns that become "my" experience. The assumptions of my mind form an energy field that rushes out continuously in streams to shape and mold the reality that will become my experience.

To put it a bit differently, each one of us sees and experiences life through a lens, a set of assumptions enculturated in us as we grew up, then modified by the decisions we made over the years about where to focus our attention, with whom to spend our time, and what we would believe—and disbelieve. This lens is our worldview, the way we understand who we are and what life is about. It is the underlying framework within which we make our decisions and understand our lives—and it is the prison that keeps us from seeing and knowing our world and ourselves in a more complete way.

This book, then, considers the most basic questions: What am I doing here in this life, on this earth? Is there a meaning to my life, and if so, how do I find it? How is my worldview aiding and how is it hindering my journey? Where do I look for guidance, and how do I make the best possible decisions for living? How do I deal with conflicts—both those with others and those within myself? In short, what will I do with my remaining chips, the remaining moments of my days?

CHAPTER 2

Do Stories Create the World?

All human beings should try to learn before they die what they are running from, and to—and why.
James Thurber

Since my earliest days, I have had questions; questions seem as much a part of me as my hands and feet. Actually, more so, for I can imagine life without some body parts, but not without questions. Perhaps we should define humans as bipeds with questions. (But then again, perhaps other species have questions, too. How would we know?)

In my early years, the range of questions was somewhat limited, for there was an inner force that pushed me to action—to seek romance, adventure, excitement, money, power, success, achievement. Thus the questions that received attention were associated with these drives and ambitions, while other things were pushed aside.

In my middle years, however, a gnawing uneasiness began to creep around the edges of my life, an old song echoing in the breezes of my mind: "Is that all there is?" A number of people have reported such experiences, either when early goals have been fulfilled or when a voice whispers, "It is time to reconsider the goals and images of youth." Submerged questions then take on a new vitality, and new questions are given birth.

Searching for Answers

Propelled by these emerging questions, one day in midlife I found myself in a workshop in Switzerland devoted to, of all things, fairy tales. Because fairy tales were not considered relevant in my family of origin (and certainly weren't considered significant for an adult life), I wondered, "What on earth am I doing here?" Thus, on that fine spring day, I was not looking forward to the program. Should I skip out and explore the beautiful Swiss countryside? Before I could make my escape, however, things took a turn for the worse (or so it seemed from the perspective of the moment). The "world expert" on fairy tales who was to be presenting that day was ill, to be replaced by a man no one in the group had heard anything about. Not an auspicious beginning to an already uninviting day.

I sat there, mustering the courage to walk out, trying to overcome an old demon—the self-doubting voice that whispers, "What will people think?"—when a quiet British gentleman unobtrusively appeared in the room, as if materializing from within the questions we were asking about him. With little introduction, he began to read a fairy tale in a low, flat voice—confirming my fears of looming boredom. But since he had begun, I was trapped; I didn't want to hurt his feelings.

He finished reading and began to ask about the possible meaning of the fairy tale in our lives. In *our* lives? What was he talking about? But then the strangest thing happened. Under his quiet, skillful guidance, the room was soon bursting with energy—with ideas and feelings and personal connections pouring forth from everyone in the room, myself included. The room remained vividly alive all day; it was a magical experience.

A magical day with fairy tales? Yes, and if you resist this notion, consider the fact that fairy tales have been used to shape the values and mold the lives of human beings since before history began. This, of course, does not prove their value, but after my day in Zurich, I began to consider more seriously the possibility that they had an important role to play in my life.

Beyond fairy tales, I began to realize that stories of all kinds had always had a much greater significance than I had understood. Stories about George Washington, Thomas Jefferson, Abraham Lincoln, and Benjamin Franklin had formed my early views about politics and government, about the interaction of principles and power. Stories about sports heroes and business heroes had given me images of what I might be when I grew up. Stories in movies and novels had played a significant role in forming my images about romance and relationships. Stories about real people I had known—family members, people from my home town—had made it seem possible to do the things they had done: If people I knew or people from my town could do these things, perhaps I could do them, too.

A bit later, stories in my college years about what was "in" and what was "out" dramatically affected my values and beliefs, and stories of rebels—people who saw things differently from the accepted norm—brought an awareness of a greater range of possibilities to my own life. The more I reflected, the more I realized that my very identity was the product of stories. Furthermore, my conscious sense of self—who I believed myself to be—was simply the story I was telling myself about myself, framed by the stories about who I had been and who I would become.

It also became clear that stories are how we understand others, as well as how they understand us. The stories others have pieced together about me create their understanding of who I am, no matter the reality. Applying this to your life, consider the difference in the stories two people would tell—one who liked you, another who was angry with you. Compare the stories they would hold about who you are, and you will get a sense of how your identity with each person is created by the stories they tell themselves about you.

Broadening out, think of your whole array of friends and acquaintances; in your mind's eye, think of the very limited stories each would be able to tell, compared to the whole sweep of your life, the vast array of information available from which to choose. Obviously, a few facts would have to be selected by each one, out of all that are available, with many things being left out. In addition, each would select different facts, and of those facts, some would be emphasized, while others would be given a minor role—all of which would dramatically affect who you would seem to be to each person.

> **Thought Experiment—Which Story Is True?**
>
> Imagine being in a class where you are given the assignment to tell the story of your life as a success. The next week, the assignment is to tell the story of your life as a failure. How would you organize the facts of your life to tell each story? If you can do both (and most of us can), which one is true? If neither is "the truth," what is the true story?

Do Stories Create the World?

Following the thread of story, I attended a conference in Boston titled "Storytelling, Myth, and Dreams," with a marvelous group of tellers performing humorous and serious teaching stories for a small group of captivated story listeners. Absorbing these stories of wisdom and compassion, and reflecting on the role of story in human history, I realized that as far back as we can trace, stories have been with us.[b] In every land, there have been stories of how the world began; of how cultures came to be; of the tribe's relationship to nature, to others, to the gods.

Why so many stories? Were they simply designed for entertainment on a winter's night around the campfire? Were they created simply to educate the young? These functions are certainly part of the role of story. But is there more? Do some stories carry hieroglyphic meanings, still relevant today, that we somehow intuit but find difficult to unravel?

---

[b] Excavations at the Shanidar Cave in the Kurdish region of Iraq by Ralph Solecki and his team suggest that Neanderthals might have had stories as well.

Consider the epic stories of India, Scandinavia, Sumer, or the American Indians—actually, of any land—and it is clear that suggested answers to life's important questions have always been carried by story. Even today, anyone who reads or is lucky enough to hear a well-told Zen, Jewish, or Sufi teaching story will know that stories can help us wrestle with the central questions of life. Or consider the great plays of the Greeks, Romans, and Elizabethan England. In each case, we are in the presence of stories grappling with the most fundamental issues—love, honor, courage, purpose; what is right, what is true, what is good.

In my own life, the parables and stories of the Bible shaped my early beliefs about what was important, how I should act, the major issues of life. In every culture, stories have always carried the beliefs of humankind and have been the vehicle for passing on the central meanings of the culture to each new generation. Capturing this reality, American poet and political activist Muriel Rukeyser declared, "The universe is made of stories, not of atoms." This thought seems strange at first, but consider: How does the mind put together an understanding of the world? Basically, we organize the information that arrives in our minds on the basis of the assumptions we have already made, on the basis of how we currently understand the world. And where do our assumptions come from? From the stories we were told as we grew up. In this light, the idea that the universe is made of stories makes a great deal of sense.

This understanding also aligns with one of the crucial insights of philosophy. The brilliant Scotsman David Hume led the way, and Immanuel Kant, the philosophical giant of the eighteenth century, developed the insight. The world we see is not some fixed, objective fact, but what we see and experience is greatly determined by the innate structure of the mind. The insights growing out of this Kantian revolution have made it increasingly clear that the assumptions and beliefs we hold at the moment of each new experience dramatically affect what we will perceive.

In other words, our minds are not passively recording facts received from the outer world; instead, they are continually selecting facts that support our current understanding. Equally important, the mind organizes the facts into a meaningful sequence based upon what we currently believe (often happening prior to conscious engagement). Thus, what we believe about reality at any given moment greatly determines how we will experience and understand the next thing that happens to us.

To get at this in a practical way, how do I deal with the simple question: "What will I have for lunch?" I might think, "I would like apple pie with ice cream," but there is already a lot of background to this thought, a whole series of stories, for what I "like" comes from stories I was told throughout my life about what is good, merged with memory stories of enjoyable moments with food. Further, these memory stories are not just about taste but are greatly affected by the setting (the people I was with, what they were saying about the food, the mood I was in at the time, and more). Although I seldom bring all this to consciousness, it is always there as I decide what I "like."

But back to deciding about lunch. I think of something I enjoyed in the past (apple pie and ice cream) but then have the thought: "That is not healthy." Behind this thought is a series of narratives, stories about what is and is not good for me, and behind those stories are my self-stories about my weight, my looks, or the health conditions of relatives and friends (and how diet contributes to health problems). Such stories are far from trivial; they cut all the way down to issues of life and death. I have read of people who starved to death when food was available simply because their stories said the available food was taboo or inedible.

But I keep digressing, and I am hungry, so I must decide what to have for lunch. More stories kick in. I discover I don't have the right ingredients for what I would like to have (at least what my stories say the dish should contain), which triggers a whole series of stories about why I did not go shopping yesterday, including stories about time and how busy I am. There are also stories about money: what

I can afford or not afford. Finally I settle on something for lunch and begin the preparation, at which point another set of stories begins, memory stories about how food should be prepared (and because methods of preparation vary with each culture, these stories embed me in my culture).

Again, I do not consciously think about most of these details in deciding on a meal, but this is how stories make up the background and context within which we make the decisions of our lives. Our memories structure and organize the living of each new moment, and memories are packaged as stories. Penetrating through to these underlying layers helps me understand how Marcel Proust could write a seven-volume memory/novel inspired by the "taste of cake soaked in tea." Called by one reviewer "one of the great novels of all time," it is an exploration of the way memory, and therefore stories, interacts with and affects our lives. (The book used to be called *Remembrance of Things Past* but is being changed in new English editions to *In Search of Lost Time,* which is a story in itself, but not for this time and place.)

Surrounded by Stories

What all this means is that from our earliest days, we are surrounded by stories. Think of how young children learn about the world: They hear stories of all kinds, many containing guidance. We tell them stories to keep them from doing things ("Do you know what happened to so and so when they did 'that?'") or to guide them toward actions we consider positive ("If you do this, then good things will happen to you."). When administering punishment, it is usually with a story (you did "this," and it is bad "because," and the consequences will be "these"). Or when we wish to encourage, we praise with a story about the merits of the accomplishment or our pride in the victory. The very atmosphere of a child's life is made up of stories: tales of successful people we hope they will emulate or those who failed—and our interpretation of why. (In telling these stories to children, we are always selecting one story over others that could be told and are giving our interpretation, which is never the only way the events could be understood.)

Children learn quickly. Have you watched youngsters at play? At a very early age, they play within stories: cowboys and Indians, war games, games with imaginary figures, or stories with dolls (this is Daddy, this is Mommy, this is Sister Jane, this is Fido—and this is what they are doing). Not long thereafter, they graduate to video games built around stories: escaping from monsters, fighting wars, or creating a family. For those interested in sports, there are endless stories of the exploits of sports heroes and heroines, fueling the dreams of aspiring athletes.

In our teen years, another layer of stories develops around the groups with which we identify. Remember how it was as a teenager? Whichever group you were a part of, that group had stories about why it was good to be a member of the group and why other groups were less desirable. The hard-rock group looked down on classical-music types, while the classical-music aficionados felt they were superior. The sports types made fun of the studious ones, while the studious group had their stories about why their way was cool. The social types had their "in" language, and the computer types had their jokes about outsiders. And every group was constantly telling its defining stories to each other in the group, establishing and maintaining a sense of belonging and reinforcing that it was worthwhile to be a member of the group.

This process does not end with adolescence. Adults don't get away from stories; the stories simply change. Movies, novels, the theater; stories about what is going on in the world, stories about famous people, stories about what is happening with loved ones; gossip about friends and neighbors—these stories permeate our adult lives. Our communication is not with raw facts but with stories in which facts are organized into meaningful patterns that give them significance to us. We often take this organization of the facts to be the way things are, but such is not the case; it is always an interpretation that includes some things, excludes other things, and emphasizes one thing at the expense of another.

Also, as in our teen years, every adult lives within one or more identity groups held together by stories. There are many groups to choose from: family, political party, neighborhood, intellectual circle, sports interest (the bowling and the tennis circles have different identity stories), churches, hobby groups, Internet groups, civic groups, activist groups, music-interest groups, and on and on. Each group has a set of stories about itself, and each initiates its members by telling and retelling stories about what the group is like and why that is good.

At another level still, the intellectual fabric of our lives is carried by stories. History is obviously composed of stories in which some facts are chosen and some are left aside in order to put together a sequence that has meaning for the intended audience. The same is true of the news, which is not made up of bare facts, but selected facts packaged to carry forward a particular narrative. Investing involves buying into a story about the prospects of a company, industry, country, or investment manager. Equally significant, politics rides on stories. What is a political campaign but competing stories about how we got to this place, what is good or bad about it, and what each candidate intends to do to fix the problems or accentuate the positives? Each candidate selects a few facts and tells a story about what those facts mean: Here is my life story (with selected details), which means I will act in such-and-such a way if I am elected. (In an age when we often do not personally know the candidates, it is little wonder that these stories often disappoint; they are constructed to be self-serving, not for accuracy). Then there are the endless stories saying "My opponent once did this" and "This means that he or she will do so-and-so" if elected. (Isn't it fascinating how candidates always seem to know what their opponents will do in the future and that what they "know" is always unflattering?)

Perhaps it is not extreme to say that political campaigns are nothing but competing stories about reality, and voting is to make a choice about which story seems most true or which story will benefit the voter (or the group about which the voter most cares). And because we each identify with several groups—family, neighborhood, region, ethnic group, socioeconomic group, the nation, or even the world—the difficulty in deciding whom to support in a campaign often arises because a candidate's ideas seem good for one circle of interest but not another.

Even science is created by stories. Scientists don't go out and collect random facts; they look for facts within the framework of the existing stories of science in which they are functioning. The ongoing story of science includes what the "in" group knows, what questions need to be answered, and the role science is supposed to play. There is a reason it takes many years of study for someone to become a scientist—the aspirant must learn the stories about how science got to be the way it is, how one goes about doing science, and what the great scientific discoveries of the past mean in the science story, which is always changing.

Another way to approach this is to realize that science rides on theories, and the word "theory" comes from the same Greek word as "theater." A theory, like a play, is a way to organize facts into a meaningful sequence; it doesn't capture everything but helps us organize part of our experience into useful or actionable components. This means that we select and organize the facts according to the meaning they have for the story we are trying to tell (philosopher of science Karl Popper suggested that most every scientific theory started as a story). Newton put together a theory, a meaning story, with selected facts. The ancient Chinese, and Einstein, did the same. The Big Bang theory is a story of how the universe developed. Depending on the goal, some stories work better than others, but they are all stories. (The great value of modern science is the importance it places on the testability of its stories by anyone trained in the field rather than relying on facts selected to support personal prejudices. This is a hard master, but a commitment to this ideal gives science enormous power when dealing with anything that can be put to a test.)

Stories as Answers

Our lives start with questions, and we find the answers in stories. From the rich matrix of stories in which we are embedded in our early days, we begin to put together our personal identity stories, such as the following: "I am smart but not very athletic or good-looking, so I had better learn to use my brain." "I win all the athletic games, so I will be a star like Michael Jordan and don't need to study math." "The world is a dangerous place, so I must be careful, protect myself, and take no chances." "Family is the most important thing, so I must sacrifice everything else for family." "Close relationships are not safe, so I have to be very careful with the people around me."

Through our stories, we create an understanding of who we are and what our lives are about. Of course, there are thousands of stories to choose from and unlimited ways to put them together, so in some mysterious way in youth (often below the threshold of the conscious mind), we put together a handful of stories around which to organize. For most of us, though, there is an immediate problem: Some of our stories conflict with others, so difficulties and struggles soon arise.

Are our stories true? No! Are they false? No![c] We each put together the best set of stories we can from the material we were given. But because each of us knew some people in our early lives who were unhealthy, some who were mistaken about important things (but we cannot easily know which things), and some who meant well but gave harmful messages, one central task of life is to sort through the stories that surround us and find a healthy relationship to them rather than being enslaved by them.

---

[c] One could, of course, ask if there is such a thing as *true stories*, but much more circling of how stories affect our lives and how identity and reality are created will be necessary before we can consider whether there is such a thing as *Truth*.

To get a sense of the power of stories to create one's reality, imagine a young girl who is born with the greatest potential opera voice the world has ever known. Then imagine that she lives in an unhealthy family, one that is always critical of her and even takes out the family's unhealthiness on her, making her the scapegoat. Now imagine that any time she spontaneously starts to sing as a child, someone shouts, "Shut up, you sound like a sick cow" or something equally insulting. What do you think her identity story would be with regard to singing?

But because this is a fairy tale, imagine that one day, when she is fifteen years old, she is walking all alone along a stream in the woods. It's a beautiful day, the birds are singing, sunlight is drifting through the leaves, and without a thought, she begins to sing. And on this day, by an amazing coincidence, on the bank of the stream, but out of sight, is the greatest voice coach the world has ever known. (If you feel an urge to protest the unlikeliness of these events, remember, this is an imaginary story, a mind experiment, like Einstein used to help create modern physics.)

The voice coach hears this beautiful voice and rushes up to her, saying, "Your voice is incredible! Would you let me be your coach?" The girl is shocked and embarrassed. She protests that she cannot sing at all, exclaiming, "Why are you making fun of me?"

Is this story exaggerated? Perhaps, but it is also true—and it is true about you. And about me. About each one of us. We were each told things when we were young involving talents and possibilities, things we have incorporated into our identity stories that are simply not true. But how do we discover and reclaim those possibilities? This is the challenge—and the opportunity.

As for the imaginary girl, let's assume she mustered the courage to visit the voice coach and take a few lessons. Would she be able to realize her potential? It is hard to say. Perhaps with enough grit and determination, and a willingness to fight through the old stories, she would learn to fully use her talents. Failure or success, however, would not be determined by talent but by her ability to change her relationship to the stories she had been given when young.

> **Thought Experiment—Identifying Your Stories**
>
> Can you recognize the four or five main identity stories you operate within in your life? If so, and you would like to work with them, do not start by being critical of them or by trying to change them, but simply begin to notice how they affect your life. This is the best way I know to more consciously participate in the ongoing creation of one's life.

What-the-World-Is-Like Stories

As with our personal-identity stories, we each have stories that answer questions about the nature of the world. However, many different stories are available, so depending on a person's underlying nature and the messages received while growing up, different people end up with different what-the-world-is-like stories. Imagine two young men, both first-year college students, who have exactly the same intelligence, abilities, and aptitudes. One, however, is told throughout his youth that the world is a hostile and dangerous place and that people always take advantage of the gullible. The other young man is told repeatedly that the world is a friendly place, that most people will be helpful and kind when approached courteously. Assume that these two young men arrive at college and are assigned to the same dorm, meet the same people during their first week, and take the same classes with the exact same professors. After a week, each calls home to describe what has transpired. Now imagine what each would report. (My guess is that the reports would be quite different.)

To see how deep our stories go in shaping our realities, consider how stories influence the experience of fear. When I mention fear as being created by stories, many people protest, saying fear is visceral, automatic. Perhaps some fear reactions are, but if so, the number is very small. A young child is not automatically afraid of many things. Consider a hot stove; we have to warn her because she is not naturally afraid; and she learns to be careful only because we tell her vivid stories about the bad things that will happen if she touches the stove. Or if she touches a hot stove, she then puts together a meaning story for herself about what will happen if she does it again, and in this way, she develops fear. But she did not start with it.

Imagine how three different people would respond to a snake on a trail in the woods:

1. Someone raised in a family of ophiologists (those who study snakes) who goes with the family on vacations to rain forests and deserts to look for all kinds of snakes, and everyone in the family is excited to find a poisonous one
2. A second person, raised by a tribe that eats snakes and considers them a great delicacy, a tribe that teaches the young how to catch snakes safely, even the most poisonous ones
3. A third person, growing up in a family that was terrified of snakes of all kinds and who was constantly warned about the danger they posed

Now imagine how each person would respond to seeing a snake on a trail in the woods.

Or consider how some people are afraid of black bears. Small children are no more naturally afraid of black bears than horses; in fact, they might run toward either with excitement. Over time, however, how children will feel about each will be determined by how they are conditioned, by the stories they are told about each. Some people are afraid of horses as adults, but many more are afraid of bears. Why? Because of the stories they have been told. It certainly is not because they have been injured by a bear, for that number is minuscule. (And come to think of it, many more people have been killed by horses than black bears, yet most of us have not been told to run from horses, so most of us are not terribly afraid of them.)[d]

For that matter, cars are 100,000 times more dangerous than black bears, but we don't run from cars every time we see one. We might choose to stay out of their way in certain circumstances, but most of us don't run from them (although we might be safer if we did). What accounts for the difference? The stories we tell ourselves about cars versus bears. (Of course, even if we are not afraid of bears, we might wisely keep a safe distance from a mother bear with cubs, but that does not mean we need to be afraid; we just need to be mindful of the circumstance.)

A story about how we project our views onto the world:

A woman sitting at a kitchen table sees a new neighbor hanging out the wash and says to her husband, "That laundry is not very clean. She doesn't know how to wash."

Her husband remains silent.

Every time the neighbor hangs her wash out to dry, the wife makes the same comment.

About a month later, the wife is surprised to see a nice, clean wash on the line next door and says to her husband, "Look, she has learned how to clean clothes correctly. I wonder who taught her."

The husband replies, "I don't know, but I got up early this morning and cleaned our windows."

The Opportunity of Story

Stories create our identities, build our values, propel us toward or dissuade us from actions, supply images of what is worth doing, stimulate our longings, and provide the building blocks for how we will see and understand the world. Stories also give birth to our fears. I have awakened in the night with a worry story running in my mind: What if this physical problem I am having right now is cancer? What if

---

[d] Since 1900, only forty-five deaths caused by black bears in North America have been reported.

such-and-such a bad thing I am imagining happens tomorrow? With the light of dawn and a cup of coffee, I can let go of most nighttime worry stories, but what about the worry stories that are running in me that I do not recognize as such, that I take to be "true"?

To come to terms with what it means to be a human being, we must understand the stories that shaped and molded us and come to a more conscious understanding of our relationship to them. This is not an easy process. We are complex beings, and the world is complex as well, so complexity multiplied by complexity gives rise to complex and conflicting currents. Further, our stories about ourselves, as well as about others, are constantly changing as experience grows and moods shift. Given all these factors, it is little wonder that life can be difficult, confusing, and complicated.

If, however, we can begin to watch how our minds create and maintain our stories and how our stories determine a great deal of our experience, we can start to recognize which stories are serving us and which are creating the boxes in which we are imprisoned. From this place, we can make the conscious choice to give our time and attention to the stories that lead to well-being and fulfillment, and in so doing, participate more fully, more consciously in the ongoing creation of ourselves and our world.

CHAPTER 3

10,000 DECISIONS CREATE A LIFE[e]

It is an extraordinary blindness to live without investigating what we are.
Blasé Pascal

The phone rings. Should I answer? My work is going well, and it will be hard to get back to this state of mind. Reluctantly I pick up the phone. A friend is on the line asking for a favor *that I do not want to do*. Should I agree, simply because it is a friend, or say no, respecting my inclination but hurting my friend's feelings (and perhaps even harming our relationship)?

On the desk before me is a list of possible trips, and I will have time for only one this year. Which shall it be? Each trip has a strong appeal, with a different feel and flavor. How do I choose among them? (And how did I decide there was time for only one trip?)

Each of us has thousands of such decisions to make, and how we decide will determine the kind of persons we will become and the kind of life we will live:

- Who will I date, hook up with, marry? Will I have children? How many, and where will they go to school? Will I divorce or stay with my spouse even if things aren't working? Should we go to therapy?
- Which career path, what company? Should I work for myself or someone else? How hard will I work? Should

---

[e] The Chinese speak of the "10,000 things" meaning, simply, "many."

I change jobs, change careers? How much time to take off? Do I ask for a raise?
- Which city will I live in, what neighborhood, which house? Do we need a bigger one? Do we undertake major repairs? If so, which contractor; how much to spend? Do I move? Where?
- Should I go to the doctor for this problem? Which doctor? Do I have the operation, take the new medicine, or wait and watch? What about alternative treatments?
- Where will I vacation, for how long; with whom; how much can I spend?
- What about free time? Which hobbies, books, entertainment? Which restaurant? Which movies? Which TV shows are worth my time? How much time on the Internet? Do I answer all those e-mails?
- Will I exercise? Which ones? How much time and money will I spend?
- How about sports? Which ones do I like? How will I decide the ones on which to focus?
- Which social groups will I join, and how much time will I spend? Do I join a church? Which one? Do I help others? In what way? How much time will I spend on service to others?

Nine Motivations

Creating this list makes my head swim, a major reason so many decisions do not reach conscious awareness; it is easier to let conditioning and enculturation, "habits of mind," deal with them. Nevertheless, whether we are conscious of them or not, we are making decisions continuously. And these decisions are creating the life we are experiencing.

To sort out the many currents that make up our realities, and to recognize the motivations that affect us as we make our decisions, here are nine of the primary currents that push and pull on us as we move through life. This is a map, though, and not the system itself, which means that the categorizations are not hard and fast things but arbitrary divisions of a fluid system that is interconnected; there could, therefore, be ten categories, or seven, or twelve. (I have settled on nine for myself, but feel free to create your own list if you are so inclined.)

How each of these motivations arose in the first place could be (has been) debated endlessly, as well as the appropriate time and energy to be given to each. What is not subject to debate, however, is that each of them has affected many people through history, and each remains a force in the lives of many people today.[f]

The three basic levels that focus on maximizing individual experience:

1. **Necessities of life:** There is a drive to fulfill core physical needs: food, fuel, shelter, clothing, and protection from physical harm.
2. **Sex and pleasure:** There is an urge for sexual fulfillment, for sensual pleasure, for pleasurable sense experiences of all kinds.
3. **Power:** There is a drive for power, to be able to do what one wants, when one wants to do it, and this includes the desire for other people to do what one wants *them* to do as well.

---

[f] Many systems for understanding these motivations have been put forward in the past, to which this list is greatly indebted: the Great Chain of Being, the chakra system of India, Abraham Maslow's hierarchy of needs, the Sephiroth of the Jewish Kabala, Dante's seven levels in the "Divine Comedy," Theresa of Avila's Seven Mansions, and Thomas Merton's *Seven Storey Mountain* (some of the important ones for me). Each is a map, an intellectual construct to help in understanding our inner experience, and, while all are different, there is a great deal of overlap among them.

The three levels of communion: Some people spend all their time and energy on the basic drives, but at some point many begin to expand their circle of interest to include a deeper connection with others, using some of their life energy to explore and develop relationships of mutuality:

4. **Accomplishment and achievement:** One expression of relationship is the urge to do something in life, to make a mark, build something, feel worthy, be "somebody"; to express one's talents and gifts and be recognized in the community for one's contributions. This urge takes us into engagement with the world, testing our skills and abilities, discovering what we do well, and investing life energy in shared activities. This current is a fluctuating mix of self-centeredness, concern, and care for others, a blend of personal ambition along with a desire to serve, carrying us into engagement in societal life.
5. **Love and personal relationships:** Most of us discover within ourselves a need for close relationships, to share our lives and stories with others, to find and share love beyond its expression at the sexual level. This current leads to long-term relationships: deep friendships, marriages, families. At times this motivation is stronger than any other, leading some to sacrifice security, safety, pleasure, and achievement for the good of loved ones (sorry for the disagreement here, Sigmund, but at times these motivations are stronger than sex).
6. **Community:** We humans are communal creatures, seeking a web of connections beyond close personal relationships. Transcending, at times, the drive for achievement within a community is the urge to simply be part of a community and to further its aims, and even to serve the group without thought of recognition or reward. It is not uncommon to find those who have served their community at a high cost to themselves simply because they felt so connected that the well-being of the group was a higher goal than personal needs and desires.

Then there are two currents that touch something broader than personal relationships or communal concerns, currents that move into what seem to be universal waters:

7. **Creativity:** Our creative juices can be used to further the six preceding currents, but sometimes there is an urge to create for its own sake, explaining why some creative folks abandon safety, security, fame, fortune—even family and community—to express images or feelings that have welled up within. This current can be so strong that it overrides everything else, becoming the defining current of a life.
8. **Knowledge and wisdom:** There is an urge in many of us to acquire knowledge about the world, about others, and about ourselves. At one level, this knowledge involves usefulness in pursuing the seven previous currents. Sometimes, though, a threshold is crossed, and the desire to know goes beyond the practical or the utilitarian; an urge for knowledge for its own sake takes hold. At the outer reaches of this urge is the search for wisdom—an ultimate motivation in itself. For some, the sharing of wisdom is the ultimate meaning and fulfillment of life.

There is one final current:

9. **Transcendence:** This is hard to pin down, but it has to do with a connection to something beyond the everyday experience of who we usually think we are. Sometimes we experience moments of feeling at one with nature or being totally absorbed in music or meditation. Those who journey further speak of enlightenment, salvation, or union; of entering into the field of Love, experiencing "Being" itself, or merging into the Divine. Many have felt some version of this experience, and a few have given their lives to its pursuit.

Here's the Rub

This, then, is one basic diagram of the internal workings of a human being—not simply the body, but the experiencing interior. These nine currents are not a simple hierarchy, for most of us move up and down, back and forth between them. But there is a general directionality here: The most respected among us through the centuries have tended to spend more time on the upper reaches of the list, and they have encouraged us to do the same. The general movement seems to be from self-centeredness to greater concern for others; from individual drives to broader fields of concern; from the personal to the universal; from the turmoil of striving to peacefulness and equanimity; from a focus on details to a concern with patterns and wholes.

There is a major problem, however: Many of these currents conflict with each other, point in different directions, compete for our time and attention. At any given moment, each is competing with all the others for our energy, and our decisions are being influenced by a confusing mixture of them all. In such an internal environment, it is difficult to sort out the contribution each is making, or should be making, as we decide. Further, as our moods and thoughts change, the internal weight given to each changes, so our inner workings are tremendously fluid and complex.

Within this flux, how on earth do we make decisions? Observing myself, I notice that sometimes I make decisions mostly out of one current—pushed along by its attendant emotions such as fear, anger, excitement, sympathy, greed, lust, or frustration—while paying scant attention to the other currents within. When I do this, however, problems almost always follow. For instance, I might make a decision about a relationship when I am upset—when the stories in the front of my mind about a person are mostly negative. Organizing around these negative stories, I see a very limited picture and act from that. Not a good idea. The opposite also happens: I feel good about someone, and I organize around a positive story in which my mind selects a string of positive memories, to the exclusion of not-so-pleasant ones. Not such a good idea, either.

Adding to the complication: When I make a decision, sometimes it sticks, sometimes it doesn't, but at the moment of decision, I do not know whether it will stick or not (as T. S. Eliot says in *Prufrock*, "In a minute there is time, for decisions and revisions which a minute will reverse."[4]) This means that I am frequently operating out of a decision that will be reversed, leading to actions that will have to be undone or will make life especially complicated when I try to undo them. Not a very efficient process. Would it be better to stay with bad decisions? Maybe, but sometimes, seeing the mistake, that looks like a terrible idea. Maybe I should refuse to decide until I am sure about things. But waiting freezes life, fostering inaction for long stretches of time, and there is no guarantee surety will ever come. No wonder decision making is hard.

Continuing to observe what's going on within, I notice that when I focus on one aspect of myself (a desire, an image, a belief), it will dominate the center of my attention, and I will want to make a decision based on that. If I take action, though, later I will remember something important that was not in my awareness at the moment of decision. It can even be something that clearly seemed important in the past. For example, a few years back, in deciding which car to buy, I looked at several models, made lists of the advantages and disadvantages of each, and finally decided. The purchase was made and the new car came home with me. That night, though, I remembered something I had read a month earlier about a particular problem with this model. If I had remembered that detail, I wouldn't have bought the car. Where had my awareness gone? And why did it come back now—too late to be of value?

As my awareness of these problems increases, I try harder, making more lists, making a concerted effort to put all the relevant information on paper. Sometimes I work at this for weeks. The lists are helpful, but I begin to notice that they lull me into thinking that all the items are equal, when in fact their relative importance varies enormously. I make a pro and con list, trying to be objective, but find myself leaning toward the side with the most items on it, even though I know it is not the ***number*** of items on each side that is important, but the ***weight*** given to each. But assigning weight is totally subjective, defeating the attempt to be objective. (How does the color of a car compare in an objective way to the quality of its transmission, the quietness of the ride, or its price?)

To be painfully honest, the more objective I try to become, the more time I spend collecting information and worrying over decisions that are of little importance (where to eat dinner, what clothes to order, which model of car to buy), and less time on things that will have a greater impact on my life. I think I do this because the small decisions are easier to manage, are easier to make objective; it feels like I can get my mind around them. On the other hand, the important ones are more difficult, causing more anxiety and involving so many factors that it is impossible to be objective about them. The result: If I am going to be objective, I avoid the hard issues and focus on the trivial ones.

Given these difficulties, it is amazing that we make decisions at all. But we must, either consciously or by letting them happen unconsciously (and if they turn out badly, by disowning responsibility, blaming someone or something else for the outcome). There is another possibility: We may work consciously with the unconscious. This is one of my favorite decision-making strategies, and it goes like this: As I am about to go to sleep at night, I focus on a question or a decision I need to make, and on waking, I sometimes have a clear answer that feels right. I then consciously weigh it against everything I can think of concerning the issue, and if it still feels right, I act. This process has worked many times in my life (and sometimes it hasn't). But when it works, it has the best chance among all the strategies I know of, producing a good decision, one that will resonate harmoniously with the overall pattern of my life. (But I do wonder where the answer came from.)

> **Thought Experiment—How Do You Make Decisions?**
>
> How do you make decisions? Try to watch how the decision-making process happens in you. See if you can watch yourself in the process. How does it work?

Three Major Life Decisions

Although we must make millions of decisions during our lives, there are three that are of utmost importance, and if resolved, create a framework for all the others and create a context within which all other decisions can be made:

1. What is worth doing with my time?
2. By what values will I live?
3. Toward what goal will I aim?

These three cannot be fully separated, of course, for they overlap in numerous ways. But they can be considered somewhat independently because the first involves hundreds of daily decisions about the allocation of time, the second creates the framework within which goals can be acceptably pursued, and the third provides an overarching goal toward which to move, a goal against which to measure every decision.

This third factor the ancient Greeks called *"telos."* Discovering (or choosing) one's *telos* can be very difficult, but once in place, it makes all other decisions easier, for all can be weighed in relation to how they serve the overall aim. Finding a *telos* in the modern world is especially difficult, however, for there are dozens of claimants to the throne, as well as persuasive arguments against each.

The claimants are numerous because every motivation we humans feel has been enshrined by someone as an ultimate goal: Some have given sex and various other pleasure a central place; others have advocated power, achievement, or prestige as the goal; some have posited the primacy of romantic relationship; others have given family or community the central place. The list is quite long. Some make creativity the goal, while others enshrine protecting the natural world. There are even those who advise that there is no *telos*. Little wonder, then, that finding a *telos* has become the "hard problem" of living today.

One reason for the difficulty in finding a *telos* might be that each person's is different. We move within many currents, and their interaction affects the flow of each life stream, so the example of one life does not necessarily apply to another.

There is a clear, powerful movement in life toward **complexity**. Through the eons, more and more complex systems have arisen in the universe, going from amoebas to elephants, from small huts to great cities, from simple communication between adjoining cells to brains with a hundred billion interconnected neurons.

There is a related but somewhat separate movement toward **growth and development**. Every child goes through growth stages, as does every organization, culture, religion, and field of knowledge. That this should be so is not given by any laws we know; in fact, this movement, as well as the movement toward complexity, seems to defy Newton's Second Law of Thermodynamics, which says that systems tend to wind down over time if left to themselves, that they will move toward dissolution rather than growth and development. What is the source of this movement toward growth and complexity, and how does it relate to each of us?

There is a clear, powerful force in life toward **health and healing**. Cuts heal, as do broken bones and injured nerves. When we cut ourselves, there isn't just a 50/50 chance that it will begin to heal, but almost a 100 percent chance that it will do so. (The process might be thwarted, but it will try to heal.) We don't consciously have to do anything; the cut will start to heal on its own. Why should this be so?

There is an energy toward **emotional healing** as well. We suffer great sorrows: the death of loved ones, physical infirmities, losses and failures of all kinds, but something in us begins to heal the wounds, begins to restore us to life and well-being. The grief process itself seems to be a natural system that moves gradually toward healing. This healing can be stymied, but there seems to be a push in us toward healing our emotional wounds, in contradiction to those who suggest that the main motivations in life revolve around procreation of the species. This drive extends far beyond reproductive and child-rearing years, going strong into old age—for many, up to the point of death.

Where does this energy toward healing come from, and what does it have to teach us about the meaning of our lives?

There is also a clear, powerful urge in us toward **communication**. We have developed language and other tools far beyond any practical benefit: literature, music, poetry, the theater, and so much more—all having to do with the drive toward sharing our yearnings, hopes, dreams, and fears with one another. This urge toward exchange goes far beyond sex. We form clubs, groups, and spontaneous gatherings; sit up all night talking; and spend hours on the phone, writing letters, e-mailing, and texting, in order to share our thoughts and feelings with one another.

There is a strong drive toward **order** in the universe. Science is based on the belief that everything is governed by orderly laws, but what is the source of this order? Systems within systems within systems are coordinated in orderly ways (a human cell within an organ of the body, organs within the whole body, the body within the environment, the environment contained by the earth, the earth in the solar system, that within a galaxy, and so forth). Why do all these systems work in such an orderly way, one within another? How did the undifferentiated flux turn into sophisticated order? There seems to be a drive toward interconnectedness on every level of existence, from the smallest to the largest systems.

And there is a push toward **existence** itself. There is nothing logical or inevitable about the existence of a universe. Why does this universe exist at all? If there were once nothing, wouldn't the most reasonable assumption be that there would be nothing still? Without some energy toward existence, how would a universe of incredible complexity and expanse…just appear?

A Telos of One's Own

This brings us to one of the ultimate questions—one among a handful worth time and attention: Is there some *telos* under which we all live, a *telos* all humans share? Attempting to answer this query has been the stuff of religious theology, spiritual inquiry, and philosophical speculation through the ages. Various answers have been given: Plato suggested the existence of a world of forms toward which we move. All religious and spiritual systems present a *telos:* perhaps that is their main reason for being.

Christianity says life's purpose is to seek the Kingdom of God (or Heaven), and to live while on earth in such a way as to end up there (either in the future, or in the present moment, depending on one's interpretation of the tradition). In Buddhism, the *telos* is to awaken, to realize that one's true nature is not different from Buddha Nature; the goal is to live in such a way as to have that realization.

In Hinduism, the goal is to recognize oneness with Brahman, to realize that at the deepest level, the level of the true self, there is only Brahman, and *"Thou art That."* In Judaism, the goal is to abide by the covenant made with God, or for some it is *"tikkun olam,"* "to repair the world." In Islam, the goal is to surrender to the will of God, and in some branches of Sufism, it is to achieve union with the Beloved. Taoism says the point of life is to live in harmony with the Tao, and Confucianism says it is to embody *"jen,"* which is "dearer than life itself—the man of *jen* will sacrifice his life to preserve *jen,* and conversely it is what makes life worth living."

There are many other examples, of course, some of modern origin. Hegel said there is inherent in the universe a force toward the awakening of humanity to its unity with Spirit. Teilhard de Chardin suggested that the goal of life is embedded in evolution, and by recognizing that there is a final end toward which we move (he called it the "Omega Point"), we participate in the process of arriving there. Carl Jung said there is a call from the collective unconscious to individuation, and following that call will bring about a conscious relationship to the higher Self. Nietzsche proposed the Übermensch, the Overman, as the goal toward which we should move. (Or perhaps he meant toward which we are moving; I can't discern in his writings whether he meant *were* or *should,* but in either case, this is the *telos* he proposed for human life.)

One formulation that is particularly inspiring was given by the great twentieth-century mathematician and philosopher Alfred North Whitehead, who suggested that perhaps the foundational current of life is "an all-embracing chaotic Attractor, acting throughout the world by gentle persuasion toward love."[5] Another quote I find moving is by Albert Einstein: "A human being is part of the whole called by us 'the universe,' a part limited in time and space. He experiences himself, his thoughts and feelings, as something separate from the rest—a kind of optical illusion of his consciousness. This delusion is a kind of prison for us, restricting us to our personal desires and affection for a few persons nearest to us. *Our task must be to free ourselves from this prison by widening our circle of understanding and compassion to embrace all living creatures and the whole of nature in its beauty.*"[6] [Italics mine.]

It is not my intention at this point to praise one *telos* over another, but only to point out that all spiritual and religious traditions, as well as many philosophical ones, have posited a *telos* for human life. The reason they have done so is the overwhelming feeling among the wisdom figures through the centuries that there is an overall directionality to life, that there is a harmony about which we can gain understanding and with which we can find attunement. If this is the case, every life will not necessarily be the same—perhaps we are each instruments in the orchestra of life, each of us playing a unique part in the overall symphony. But if there is a harmony, discerning its direction and discovering how to move in attunement with it is a major task of life.

Of course, we are also free to reject the idea of a *telos,* making an act of faith that no such goal or purpose exists. We are even free to select as our *telos* the goal of refuting the existence of any *telos.* For me, however, the existence of so many currents moving toward complexity, growth, healing, communication, order, emotional connection—toward existence itself—suggests that there is a directional flow in life, whether I am consciously aware of it or not, and giving time and attention to discerning its direction seems worth the effort.

An analogy from ancient India: Holding an acorn, you know there is a force within that small acorn toward becoming a great oak tree—a force that can and will push aside rocks, push through soil, overcome obstacles to fulfill its goal. That purpose can be thwarted if the obstacles are great, but the force is there, moving toward a given end. Further, within that acorn resides all the knowledge necessary to become a great oak tree. If this is true for an acorn, perhaps it is true for you as well.

If so, the unique human *telos* is likely to be quite different from that of an acorn because we are in possession of the magic elixir of consciousness, a faculty of great mystery. (Besides, I don't think I would make a very good oak tree.) But insofar as a *telos* does exist in me (either for my individual life or the larger life of which I am a part), if I can become conscious of it, then I can help it along, or at least attune with it—rather than interfering with its unfolding. If that *telos* is fixed and eternal, then my task is to learn to move in harmony with it. If it is unfolding over time, then my task is to make choices that support and encourage its highest and best development.

Given the mistakes I have made and the time I have wasted (assuming one can actually "waste" time), an especially encouraging thought for me is the near-unanimous verdict among the wisdom figures of history that the fulfillment of life does not depend upon what one has done up to the present moment; one's fulfillment will be determined by the actions taken (or not taken) from this moment forward. As T. S. Eliot puts it in *Four Quartets*: "Right action is freedom from past and future." No matter what has happened prior to this moment, we are undefeated if we are willing to go on trying.[7]

For many of us, though, finding a *telos* of our own is life's hardest task. Yet difficult does not mean impossible, nor does it suggest avoidance. On the contrary, one of the great adventures of life is wrestling with the questions the possibility of its existence poses: Is there a current pulling, or pushing, or guiding me toward some end? If so, where is it headed, and what role am I asked to play in the process? What is pushing to be fulfilled in my life or pulling me toward its embrace? All these are interesting and worthy questions, requiring our best effort.

Four Ways to Decide

Moving from the theoretical to the practical (ideas without practical application having little use), here are four primary ways one can go about making life's decisions:

1. **Whim:** Simply follow each urge as it arises.
2. **Culture:** Follow the dictates of your birth culture or another culture you join.
3. **Reason:** Use your rational mind to try to understand life and make decisions.
4. **Intuition:** Try to get a sense of the flow of things, a feel for what is right, and follow that guidance as best you can.

Each of these four approaches has value, and we are moved and guided by each at various times in our lives.

Therefore, the next four chapters explore how whim, culture, reason, and intuition play out and interact with each other in the course of our lives, and how we can use them in concert with each other to arrive at the best possible decisions. Only then will we be able to delve further into finding a *telos* of our own.

CHAPTER 4

WHIM

After graduating from high school, I worked as a caddy the summer before starting college. After caddying eighteen holes, we could play a round of golf for free. Late one afternoon, I hooked a ball out of bounds across a barbed-wire fence. Suddenly, an image of vaulting the fence came to mind (as opposed to the safer route of climbing through). In an instant, I was vaulting through the air, almost flying—until a shoe cleat caught the top rung of the wire, sending me sailing downward. Extending my left arm to break the fall, my elbow was shattered, requiring major surgery. Major nerves in the arm were damaged, and the prognosis was grim: no college for at least six months and I might lose significant use of the arm. I experienced tremendous pain.

Where did this whim come from, to vault over the fence? I have thought about it many times. It was partly an urge to impress the other members of the group—even though, in retrospect, they were too far away to notice. There was a sense of testing the limits, to see what was possible. There was a devil-may-care feeling of invulnerability because I had never had a serious injury before.

☙ ☙ ☙

As this experience suggests, following whims can cause problems. Many problems. I have awakened at night numerous times with a deep concern (having acted on a whim the day before), thinking, "How could I have said that? Or suddenly realizing how an action was perceived by another, having a wave of regret: "Why did I do that?"

Besides the problems they can cause, whims tend to arise one after another in rapid succession, so trying to act on each is exhausting (and crazy-making for the "whimee," as well as everyone else around). There is also the fact that new whims arise before prior ones are completed, which means that trying to follow every whim leaves a trail of unfinished actions instead of a coherent life. In addition, there is the fact that if everyone followed each new whim that arose, families, communities, and human culture would collapse. Why, then, are whims there, seemingly sitting at the center of our life experience? Why haven't they been enculturated, or naturally selected, out of us?

Having followed the gubernatorial primary in Tennessee while working at the White House on the National Security staff in Washington, I saw in the paper the morning after the primary that the candidate I favored, Winfield Dunn, had won the Republican nomination for governor. I picked up the phone immediately and called a friend to express interest in joining the general election campaign. It was a snap decision, perhaps a whim. Ten days later, I was the campaign co-coordinator, a life-altering change that seemed to arise from a whim.

Taking Whims Seriously

Because whims get us in trouble, they often have a bad reputation, and many moralists would banish whims if they knew how. Yet there is much to be said for their value: They break us free from rigid rules and regulations, from the stultifying embrace of too many "shoulds" and "should nots" that can deaden life. Although dangerous, they can also give a fresh glimpse of the direction in which our energy is flowing, provide a motivating spark when we are stuck or stagnant, and propel us forward into new and exciting adventures and opportunities.

> **Thought Experiment—To Act or Not to Act**
>
> How do you decide in a split second whether or not to follow a whim? (All whims are not resolved in a second, but many are; you either act or the moment is gone.) Examining yourself, how do you decide whether to act in those moments? We do not always follow our whims, so how does a decision to follow, or not follow, happen?

Whether positive or negative, whims are a serious matter, for they are the urges and desires that propel us into life and living, the instinctual urges impelling us to take care of ourselves, as well as snatch the momentary pleasures presented with the day. Dressed up in intellectual garb, they are the "id" of Freud, those primal urges (mostly sexual, in his view) that drive us to undertake actions and activities. (In the Freudian model, these sexual urges are sometimes sublimated—directed toward substitute objects—as when a person directs energy toward winning a contest rather than winning a lover. And they are sometimes repressed, hidden from our conscious awareness, as when we cannot admit to ourselves a physical attraction for someone who is forbidden to us by custom.)

This idea of basic drives did not begin with Freud, of course. Almost 2,500 years ago, Plato saw the human psyche as having three primary levels, the first being that of instinct and impulse. Schopenhauer, influenced by Plato, called this primal energy "Will," by which he meant those blind, insatiable drives that arise out of living in a body. Nietzsche picked up the theme from Schopenhauer and spoke of the Dionysian energies that flow through us. Unlike his predecessors, however, Nietzsche made these energies a primary virtue, saying that we should live them fully rather than letting them be socialized out of us.

This Nietzschean focus on instinctual energies was probably a key stimulus for Freud's development of the "id" (although there is controversy here, for in his later years, Freud tried to disassociate himself from Nietzsche). But Freud knew a great deal about Nietzsche and his ideas, and several major Freudian themes appear in Nietzsche's writings years before they appear in Freud's.[8] Further, in a biography by his childhood friend Ernest Jones, Freud is reported to have said of Nietzsche, "He had more penetrating knowledge of himself than any man who ever lived or was likely to live."[9] (It is important to emphasize, however, that Freud did not come to the same final conclusions about values or how one should live as did Nietzsche.)

So whim, as id, is the starting point for Freud's theory of how we humans function. Further, the superego, another crucial Freudian concept, is made up of the societal rules that arise to control the whims of the id, to curb the unrestrained expression of urges and desires. In fact, Freud's view was that civilization arose primarily to "civilize" us out of acting too quickly and too often on our whims, going on to suggest that containing the id has been the driving force behind the development of civilization, including art, philosophy, and religion.

Another great thinker, Immanuel Kant, maintained that the most important value in life is to follow the dictates of duty—his proposed defense against being led astray by the evils of whim. Duty was necessary, in his view, because whims are so powerful that, if left unchecked, they pose a great danger to a good life. So whims are quite important, not only in providing a significant part of our energy and vitality, but perhaps because they provide the reason for the creation of human civilization. Pretty heady stuff for what we sometimes think of as the lowly whim.

In some ways, Nietzsche and Kant are on opposite ends of a spectrum. (Nietzsche's ideas burst forth as a rebellion against the repressive nature of life in a culture pervaded by Kantian duty and morals.) The danger of Kantian thought is that if we severely repress and demonize our whims, we drain the vitality out of life and create neuroses (as

Freud saw happening in his patients in the repressed Victorian society of Austria). When repressed too long and too hard, whims eventually break out into acts that seem to be "out of character": sexual escapades, binges of all kinds, bouts of gambling, or even cruelty and warmongering, as we see in some politicians, preachers, neighbors, and friends—and even in ourselves. The Nietzschean danger is a life racing from one whim to the next, with no coherence or restraint, and no basis upon which to build a society of mutual care and concern.

One does not have to fully agree with early and middle Freudian thought (during a long period, he believed the sexual drive in the id made up most of the life force), to realize that whims must be taken seriously. Nor does one have to go all the way with Nietzsche (who gave whims the dominant role in decision making) to acknowledge the significant role they do, and should, play in life. On the other end of the spectrum, one need not become as rigid as some have interpreted Kant (suggesting we must fiercely resist all whims), to recognize that some rules, laws, and moral guidelines are necessary to contain and mitigate the dangers of whim given free rein. Holding all these views simultaneously, the central question becomes: How does one find the right balance among all these forces?

> **Thought Experiment—Balancing Nietzsche and Kant**
>
> Imagine what life would be like if duty were your central motivation, with all urges and desires totally subordinated to duty. Then imagine what it would be like if you followed each and every urge or desire that arose. Now consider what a path between these extremes might look like.

Riding the Tiger

There is more to be considered regarding whim, though Freud might not approve of what follows. In some spiritual traditions, desire is not to be gotten rid of but used to carry an aspirant into higher states of awareness, even to spiritual awakening. Such is the goal of various tantric traditions, to ride the tiger of urges and desires, using these powerful energies to break the seeker open and into spiritual realization. Riding a tiger is, of course, dangerous, and falling off during the ride is not recommended, for the tiger is usually hungry. In other words, such a path is subject to much abuse and misuse.

Yet turning the energy of desire toward spiritual development has been recognized and used by spiritual traditions for centuries. Some lines from the biblical Song of Songs give a taste:

> Let him kiss me with the kisses of his mouth: for thy love is better than wine.
> He shall lie all night betwixt my breasts.
> By night on my bed I sought him whom my soul loveth.
> I held him, and would not let him go.
> How fair and how pleasant art thou, O love, for delights!
> I am my beloved's, and his desire is toward me.[10]

Joseph Campbell makes a persuasive case that these poems were not written by King Solomon but were a composite of erotic poems from the fifth century B.C. dealing with the overlap between desire and the search for the divine. This same theme has been taken up by many Christian mystics, using the language of love and desire to express spiritual longings (and sexual imagery is not banned, but embraced). Jesus is often declared the "Bridegroom," with the aspirant as the bride, so Mechthild of Madgeburg in the *Flowing Light of the Godhead* cries: "Everything I think—and am—runs after You like a bride hungry for her husband." Julian of Norwich often refers to God as "our Lover," saying, "Our natural will is to possess you."[11]

Teresa of Avila says the goal is to "Take God for your spouse," and John of the Cross ends his most famous poem, "*Dark Night of the Soul,*" with his soul (spoken of as feminine) encountering the Beloved:

On my flowering breasts
Which I had saved for him alone
He slept and I caressed
And fondled him with love.... I lay, forgot my being
And on my love I leaned my face. All ceased. I left my being
Leaving my cares to fade
Among the lilies far away.

    Many other traditions recognize the sometimes shared ground between desire, love, and spiritual awakening. The love between Sita and Rama carries the story of the Ramayana, one of the great religious epics of Hinduism, and Krishna's appeal to his female followers is often depicted in sexual language and imagery. It is not too surprising, then, to find a great Indian temple complex covered with images of sexual engagement (at Khajuraho) whose purpose is to help seekers on the spiritual path.

    Likewise, alchemical texts from medieval times such as the *Rosarium Philosophorum* depict sexual union as a step on the path to transcendent realization, and in the "*Divine Comedy,*" Dante uses the figure of his childhood love, Beatrice, as the image that leads him to final realization. Out of these traditions, the troubadours of the late Middle Ages created the Arthurian Romances, in which intense love for a lady (almost never one's wife) was the energy that gave rise to adventure and finally to full awakening into spiritual realization.

    Or consider Sufism, in which the goal is union with the Beloved. From the great Sufi poet Rumi, we learn that, especially at the beginning of the quest, we must be open to these energies however they arise:

Advice doesn't help lovers!
They're not the kind of mountain stream
    you can build a dam across.
An intellectual doesn't know
    what the drunk is feeling!
Don't try to figure
    what those lost inside love

will do next!
Someone in charge would give up all his power,
  if he caught one whiff of the wine-musk
  from the room where the lovers
  are doing who-knows-what![12]

In Rumi's poetry, it is hard to know when the shift from physical passion to spiritual passion takes place—there is no clear line of demarcation. In *The Essential Rumi*, Coleman Barks speaks of the merging of these wantings: "From the urgent way lovers want each other to the sannyasin's urgent search for truth…every pull draws us to the ocean." Thus Barks concludes, as did Rumi, that "it's important to live the wantings as they come, and not get stuck *somewhere*, stagnant." When asked what to do about a young man who had exceeded the sexual mores of his time, Rumi replied, "It just means he's growing his feathers. The dangerous case is a kid who doesn't." That one "leaves the nest without feathers. One flap and the cat has him." No wonder many cultures have initiatory traditions, some quite shocking to our conditioned sensibilities, to introduce the young to the world of passion. At least in most cultures there are elders to assist the transition, rather than throwing unprepared youth to "the cat" the way our culture often does.

There is great danger here in both the casual immersion of young people in the energies of passion, and on the other side, of over-protectiveness that leads to repression. If a child is shamed for his or her passions, and thus becomes repressed, that child will likely break out at some later point in ways that will be harmful to all involved. (If the parents of spiritual leaders who have suffered a downfall because of illicit sexual escapades had understood this, such a fate might have been avoided.)

Coleman Barks, again:

The nafs [another nice word for whims] are energies that keep us moving, stopping nowhere. Union with the divine continually unfolds. Next to the glowing drive-in movie, the junkyard's rusted stacks of old desire-bodies. Let the beauty we love keep turning into action, transmuting to another, another…exchanging one set of nafs for the next.

Particles of praise shine in the sunlight. Anything you grab hold of on the bank breaks with the river's pressure. When you do things from your soul, the river itself moves through you. Freshness and a deep joy are signs of the current.[13]

This idea is the real meaning of Joseph Campbell's oft-quoted and oft-misunderstood phrase, "follow your Bliss." If one continually opens into the deeper currents of desire, not getting stuck at surface levels, desires will lead all the way to spiritual awakening, for that is the deepest desire of all. The phrase Campbell was referring to is from the Sanskrit, and it did not include the word "your," did not have a personal, possessive pronoun in it. The meaning was ""follow Bliss," the universal spiritual energies, to their complete realization. It wasn't about "your" bliss, but becoming one with the universal Bliss.

Thus what Rumi and so many others are saying is that if you try to close off these energies too quickly, rather than using them and directing them with wisdom, you will subvert the movement to the completion of life: "Life freezes if it doesn't get a taste of this almond cake." Yet it is crucial to remember that riding these energies *is* very much like riding a tiger—which is why so many cultures and religions attempt to deny and contain them. Containment is necessary for the health and sanity of the individual (as well as for communities to function), which is the reason many organized religions follow the Kantian path, warning of the dangers that uncontrolled passions present to the individual, church, and society. And they are partially right; individuals and communities must have a framework within which these energies are contained, or they will wreck both lives and communities.

Containing is only half the necessity, however, for it is also crucial that these energies find their way onto the table of life's banquet—if we are to find fulfillment, and perhaps even spiritual realization. As Bede Griffiths, a Christian monk said, "Sexuality is too powerful a force to deny or put aside on the one hand; but it is also too powerful a force to let run our lives on the other."[14] What then to do? We must find the right relationship between these energies and our higher aspirations, perhaps even find a way for them to aid and abet each other. How might we do this? "We must consecrate" them, says Father Bede, which I take to mean give them a defined and meaningful role in the journey of life.

Plato dealt with this extensively as well, seeing the final aim of Eros as leading to an awakening to the ultimate Beauty of the cosmos itself. In his speech "*Symposium*," Socrates relates his initiation by a wise priestess through the stages of the "ladder of love." First, he experienced passionate love with a unique person; he then began to see that the beauty he had experienced in that relationship was not limited to one person, but resided in all; his next realization was that this feeling did not mean sexual involvement with the many, for real beauty is not primarily in the body, but in the soul.[g] With this step, he was ready to discover the beauty of knowledge, followed by the "final secret," a vision of pure Beauty, which is "ever-existent and neither comes to be nor perishes." This direct realization, says Socrates, had been the deepest urge of Eros all along and is what makes living worthwhile.

Thus an experience of passion for another can wake us to ever-greater realities, leading beyond our limited view of who we are to the recognition of our fundamental connection to the soul of all, and of the world. This is why Rumi could say, from his tradition, that when the lover speaks, "everyone around begins to cry with him, laughing

---

[g] This does not necessarily mean that one would cease to value personal love, but rather come to see that it is not the final goal of Eros. After his initiation by the priestess, Socrates remained married throughout his life and did not seem to be attracted to the adventuresome sexual escapades going on in the culture around him, even among his friends.

crazily, moaning in the spreading union of lover and beloved. This is the true religion. All others are thrown-away bandages beside it."[15]

This connection between our passions and spiritual development has been appreciated and used by many traditions in many different ways, at times going to the furthest extremes in opposing directions: On one end of the spectrum, traditions have used extreme asceticism in an attempt to purify the spiritual seeker's soul. Along this path, aspirants have been required to avoid all pleasures, eat bland food, fast to exhaustion, avoid all contact with the opposite sex (sometimes never to look at exposed flesh), wear restrictive clothing (even wear chastity implements), go long periods with little or no sleep, and attempt to control all thoughts that involve the passions. Some traditions have gone even further, with seekers intentionally inflicting punishment on their own bodies to help them detach from identification with things of this world and from personal desires, so as to be fully present for the Divine.

There is no question that many of these practices have caused harm, and they have at times almost certainly been inflicted by spiritual leaders who were themselves obsessed, depraved, and perhaps even sadistic. But the fount from which these practices spring is the recognition that there is enormous energy in the passions, and if by these means they can be mastered, the result will be a spiritual connection that is powerful, unshakable. This was the path of the Buddha for six years; one of the greatest Christian saints, St. Francis of Assisi; as well as one of the great Hindu teachers of the last century, Ramana Maharshi. There have been many others in other traditions. And the vehicle for this result is to organize the will against a great opponent, the passions, and by overcoming such a powerful opponent, open into freedom, clarity, and/or pure presence with the Divine. I have never felt called to this path, nor do I think most of us are, but perhaps it is because of my lack of will, dedication, or discipline. But it certainly does not seem my place to judge it to be unworthy for some of the great figures of human history.

At the other end of the spectrum, some traditions have used controlled sexual engagement to bring aspirants to spiritual awakening. Arousing passion, they then turn its energy away from the body toward the spiritual dimension. Of course, this is not just riding a tiger, but an incredibly wild tiger. Under the guise of "Tantra,"[h] teachers have sexually exploited the naïve or pursued personal financial gain. This is certainly cause for concern but does not mean we should dismiss all reports (mostly Hindu and Buddhist) that there is an authentic way to harness and use the energies of desire for spiritual purposes. Again, this is not a path about which I have much personal knowledge, but Georg Feuerstein provides a valuable glimpse into its heart in *Tantra: The Path of Ecstasy*. The crucial elements for any chance of success on such a path seem to be extensive preparation, the guidance of a teacher whose motivations have been cleansed of self-seeking, and strict adherence to a framework guided by a clear internal morality.

The dangers the passions present to both communities and a spiritual life are indeed enormous, which is why both religions and cultures spend a great deal of energy trying to contain and limit them. The crucial question is how to contain them without creating excessive fear, anxiety, and even neurosis, and beyond that, how to direct the energy of the passions toward the highest purposes of life.

> **Thought Experiment—Following Whims**
>
> Have you ever followed a whim and had it turn out well? Have you ever followed a whim and had it turn out poorly? Did the different results arise from chance, or was there a difference in the nature of the whim? If so, how can you tell the difference between a valuable whim and one that is leading you astray?

---

[h] A term that, in its broad sense, means coming to understand that all things of this world are nothing other than manifestations of the divine so that the energies of all and everything can and should be lived in such as way as to realize the Divine for oneself.

Emotions and Feelings

At this point, let me introduce you to an old friend who often asks questions and sometimes challenges what I am writing. I call him Skeptico, and he is often found in dialogue with Wisdom Seeker.

Skeptico: In all this talk about whims, urges, and desires, you haven't mentioned emotions once. Or feelings. Why is that?

Wisdom Seeker: I suppose because I was trying to get your attention by stretching the meaning of the oft-maligned word "whim." In the broadest sense here, I am including emotions and feelings within whim.

Skeptico: But aren't they different?

Wisdom Seeker: They can be defined as different. So much rests on what we mean when we use the words "whim," "emotions," "feelings," "desires," "drives," "passions," "id," etc. Perhaps it is a bit of a whim to use the word "whim" to encompass so much, but I cannot find a good way to separate what most of us mean by whim from what we think of with all the others. We could create precise definitions to separate them, but such definitions would be arbitrary and fail to match normal usage. A better approach is simply to recognize that all these words point to a set of energies at the very core of our lives, in the same way that many different words can be used to describe a sunset (yet sunsets are very different from each other and affect us differently depending on the mood of the moment).

Whatever words we use, though, this vortex of energies is central to life and living. Even in traditions that severely condemn the passions, passion is still the central driving force. For instance, the ascetics who went off to the desert or became martyrs in the early centuries of Christianity were considered crazy by the "normal" people of the time. They renounced many passions (for sex, for good food, for physical comfort), and even willingly chose to confront deep fears of pain and even death, but still they had passion—a passion for connection to or realization of God. How many of them did this on a whim? How many tried it and came back, talking about what a mistake it was to go into the desert and starve oneself? We don't hear much about those who turned back.

But a few stayed the course with their burning passion and left accounts of profound experiences that have shaped the beliefs of millions for two thousand years. Yet we cannot know, today, which of these ascetics started their journeys on a whim, then somehow rode that whim to a transfiguring experience during their long years in the desert or on a mountain.

Or consider the case of the Buddha: He is said to have forsaken passions in his search, but some intense passion had to be driving him on the incredibly difficult journey he undertook. How do we know it was not a whim? Maybe it started as a whim and then transformed into something more as he matured. If someone you know decided to do something radical in his or her spiritual search, how would you know whether it was a deep calling or a whim? How would that person know for sure? What advice would you give a friend who thought he or she had to renounce everything and live in the desert? How would you know whether that friend was about to be the next Buddha or St. Anthony—or was merely lost in a whim? One thing you could know for sure, though: A strong energy was at play, whatever its source and wherever it was leading.

Skeptico: I take it that you are saying emotions are important?

Wisdom Seeker: Yes, absolutely. Whatever name you wish to give these currents within us, they are centrally important. They are the energies of life, providing a great measure of the motivation for life and living. The problem is, there are so many—whether you call them emotions, passions, desires, urges, or whims—and they often conflict with each other so that a central issue of life is to sort through and decide which to pursue and which to ignore or redirect. To a great extent, our life decisions revolve around the effort to decide which currents will be given priority and the best means of fulfilling those that are chosen. And this is made especially complex by the fact that many of our emotions, urges, and desires are not very conscious, so they are pushing and pulling us without much awareness of the effect they are having.

Skeptico: That is pretty scary. What can I do about it?

Wisdom Seeker: It is the central reason so many wisdom traditions have urged: "Know thyself." Only if you become fairly conscious and clear about the goals you are pursuing, and how they relate to the other currents within, will you be able to work intentionally toward a fulfilled life.

Skeptico: You haven't mentioned love in all this. Is it a whim? An emotion? Or what?

Wisdom Seeker: Very good question! But I will have to save my best shot at an answer for later, for "love" is just about the most complicated word I know.

Skeptico: You don't get off that easy. Give me the short version.

Wisdom Seeker: Sigh. OK. Love is sometimes a whim, as in, "I just love that dress." Sometimes love is a very deep emotion, beyond what is usually thought of as whim. Love can be an intentional decision and not an emotion at all, as in deciding to sacrifice for a person you are angry with or care for a person in need for whom you are actually feeling revulsion. Love can even be the most profound of spiritual experiences, sometimes to the point of subsuming every other thought and feeling. There is more, but will that suffice for now?

Skeptico: I see the difficulty. I will wait for a while.

Decision Making and Whims

We have come a long way from thinking of whims as trivial and unimportant. Hopefully this exploration has made clear that these energies can be interpreted as good or bad, can be thought of as leading to heaven or to damnation, but they cannot be dismissed or seen as irrelevant. Nor can they be banished, even by the most disciplined among us, for it is impossible to delineate between basic whims/desires and the energies that lead toward the highest goals we can imagine. A spiritual passion or high calling arises out of some unknown place; it is just there, as is a whim.

Whatever the name, these energies can be used to fuel actions at many different levels of life and living. Sexual passion can be directed toward spiritual fulfillment, and the same pattern holds for other passions. An artist might at first be driven by strong self-centered ambitions but then gradually be pulled into the expression of a profound creativity, for its own sake, with no regard for ambition. Or a politician's desire to succeed in the world might gradually be transformed into a passion to serve, replacing the earlier desire to be recognized and praised.

With all the passions, perhaps the best option is to live the energies given to us while seeking the highest and deepest expressions possible, trying not to get stuck at ultimately unsatisfying, superficial levels. The trick is to curb the excesses without destroying the energy and vitality, to acknowledge the burst of fresh air that passions bring, while recognizing that enslavement to whim does not bring happiness or fulfillment, but rather chaos, enmeshment in trivial pursuits, and empty debauchery.

Skeptico: Wouldn't it be easier to just get rid of our passions? Life would be much simpler.

Wisdom Seeker: Some spiritual circles do pursue the idea that we can and should get rid of our whims/passions, but this seems to me to arise from confusion. I doubt we can get rid of all passions, and if we did, what would be the motivating energy for life? What we can do is choose between passions; we can work to replace one passion with another; we can pay attention to how our passions are affecting us and work to overcome the ways they control our actions at the unconscious level. But get rid of them completely? Not likely!

There are stories of a few great beings who seem to have left all personal goals and desires behind, transcending all whims. This might be so, but the stories suggest that all came to such a place by pursuing a great passion, by concentrating all their attention on one great desire, not by trying getting rid of their passions. They were, rather, able to direct their passion toward a chosen end.

Skeptico: I have read about several folks recently who have done that!

Wisdom Seeker: Maybe a few have actually accomplished it, but for every one who truly reaches this fulfillment, there are many who claim to have done so, while busily using that claim to gain fame and fortune for themselves. There are also those who project their ambitions onto the religion or movement with which they are identified—and try to fulfill their ambitions by claiming their group to be the best. They build their human organizations as monuments to their pride and elevate their group in their own minds above everyone else, claiming they are the only ones who have "the truth."

Whims and Ultimate Fulfillment

Looking closely at the lives of the handful of great spiritual teachers who seem to have left behind all personal ambitions and desires, the example their lives leaves us is that much effort, serious discipline, and a fierce commitment to a moral and compassionate life is required.

However, having arrived on the farther shore of the journey, the reports suggest these souls could now follow whatever actions arose spontaneously within—in a sense, they could follow their whims, but with this profound difference: Their whims were now in harmony with a larger pattern, rather than being driven by personal goals and desires. As St. Augustine put it, when you reach a certain point of realization, you simply *"Love, and do what you will."* Which I take to mean that you follow each spontaneous urge that arises, knowing that if you are centered in the profoundest Love, each of your desires will automatically serve the highest Good.

In the same vein, Confucius said, as he moved into maturity, that he had begun to know "the biddings of heaven." After reaching the age of seventy, he reported: "I could follow the dictates of my own heart, for what I desired no longer overstepped the boundaries of right." In other words, his personal urges and desires had merged with the biddings of heaven.

In more modern times, Karlfried Graf Durckheim says in *Zen and Us,*

> When the inner eye has been opened, a person continues to live normally in the here-and-now, but transcendence enters the here-and-now. Having awakened to Being, that person lives from true nature, as a self poised between past and future, in an everlasting now. And because he or she lives in this everlasting now, space and time are transformed.[16]

In this place, "Daily life is now rooted in Life become conscious of itself." Here, there is:

> No clinging, no cleaving to anything. Stillness in the very heart of tumult. Every moment as fresh as dew, and as deep as a well reflecting the stars and all eternity with them.[17]

What does life look like when living from this place?

> Everything conscious, alive, and direct, with never a breath between thinking and doing. No holding back, just letting life flow from the center—as free and light as a wingbeat, as true as an arrow flying to its mark, as weightless as a dance step, as devastating as a sword blow, as precise as a sculptor's chisel, as liberating as the breath of spring, and always suffused with love.[18]

Thus centered in Being, "with never a breath between thinking and doing," each spontaneous movement arises as a sacred whim, in harmony with the highest Good.

Beyond Whim

Whims, then, have been understood as the energy that motivates all of life, the reason for the creation of culture (so dangerous passions could be controlled), drives within that will lead to disaster unless contained by duty, the sublimated force behind art and creativity, and the energy that can carry us to spiritual fulfillment. Many names have been used, but no matter what we call these energies, we must come to terms with whatever is being pointed toward in order to live a human life.

Needless to say, whims are one of the central currents in decision making, because we are constantly following them, trying to contain them, or attempting to redirect their energies. However, whims are not the only way we make decisions, not by a long shot. Other means are absolutely essential, if for no other reason than to determine which whims to follow, and when. Other questions arise: Do whims differ from intuition? How do they relate to reason? How are whims affected by culture? And are there other forces at play beyond these four? Let's plunge forward into a consideration of the second tool we humans use to make our decisions: culture.

CHAPTER 5

Culture and Community

At eighteen, traveling with a college group, standing beside the coliseum in Rome (where gladiators fought and Christians were fed to the lions), I wonder: "Would I face death for what I believe? Should I be willing to do that?"

Standing in St. Peter's Square, surrounded by thousands of devout Catholics, I remember having heard that "their" Christianity is not Christian at all. But who gets to decide these things? And if Roman Catholics are not Christian, who carried the teaching through the centuries when "my" denomination did not exist?

Then there is sex, an especially important topic for an eighteen-year-old! Sweden appears an admirable nation, with deep Christian roots, yet the rules for sexual behavior (drilled into me as "God's will" during my youth) seem irrelevant to the kids there. Are they all going to hell? That seems a bit strange since they appear to be pretty good people: well intentioned, friendly, and considerate.

At eighteen, it is mind-boggling, soul-wrenching—and quite liberating as well—to discover that people around the world understand things quite differently from the ways of my "tribe." To realize that many things I was taught as "givens" are not given at all, but simply cultural patterns, including core beliefs about religion, sex, the reasons for various wars, and even which form of government is best. (Everyone, it is clear, does *not* agree with my high school civics teacher concerning things authoritatively judged "right" and "wrong" on her final exam.)

Encountering Europe for the first time, with one after another of the truths I had been given being challenged, my mind is racing: If the differences are this great between America and the continent—cultures with a common heritage—what about countries with completely different roots? No wonder there are dramatic differences around the world concerning right and wrong, good and bad, and how people should live.

The Role of Culture

In the last chapter we dealt with whims, which arise spontaneously and move us to action. But how could we live together if everyone acted on each and every whim? Thus Freud postulated that cultures arose to keep whims from wreaking havoc on societal life. He was right, of course, but perhaps there is more to the story. Cultures do restrain our "id" impulses, but they do more, providing answers to life's questions, so that each of us does not have to deal with an overwhelming number of options and decisions each day. In this sense, cultures are a set of answers to the important questions of life, providing an integrated way of living for a given time and place, a set of rules and customs that minimize problems and establish order. At a still further level, cultures create a structure within which greater complexity of human functioning is possible, becoming the foundation upon which our highest achievements are possible, even going so far as to suggest possibilities for a fulfilled life.

Make no mistake, everyone is dependent on culture. If young children had to find answers to all life's questions for themselves, none would survive. Adults, too, are dependent on culture. Its absence would make human life as we know it impossible, and we would be spending all of our time reinventing that wheel. Each of us lives by riding the wave of a culture, or switching metaphors, we stand on the scaffolding of the accumulated wisdom of those who went before—the scaffolding of culture.

What this means is that from birth, every child is thrust into an answer system that provides guidance concerning the following:

Practical questions: What is safe to eat? Where do I find it, and how do I prepare it? How do I shelter myself from the elements? How do I build things, following what model, and with what tools? What clothes should I wear; how do I make them? What is dangerous, and how do I protect myself from those dangers?

Questions about relationships: What is an acceptable way to fulfill my emotional and sexual needs? How do I show love and affection without causing problems, and how must I act to receive these things? What is the best way to behave toward parents, the opposite sex, strangers, children, and adversaries?

Questions about communal interactions: What behavior will get me in trouble with others? What can I expect others to do, and what rules can I insist that they follow? What can I expect the government to do and not do? How will our leaders be chosen? Can they be replaced? How?

Questions about values: By what values should I live? What is virtuous? What do honesty, integrity, courage, and all of the other virtues mean? Which are most important, and in what circumstances do they apply? Which must I follow even if they require sacrifice?

Questions about meaning: Why am I here? How should I spend my time? Does life have a purpose? What does a meaningful life look like? Is meaning even important? How do I treat those less fortunate than myself? What will bring happiness? Is happiness the goal? If not, what is?

> **Thought Experiment—The Need for Answer Systems**
>
> Imagine for a moment what it would have been like if you had been forced, from the time you were born, to answer all these questions for yourself, with no guidance from anyone.

Cultures provide these answers, with each child spending his or her formative years being enculturated into an answer system. Of course, some systems are healthier than others, but we are dependent on the one we were given, whether healthy or not, to get started with our lives.

What is the mechanism for this process? How do cultures do their work? Primarily through stories! As Chapter 2 suggested, stories about who we are and what the world is like make up the scaffolding of human cultures.

Internalizing the Answers

As we mature, we start to internalize a set of answers, and these internal answers begin to operate somewhat autonomously within us, eliminating the need to think through every question each day. Gradually we come to a place where many of the questions do not rise to the level of consciousness but are simply dealt with through our internalized, embedded answer systems. This usually happens so naturally that many of us (especially those who have had little interaction with other cultures) live comfortably within the system we were given, functioning on a kind of automatic pilot within our culture.

In this way, many of us through the ages have simply absorbed an answer system, feeling as if we just "knew" what life was about and how we were supposed to live. Human nature being what it is, there have always been a few, the rebels, who didn't follow the guidelines, but most of us have understood ourselves and our world through the "given" answers; we have mostly followed our set of guidelines.

Communities Begat Cultures

The best evidence suggests that we humans have always lived in communities, and communities inexorably develop patterns of living for their members—develop cultures. When the cultures of today were developing many thousands of years ago, they did so among small communities separated by vast distances, with differing climates and various terrains, so many different answer systems blossomed. Sometimes the answers within these far-flung communities were similar, but often they were quite different.

Gradually through the eons, a few of these systems, adapting and changing as time went on, spread over large parts of the globe so that today, a majority of us live within a handful of these cultural systems (the largest being the Chinese, Indian, European/North American, Latin American, Japanese, African, Russian, Persian, and Arabic cultural systems). Today they have mixed and mingled with each other in various ways, but the main tenets of each can still be found to be quite active, tenets that began developing a very long time ago.

Within these broad cultural frameworks, however, everyone is part of a specific, living community, and individual communities are now the implementation devices of cultures. In their lived realness, communities involve specific people who interact with each other in personal ways. However, each community exists within the framework of a culture, and a discerning visitor can quickly establish the culture, or in some cases the mix of cultures, from which a community sprang. Within that broad framework, an observer can then begin to discern the variety, how each community has developed its unique ways by incorporating elements from neighboring cultures or from cultures that flourished in that locale in earlier times.

> **Thought Experiment—Differences and Similarities**
>
> To get a sense of the differences that can exist within a culture, imagine three communities based on European culture but located in: (1) rural Montana, (2) the castle compound of the British Royal Family, and (3) a working-class neighborhood in Rome. Each would be quite different but each would share much with one another, as compared to a native tribe in New Guinea or a rural village in Afghanistan.

Everyone is Part of a Culture as Well as a Community

Because we humans are communal and cultural creatures, everyone—always and everywhere—is part of some community, and every community is organized within a cultural framework. Even the solitary souls among us—the lone cowboy on the range, the monk high in the Himalayas, an adventurer on a solo trek—all are part of some community and within a culture. How so?

The solo adventurer is attempting feats defined by a community, using tools and techniques perfected through the centuries by those who took similar adventures before. (How would an adventurer function without the information and equipment handed down from the past?) Every adventurer also sets off on the journey with images of those who went before, and usually with the intent to return with the story of the adventure for an interested community left behind. Further, part of the adventurer's motivation comes from a desire to accomplish feats rarely done, or never done, as defined by a community.

As for the Himalayan monk, he or she went to the mountains because of ideas absorbed through a community, ideas about what is important in life and how best to achieve community-defined goals. Each monk sits in the cave or on a hillside in relation to a teaching and/or a teacher, as well as a pattern of behavior established over thousands of years by other monks.

Then there is the cowboy, who shares a worldview with those who went before and whose life is lived by a code passed down from generation to generation, developed and shared during cattle drives, business transactions, and storytelling around the campfire (and perhaps in the saloon, if the old movies are to be believed).

Solitary figures are embedded in community and culture in another way: They are dependent on the food systems, clothing systems, and even the value systems established by others during their formative years, and these systems provide essential guidance as to how to go about the role they have chosen, even if it is a solitary one.

The solitary thinker is equally enmeshed. René Descartes asserted that the only two things he could know for sure were that thinking was happening in his mind and therefore that he existed. But continually in the background (to him at least) of his "solitary" thinking was a human community that provided for him a place to sleep, food to eat, books to read, a monetary system to purchase the necessities of life, a security system to protect him, previous thinkers to shape his thoughts, and a mistress down the hall to satisfy his sexual desires and his need for human companionship. How would he have been able to come to his "I think, therefore I am" without the existence of this vast network of community and culture?[19]

If those we view as models of individualism are this deeply embedded in community and culture, it is likely even more the case with the rest of us. Thus cultures create the framework for human life as we know it, and communities implement the functioning of these patterns in our individual lives.

Thought Experiment—The Necessity of Community and Culture

Imagine yourself among a group of people with whom you share no common views about what is right and wrong, the rules and customs for business dealings, or the appropriate way to behave in romance and relationship. How would you function? How would you know what actions to take? Of course, if you were the sole outsider in an established culture, you could simply learn the ways of that place. But imagine for a moment what it would be like if you were in a circumstance in which there were no shared beliefs or customs among any members of a group of people.

Decision Making and Community

Skeptico: That would be terrible. What do I do?
Wisdom Seeker: One approach I have tried: I get up in morning and have decisions to make that will shape the nature of my life. Because following every whim is problematic, I turn to the answers my culture has provided. Millions before me have followed this path, as expressed

in Proverbs: "Train up a child in the way he should go; and when he is old, he will not depart from it."[20] Seems a valid approach, and seems to have led many to a fulfilled life. What's more, the only way to have a human life is to function within some answer system that has worked out a number of the problems involved in living. Therefore, in making my decisions, I just follow the guidance I was given, hoping everything will work out fine.
Skeptico: That makes sense. If everybody around me is following a set of guidelines, I'll just follow them too. Much less risky that way.
Wisdom Seeker: That might work for you, but in studying peoples' lives in many different cultures, it is clear that a lot of folks who are following the guidance they were given aren't very happy. Some fit Thoreau's "lives of quiet desperation"; others are abusing alcohol and drugs; some are depressed; many others are obsessed by one thing or another. Yet most do not think it is because of their cultural answers. In fact, traveling around the world, it is clear that many people believe their cultures are good, maybe even the best, while an outsider can quickly see that some of these cultures are causing the problems about which the people within are complaining.
Skeptico: That does not mean the same is true with my answers!
Wisdom Seeker: That's correct, but if it is true for people in so many other cultures, how do I know it is not true for me as well? Perhaps my culture and my community are a significant part of the problems I am experiencing. Perhaps they even constitute the barrier to a healthy and fulfilled life.

This issue is especially difficult because it is the nature of communities to encourage their members to believe their views are "right." One common mechanism for doing so is to characterize those from other places as "weird" or "strange." Almost every community has a tendency to make fun of those who do things differently. Many times, all over the world, I have heard jokes about the habits and practices of "foreigners." These foreigners might be from a different country, a different ethnic group, or simply from a different part of the same country. (Not infrequently I have been the object of the humor.) I have been in tour groups that made fun of the people in the country being visited—with no recognition that we were the ones who were "strange" in this place.

A related cultural mechanism is to glorify the characteristics of one's home ground while denigrating that of everyone else. I have been to cold areas where people can't imagine living where it is hot, and I have been in hot regions where residents can't imagine living where it is cold (both make jokes about the other). I have talked with people in cities who can't understand how anyone could live with the boredom of the countryside: "There is absolutely nothing to do!" (though many who say this have never been to the country). And I have talked to rural dwellers who can't imagine living in a city: "It is hectic, crime-ridden, loud, crowded" (though the speakers have often never visited a large city). These reinforcing messages are present in every community, often conveyed as put-downs of some sort. Countless times I have heard people make fun of the food others eat or the clothes they wear, with no awareness by the speakers that the way they themselves ate and dressed seemed quite weird to the "other" of whom they were making fun.

This tendency reaches down to the most basic level of human interaction: I have heard parents making fun of the customs their kids were adopting from friends. I have even heard couples from different parts of the country, or different denominations within the same religion, making fun of the other for differing habits, with no recognition that they were trying to enforce on their partner the cultural rules that had been given to them as a child.

Sometimes all this is harmless, sometimes not, but the tendency is so widespread, down to the smallest subcultures, that it must be a basic current in human nature. We are constantly trying to convince those around us (and ourselves) that our habits, customs, and beliefs are right and that anyone who disagrees with us is wrong. Psychologically speaking, this is probably a protection against inner doubt, an inoculation that helps us encounter different customs and beliefs without being thrown into confusion. (If we see "the other" as silly or ridiculous, we don't have to take their views or ways seriously And perhaps making fun of others is a way to strengthen the bonds within a group, helping members maintain confidence in their own answers.

But the crucial question is this: How do I know whether or not my culture is healthy if I have been indoctrinated to believe it is the best?

Changing Communities

Skeptico: Well, if my community is unhealthy, I'll go my own way, make my own decisions, and create my own path.
Wisdom Seeker: That approach can be exhilarating! For a little while. As I tried it, though, I discovered that a host of things were tied to my cultural upbringing and could not so easily be left behind. Furthermore, I found that being outside the community soon became unsettling: Where was I to find friends and relationships? Wasn't it presumptuous to think I knew better than everybody else? What if they began to think I was crazy rather than cool for leaving? What if I wanted to go back and they wouldn't have me?
Skeptico: I see a solution! Join a group with better answers!
Wisdom Seeker: So it is that those who leave one community almost always join another. There is a need in us for a group of like-minded others with whom to share our lives, our values, and our meanings (and to reinforce for each other that the path we are on is right).

Of course, people leave their home ground for many different reasons—sometimes wars, famine, drought, and epidemics cause them to be displaced; at other times, the wanderlust of our race urges an individual or a small group on to a new start, a better life, an adventure. When this happens, though, the uprooted ones tend to carry their cultures with them or adopt the customs of the new locale. (The first generation of those adopting a new culture can have a difficult time, not feeling "at home" in the new community, not even knowing where "home" really is. It is hard to trust one's instincts and understandings in a new place, if you have changed cultures.)

There also have been rebels in each culture who stayed within and questioned the "given" order. The young are especially prone to take this step, so a lot of modern literature has to do with young people feeling alienated from family or community, with a sense that they do not belong, and a concomitant tendency to try new things and form "alternative" subgroups.

This is, in fact, one major way cultures change: Rebels break the rules and ignore the boundaries, bringing transformation and innovation. Some rebels have even given rise to whole new cultural systems. But rebels often have difficult lives, finding themselves ostracized, banished, ridiculed—even killed. Because of this, most of us do not become full-bodied rebels. As Dostoyevsky suggests in *The Brothers Karamazov*, most of us don't want very much freedom; instead, we want to know what the customs are, and we will mostly fit in. Recently, studies have found scientific confirmation for this tendency—the pain of being excluded from one's group is as great as physical pain and seems to be associated with the same area of the brain.[21]

Another aspect of rebellion is indicative of the power of culture and community. Even rebels cannot break the need for communal bonds. To be a rebel is to rebel *against* something, so rebels are defined by whatever they are rebelling against. Thus, even in rebellion, their communities define them. The relationship is simply one of opposition rather than cooperation. Further, the form a rebellion takes is determined largely by the culture, based on stories of previous rebels and their actions. At a deeper level still, the community in which a rebel has been raised determines to a great extent what he or she can, or cannot, see with regard to reality, so the rebellion is always framed by that lens.

Finally, rebels almost never rebel alone. Instead, they join a community of fellow rebels or create a new community so that rebelling against one group leads to membership in another. In the broadest sense, those who leave their birth communities, for whatever reason, do not do so in isolation; rather, they carry their old cultures with them like a tortoise carries its shell. Either that, or they join a new community to support them in their new life.

Stepping Outside—The Healing Journey

There is a great longing for community in the modern world. I hear people speak of it almost every day. I think this is because so many communities are broken or dysfunctional, and the absence of strong, healthy communities creates the longing. We need others with whom to do the things we want to do and to care for us when we are troubled or ill.

Participation in a healthy community can foster individual fulfillment, but, as mentioned before, some communities are not healthy, and active involvement in an unhealthy community does not lead to fulfillment and happiness. Yet if I am embedded in a community, how do I know whether it is healthy or not, whether it is leading to fulfillment or not? The only way to find out is to break away, to step outside far enough to gain perspective, even though this can be painful, dangerous, and perhaps prevent an eventual return to the sorely missed fold.

These feelings are precisely why stepping outside one community almost always leads to joining another. In the world today, there is no shortage of possibilities, for many communities exist that are easy to idealize (when looking in from the outside), especially because the successful ones all have a good sales pitch. There is good reason, though, when one feels a need to separate from one's old ways, to resist quickly joining another community.

Speaking to this situation, a number of wise men and women through the ages advised that only by remaining outside for a time would we ever be able to find freedom, peace, salvation, or enlightenment. Mythologist Joseph Campbell concluded that the story of the hero or heroine has ever and always been the story of negotiating an escape from one's community in order to undertake the universal quest—to break free from one's conditioning so as have a direct experience of the deepest truth for oneself. (Not necessarily a new truth, but a deep personal realization of what is true, because anything accepted without such a personal experience cannot serve as the basis for a fulfilled life.)

Isn't this what Jesus said, and lived, by leaving family behind and going into the wilderness, teaching that we must let go of worldly things and choose the narrow gate (as opposed to the broad gate of the everyday world, the world of the established culture)? Only in this way, he taught, will we discover the abundant life.

The Buddha's teaching is the same: Those in the everyday world, the established community, are living an illusion, are not awake, so the seeker must leave behind the old ways to "wake up" to what is real and true. Thus he left home and family and wandered in the wilderness of spiritual seeking for many years—leaving an idyllic life as heir to a worldly throne—because he was determined to find the truth for himself.

For many others, leaving one's community in search of answers has been a common approach to finding a fulfilled life in many times and places. In traditional cultures, the vision quest was a sanctioned way of stepping outside social limits to foster a personal vision and understanding. Gaining such a vision provided a direction for life, and in some cases, when brought back to the community, helped to heal the tribe and provide a new path forward for the group as well. In America, Henry David Thoreau undertook this experiment for himself and came back from his sojourn on the banks of Walden Pond with suggestions for living that have inspired millions around the world, suggestions that include the importance of challenging the wrongs embedded in one's birth community.

Perhaps it is only by throwing off the blinders and stepping outside that we can find a perspective from which to discover how best to live. Perhaps it is only by breaking free from our old community that we will be able to grasp the nature of our communal wounds—the ways in which we are jointly stuck, dysfunctional, or unhealthy. Thus it is that frequently those with the courage to leave a community are the ones who discover the wisdom needed to heal themselves, and, if they choose to return, provide the vision for the community's healing and its new way forward.

Paradoxes Aplenty

Many heroes and heroines of history have taken this path, breaking with their birth cultures, then returning to share a new wisdom and truth. But a paradox arises here: Even the lonely hero or heroine must have a community; even the solitary pursuit of spiritual goals occurs within the teaching, guidance, and support of a community. No one goes off to sit in a cave or on a mountain without the example of those who went before, nor without a teaching that defines why such a path is worthwhile.

For instance, Buddhism is often seen as an internal process, but consider this conversation between the Buddha and Ananda, his most loyal follower:

> Ananda: Is the sangha (the community of seekers) an important part of the holy life?
> The Buddha's answer: No, Ananda, it is not a part. Good spiritual friends are the whole of the holy life. Find refuge in the sangha.

In Christianity, John the Baptist preceded Jesus in breaking from the old traditions, and Jesus went to John for baptism and blessing. Then, after his time alone in the wilderness, Jesus assembled a community of followers to share his work. Thoreau went to the woods alone in quest of his truth, but he did so under the influence of the Transcendental community of his time, and during his solitary stay at Walden Pond, visitors from that community came to support his endeavor and to share thoughts and fellowship with him.

Another paradox: Although joining a new community can be as problematic as staying in the old (it usually doesn't take long to discover the problems in the new group), learning from a new community is one of the best ways to grow and develop. The third paradox is that learning often happens best through total immersion in and commitment to a new system, but such a commitment puts one's individuality at great risk. The trick is to participate and learn without losing oneself in the new system—because of anxiety, loneliness, or fear.

Skeptico: How do I do that?

Wisdom Seeker: All I can say is that at some point you must find your own way, for there are no fixed rules when you enter the territory beyond the rules.

Which Shall It Be: Community or Freedom?

The last paradox above points to the unavoidable tension between community and freedom, for we are continually caught between the competing pulls of communal bonds and the desire for freedom and individuality. When one side of this equation is fulfilled for us, we tend to take it for granted and long for the opposite, so when living in a strong community, people do not long for community but complain about too much rigidity and a lack of freedom. Conversely, when there is great individual freedom and community bonds are weak, people long for greater connection. Yet communities become strong through sacrifice; they ride on what people are willing to give, their success depending on the fact that many are willing to invest time and energy in doing ***not what they want to do***, but what the community needs. Thus, when individuality is strong, it is hard to build and maintain a strong community.

To have community, freedoms must be given up: the freedom to act as one wants (at least part of the time), even the freedom to think as one wants (a good bit of the time). Communities require conformity to function, which brings them into conflict with personal freedom. Perhaps the lack of strong community experienced by many in the modern world lies in the shortage of those willing to make the necessary sacrifices. Each of us wants others to see things our way, make the sacrifices, do the work. Perhaps the longing to be a star that many feel—through sports, business, a career in entertainment, politics—springs from the urge to be part of a community but also to be the one who is the center of attention, with everyone in the community catering to your wants and needs. (Do many of us long to be treated like royalty was treated of old?)

The way this conflict has played out in my life is crystallized by the fact that I was raised to forgo my whims (or to fulfill them in the proscribed ways, following the rules of the community), with the proviso that this would lead to a happy and fulfilled life. It was made clear that only by subordinating my personal desires, making numerous compromises to be part of the group, would fulfillment be found. Yet I was also taught that individualism is a virtue, that every "cowboy" should blaze his own trail, that each of us should ask, with Ayn Rand, "Who is John Galt?"—and upon catching a scent of the answer, follow his example. The paradox is vivid here: I was supposed to *follow the example* of the ultimate rebel! Where, then, was my individualism to be found?

Negotiating the Rapids

Each person's relation to culture and community is one of the most complex and crucial issues of human life. We are required to negotiate the terrain between communal immersion and individual freedom from birth to death, and for many in today's world, the course is treacherous, with no reliable map. We hope for good communities, ones that will provide a structure for successful interaction with others while leaving room for individual freedom; maintain order while fostering creativity; and guide our actions while allowing, even encouraging, each of us to experience the deepest truth for ourselves. Yet for a community to get these balances right is a high art, and many do not succeed, leaving us is to make the best of a difficult situation.[i]

The lack of strong and stable communities was not a problem for many of our ancestors, living as they did within systems that provided structure (although requiring conformity). But in modern times, especially as cultures have become widely dispersed (and have run headlong into other cultures, mixing and mingling with them), there has been a breakdown in the ability of communities to enforce core ideas and beliefs. This is both good and bad (good for freedom, bad for fulfilling our need for community) and has fostered the emergence of many subcultures within large umbrella cultures. As *The New York Times* columnist David Brooks noted concerning the United States, "The country has simply drifted apart into different subcultures," and each has "developed different unconscious maps of reality." They have "different communal definitions," "different communal understandings of what constitutes a good leader," and even of "what sort of world they live in." In a sense, these subgroups "have begun to function like tribes." Because of this, the cultural groups within which many of us now live have become "infinitely complex and poorly understood," even by those who live within them.[22]

This process has been hastened and enhanced by modern transportation and communication, to the point that the primary communities for many of us are no longer village or neighborhood, but an area of interest (political party, church group, professional group, country club membership, advocacy or service group, bridge club, or quilting circle) that we share with a far-flung group of others. This means that a person's main community might be spread over a wide geographic area, with members seeing each other only on occasion—if ever. Even many families are fragmented geographically, and sometimes

---

[i] In future chapters, we will consider whether all cultural answer systems arose separately as power bases for those who controlled the common ground. We will also consider whether all systems are simply habits that have developed over time that can be changed arbitrarily, or whether there are deep currents that a system must incorporate in order to provide fulfillment for the human lives within it.

emotionally. Most people in the past did not have to travel far to visit relatives, and in some cultures entire families lived in the same house or in neighboring homes.

Some communities, and even families, interact today mostly through the web via e-mail, Facebook, or thousands of networking sites. This means that, rather than living in one coherent community, many of us are part of several, with all the pluses and minuses that brings. (The pluses include greater freedom of choice, a broader range of friends and interests, great variety, and dynamic economic systems. The minuses include conflicting values between our groups, hard choices about where to spend time and energy, split focus, lack of commitment to any one group, loss of feeling deeply connected, frail means of holding a community's operating structure in place, and the disappearance of the feeling that people will be there for us in times of difficulty.)

> **Thought Experiment—Where Is Your Community?**
>
> How would you define the main community, or communities, in your life? If it is not immediately clear, simply ask yourself: Who shares my values? What group of people do I look to for guidance and confirmation with regard to important questions? Where do I turn for help and support?

However we define our community or communities, each of us must continually decide how much time and energy we will commit to working within them, either to fulfill ourselves or foster the well-being of others.

The Next Tool for Decision Making

Each of us is moved from our earliest years by what I have whimsically labeled "whim"—our urges and desires. As we grow, these whims are molded and shaped by the culture of our heritage, by way of the specific communities within which we live, providing one major means for making decisions. Many people through the ages have relied heavily on this guidance, which in turn has led to many fulfilled lives. Yet this approach to decision making has also created much frustration and constrained many lives as well.

In the modern world, whether we would like to live in strong and stable communities or not, the ability to do so has been powerfully undermined by the fragmentation of communities the world over. Given this problem, how else might we proceed with making decisions? One alternative is to participate more consciously in the process, breaking at least somewhat free of both whim and culture. To do so, however, we must: (a) recognize our whims and develop the ability to choose between urges and desires as they hinder or support the person we wish to be and (b) discover how our cultures and communities are asserting their influence on us, and then develop the wisdom to decide which rules and customs to follow and which to reject.

That's a tall order! Is there any way to accomplish such a task? Yes, and we will explore it in the next chapter: the amazing faculty called "human reason."

CHAPTER 6

Are You Rational?

Have you ever taken responsibility for a puppy? We brought two young German Shepherd pups into our home (four years apart) and began the delightful and difficult process of acculturating Shakti and Dante to our world, teaching them to fit in, to act in ways that seemed best—to us. That's the key, isn't it, getting your canine companions to do what you want them to do, to follow the rules you lay down so they won't disrupt the life you wish to live? Being able to create the culture facilitates one's enjoyment of a dog's company and reduces the hassle for the "owner." This is best for the dogs too, isn't it?

Dante was a male, the epitome of a trustworthy and loyal friend. He almost always did what he was supposed to do and seemed to take delight in doing what we defined as the right thing, even if it went against his natural instincts. He had a fierce commitment to fulfilling his duties. Was this rational behavior?

Shakti was a female who learned fast and followed the rules, up to a point. As she learned, however, she began to manipulate the rules to get what she wanted within them—and became very skilled at this. (At times we wondered just who was in charge of the household.) She would roll over and act like she wanted to be petted to get our attention, then promptly switch and ask for a treat—the offer of letting us pet her being a tactic to get something she wanted more—a treat. Was Shakti being rational?

Much Confusion

"Reason" and "rational" are words that describe what many believe to be a central characteristic of being human. (The two words will be used here as having similar meanings. Both, however, are quite different from "logic" and "logical," as will be made clear.) Of central importance, reason and rationality suggest an ability that serves as the third great tool for decision making, offering the possibility of correcting mistakes that an over-reliance on whim and culture can bring.

Shakespeare, in a fine flourish, suggested that reason constitutes the primary basis upon which we assign ourselves a more advanced status than that of other creatures:

> What a piece of work is a man!
> how Noble in Reason!
> how infinite in faculty!
> in form and moving how express and admirable!
> in Action how like an Angel!
> in apprehension how like a God?
> the beauty of the world,
> the paragon of animals.[j][23]

Reason and rationality might be noble, but the way we use these words is highly problematic. Through the centuries (and right down to the present day) they have had many different meanings, several of which are conflicting and incompatible, yet we slide back and forth between meanings without recognizing that we are doing so. I have heard numerous people switch meanings in mid-thought, even mid-sentence, with no awareness of what was happening.

---

[j] This is from the *First Folio Edition* of Shakespeare's works, with its punctuation (but with each line separated for emphasis here). Other editions punctuate these lines quite differently. Although Hamlet spoke the lines to create a contrast to how he felt, it must have been a common view the audience held, against which Shakespeare was contrasting Hamlet's mood.

> **Thought Experiment—What Is Rational?**
>
> Before reading on, pause for a moment and ask yourself: What is this human trait we call reason? How do you know when something is rational? Is there a common understanding of these terms? What is your understanding?

Skeptico: I am having trouble!
Wisdom Seeker: You are not alone. When most of us use these words, we slip and slide in our minds between understandings, and when using them in conversation, we often have different definitions in mind than the person with whom we are talking. Truth be told, most of us have such a loose grip on what these words mean that we bounce all around without recognizing it.

Think of the irony here! Most people are quite confused about the meaning of the very words that stand for the crowning achievement of human intellectual development. Many smart folks have suggested that reason is the path to solving the problems of human existence, but there is no agreement as to how reason works or how rationality can be applied. This poor understanding is a serious problem, especially with regard to discovering how to live a fulfilled life. Let's sort out, then, some of the confusion surrounding reason and consider how we can render it more valuable in communicating with others, as well as in making life decisions.

Five Distinct Views of Being Rational

1. Reason's highest function is to grasp transcendental truth.

When Plato gave reason an exalted place in the pantheon of human abilities, he was referring to our capacity to come to a clear understanding of what is ultimately true. This idea of truth was grounded in the belief that there is a realm transcendent to the everyday world (he called it the world of Pure Forms or Pure Ideas). For Plato, and Socrates before him, truth was not based on evidence from the senses, nor did it come from an experience of the material world. Rather, they taught that the senses could easily deceive. (A classic example from India concerning the deception of the senses is that a rope lying in a corner in dim light can easily be mistaken for a snake. Yet perceiving it as such, we will act as if that is reality. Who knows, then, how many things we perceive that, at this moment, are but illusions, like the snake in the corner?)

In Plato's view, then, reason is a process of discourse and reflection that leads to an insight into the true nature of the broadest transcendental reality, beyond the material realm, and beyond the flawed perceptions of the physical senses.

2. Reason is the human faculty that allows us to understand the world God made.

Thomas Aquinas combined Aristotelian thought with Christianity to develop one of the most influential views of reason in Western history. Dominating the understanding of most westerners for hundreds of years, he said there was no conflict between reason and faith, for the human faculty of reason was precisely the tool that allowed us to understand this marvelous world in which we live, which itself is rational.

3. Reason is an inherent structure in the mind used to organize and decide about sense data.

Immanuel Kant, in the eighteenth century, attempted to establish a basis for human action without reference to Plato's world of Pure Forms or the ideas of any established religion. Contrary to the transcendentalism of Plato, Kant was focused on how we could best organize the data of our senses, and reason was the human ability that let us "make sense" of the information that came to us from the everyday world. It was a function inherent in the mind itself, thus overcoming the problem of those who, having rejected Plato as well as the dominant religious ideas of their time, were having trouble finding a way to understand how the world came to make sense at all.

Kant's rationality did not preclude a transcendent or spiritual realm—in fact, he made explicit room for such to exist, calling it "The Thing in Itself." But he did not believe we could know that mysterious *Ding an sich,* so how could we know how to live? For Kant, that was precisely our human responsibility, to sort through our experience of the everyday world and use reason to find the best way to do it. Thus, his moral writings present a "rational" argument for the behavior he saw as good and right. (He did not seem to recognize—or want to admit—that his moral assumptions were remarkably similar to the values and meanings he had been taught in his Germanic upbringing, which in turn had grown out of a spiritual tradition.)

This Kantian view of reality had a profound effect on Western thought, and his recognition that our minds shape the reality we experience has been a building block and a challenge to every system of thought since his day. (Kant did not hold that we can simply change our reality by changing our thinking; the structure of our minds was given to us, and to a great extent we have to work within that structure.)

Kant's moral ideas also had a powerful impact, and one primary belief today concerning the essence of rational behavior filters down to us with his view that *there is an inherent moral imperative to do our duty, fulfill our responsibilities, and respect the rights of others.*

4. Reason is an individual's way to know what is right, as opposed to blind obedience to authority.

The ideas of Spinoza and Leibniz inspired many thinkers in the eighteenth century to view reason as the primary tool to be used in making the important decisions of life. A group exemplified by Voltaire and Thomas Jefferson wished to shake people from a blind obedience to authority, to free them from an over-reliance on duty to a cultural heritage. Both wrote in support of revolution (Voltaire against the church, Jefferson against the English monarchy).

Agreeing with Kant, they felt a rational being would stop, reflect, think through issues, listen to the arguments of others, and consider all available evidence. Differing with Kant, however, *their rationalism gave greater emphasis to a personal, independent judgment of the right and the good. They wished to justify breaking with the ruling authorities of their time, so their view of reason encouraged each individual to discover truth for him or herself.*

This did not, however, constitute a rejection of the spiritual dimension. Although Voltaire is sometimes placed in the pantheon of materialists, he actually felt reason led to a direct knowing of the spiritual domain: "It is perfectly evident to my mind that there exists a necessary, eternal, supreme, and intelligent being. This is no matter of faith, but of reason."[24]

Jefferson too, although far from friendly to the established church of his time, felt that some human "rights" arose from a transcendent source—as he voiced so elegantly in the document that led to the formation of the United States of America: "We hold these truths to be self-evident, that all men are created equal, that they are endowed by their Creator with certain unalienable Rights."

This Jeffersonian/Voltairian view of reason is very much with us in the modern world, as well, still giving rise to revolutions and the overthrow of established authorities around the globe. There is an overlap with Kantian reason but a greater emphasis on the belief that the individual can know what is right and good and that this will, at times, be quite different from what authorities say. Rather than emphasizing duty and responsibility within an established order, this view of reason sees the individual with much more free agency. Reason is still the tool that allows us to know what is right and good, to directly perceive what has been "endowed" by our "Creator." Kant wouldn't have approved, especially upon the insistence that we had the right, even the duty, to act on our perceptions of the mysterious realm of the *noumenon* (beyond the senses), no matter what existing authorities might say.

5. Reason is being logical.

Finally, some thinkers in the late nineteenth and early twentieth centuries came to equate being rational with being logical. Mathematics had flowered, and it was hoped that all of life could be made subject to the same hard logic that prevailed in math. This led to logical empiricism, or logical positivism, which, in its simplest form, held that nothing could be accepted as true unless it could be demonstrated with logical proof.

This approach proved extremely valuable in math and science and for a narrow range of issues in daily life: If something is easily quantifiable, by weight, height, monetary value, etc., then logical analysis can often provide the best answer to a question. (Would you rather receive fifty dollars or one hundred dollars for something you are selling?) It is both "logical" and "rational" to choose one hundred dollars; this can be shown persuasively to most anyone. Proponents of this view hoped that, by forcing reason through a logical funnel, a system of thought could be developed upon which all could agree.

The proponents of this position should have consulted Ludwig Wittgenstein, considered by some the greatest Western philosopher of the twentieth century. At the end of his *Tractatus Logico-Philosophicus*, published in 1921, he presented an authoritative understanding of logic. He concluded that logic can show us the material world and that language can say what we know about it. There are areas of experience, however, such as ethics and religion, about which logic has nothing to show and rational language has nothing useful to say. If he had stopped there, he might have been interpreted as saying that nothing else existed. But he did not stop there; he went on to say that ethics and religion are more important than the things logic can consider or rational language can speak! (Although much later in life Wittgenstein revised and expanded his views about logic and reason, he did not revise this view.)[25]

As Wittgenstein would have guessed, then, little progress has been made in the last century to fit human life into a logical box, and modern philosophy has largely abandoned logical empiricism. Yet its influence lingers on in the modern mind, aided and abetted by those who want to think that their beliefs are logical and that their core assumptions are supported by "proof." *This has culminated in a fairly common "street version" of the word "rational": that being rational means there is logical proof for one's positions.*

Belief in the Five Senses

Although there are many other important ways in which reason and rationality have been understood in human history (such as those of the Buddha, Confucius, and Averroes), the five presented above illustrate the broad range of meanings, and each is still very much with us in the modern world.

Another stream of thought, empiricism, arose as an alternative to the rationalism exemplified by Plato and Kant. Stated simply, empiricism holds that everything we know comes through an experience of the five senses (sight, sound, touch, taste, and smell). This theory has roots going back at least to Aristotle and includes some of the work of Francis Bacon and Thomas Hobbes, but perhaps its best known modern exponent is English scholar John Locke, who taught that each child is born as a "blank slate" upon which experience writes all. (Even Locke, however, was not an empiricist in the modern sense, for he believed that knowledge of God's existence, which he affirmed, was gained through intuition rather than through the senses.)

Empiricism as a way of knowing has great power, for the truths that arrive through our senses seem immediate and real (the pain of a needle; the taste of food when hungry; the swift, automatic reaction to a rock hurtling toward the head; the exquisite pleasure of a passionate embrace). We move through the day reliant upon our senses, and in their immediacy it is easy to question the abstract thoughts and theories that parade through our minds. From the power of direct experience comes the wish that we could organize our lives around things that are solid and real, which the tangible evidence of our senses seems to be (at least at times).

But many things are not empirical—for instance, love, honor, courage, and meaning cannot be put in terms of quantity or sense data. (What instrument would we use to measure courage?) Trying to make everything tangible excludes many central elements of life, such as values, meanings, and beliefs. Most of us do not actually think or act as if sense data is all there is, but the influence of this view pervades much modern discourse and deeply affects how we think about our world and ourselves.

Skeptico: What does all that have to do with making decisions?

Wisdom Seeker: If, for a fulfilled life, we cannot rely solely on whim, nor the rules of our culture, wise counselors through the ages have suggested that reason can point the way. Some have even gone so far as to say that reason is the single most important ingredient in being human. Accept that or not, but reason is unquestionably a crucial part of a human life and a primary tool in decision making.

Skeptico: I try to be reasonable in my decisions.

Wisdom Seeker: But what do you mean by that word? We fling it about as if we know what it means, endowing it with great importance, yet misunderstanding each other's definitions, and even our own. I received little instruction as to what reason is; somehow it was just assumed that we all knew. But we really didn't, and most of us still don't know what we mean when we use the word "*reasonable.*" So, Skeptico, take a moment and ask yourself: Who explained reason to me? What do I understand it to be? You wouldn't try to fly an airplane without lessons, but in using our mental apparatus, we often take off with little understanding of how to use the instruments.

A Modern Error

I dwell on the meaning of these words because so many of us trip over the idea that to be a good, modern, rational being, we must reject everything for which there is no logical proof, as well as everything that cannot be demonstrated by the evidence of the senses—without recognizing that these criterion for knowledge are not given by logic nor supported by the senses. Rather, they are based on a set of assumptions, and only if one accepts the assumptions—through a conscious or unconscious act of faith—do the conclusions follow. Further, these two criteria for reason run counter to what has been considered rational by most of the great thinkers of human history; "reason as logic" would seem highly irrational to them. This narrow view requires the rejection of (to name but a few) the rationalism of Leibnitz and Kant, the idealism of Plato and Hegel, the romanticism of Goethe and Wordsworth, the transcendentalism of Emerson and Thoreau, and all ways of thought put forward by spiritual and religious traditions through the ages.

For reason to function, there must be an agreed-upon framework that determines how to arrive at "facts," as well as how the accepted facts will be processed. The conclusions reason gives depend upon the assumptions about the world (and ourselves) with which we start, the values within which we frame the inquiry, and the goals toward which we aim—none of which are given by reason. Reason is a tool that can be used in many different ways, and our underlying assumptions are the sea in which it swims. As science writer James Burke put it in *The Day the Universe Changed:*

> Every observation...is impregnated with theory. Nature is so complex and so random that it can only be approached with a systematic tool that presupposes certain facts about it. Without such a pattern it would be impossible to find an answer to questions even as simple as "What am I looking at?"

The structure is institutionalized and given permanence by the educational system. Agreement on the structure is efficient: it saves investigators from having to go back to first principles each time. The theory of the structure dictates what "facts" shall be, and all values and assessments of results are internal to the structure.[26]

This is why, he says, "theory 'creates' facts, and facts prove the theory." The Australian aborigine and the TV climatologist both predict the weather, but their facts and their reasoning are quite different. (There is disagreement as to which is better.) The facts and the reasoning of physics make sense within the framework of physics, but that framework is not very helpful in understanding poetry or romance.

Ah, romance. Emotions of all kinds are arguably the central experience of our lives: We spend an enormous amount of time and energy trying to experience good emotions and avoid those we consider bad. Reason and logic can aid in this process, but they do not control it. The reasoning of a person in love might have some similarity to someone who wants to make a fortune, but there will be great differences as well. To begin with, the goals of neither will have been selected by reason, and how they will employ reason and rationality will vary considerably, for the degree to which emotions will control the process will vary with each, as well as how much or how little the rational process will be dominant at different moments.

All of this is important because in many discussions about life, a trump card thrown on the table is the cry, "You are not being rational," or "Reason demands...!" But this trump card is actually a bluff, a raw assertion by those using it that they "own" reason and truth. Not so. All assertions about the deepest truths start with an act of faith, including by those who hold the view that we should rely exclusively on sense data and logic. All those claiming their particular beliefs to be "rational" are simply saying that we should base our lives on their acts of faith. There is no rationality here, nor reason—simply unproven assertion.

> **Thought Experiment—Is There a Logical Basis for Our Beliefs?**
>
> I have challenged a number of folks to give a logical proof for the core beliefs they considered "rational." When pressed, they have always fallen back on a claim that an authority said it was so, or else they contorted themselves into knots of circular reasoning. I have yet to discover a remotely plausible "proof" for the assumptions behind a set of beliefs.

This is not to say that sense data and logic are unimportant. We dismiss them at our peril, and all healthy belief systems incorporate the best logic, the best sense data, and the best science in understanding the world. But including the best ideas in these areas does not require passing everything through a logical filter—only those things about which logic and the evidence of our senses can speak with clarity.

Still, it is easy in our modern world to get lost going down this blind alley, cut off from the most important things in life. But it is not necessary for a rational being to be trapped in a logical prison; wise, thoughtful, "rational" people in the past have accepted many different views of what reason is and continue to do so today. Thinking always functions within a context that gives definition and meaning to how we understand the facts and what logic will be. From Plato to Einstein, and embracing countless philosophers and scientists such as Kant, Heidegger, William James, Alfred North Whitehead, Descartes, Newton, Jefferson, Voltaire, and many others, there need be no conflict between reason and intuition, nor between rationality, values, meanings, and spiritual beliefs. Nor can our emotional experiences be contained or explained by logic or reason. The lesson of most great thinkers through human history is that reason, emotions, intuition, and spiritual beliefs must be integrated in some way to form a solid and sustainable worldview.

How could it be otherwise? You can create an arbitrary concept that reason is separate from feelings, values, meanings, and spiritual beliefs, but it is impossible to have such a separation when making decisions. I do not have separate boxes in me that are the rational box, the logical box, the emotional box, and so forth, to which I refer respective decisions. When I am thinking about something, there is a stream of thought that includes all of those things and more. I have no idea how to remove all my values or feelings from my decision-making process. Nor would I want to! Any such decision would have little to do with what is important in life.

Neurologist and author Richard Cytowic has spent much of his career studying the relation between reason and the emotions, and his conclusion is that "emotion rather than reason is primary"[27] because decisions seem to arise from the limbic system, the area of the brain associated with emotions. The cortex, more often associated with reason, is involved, but it is not the final decision-making center. Information is passed back and forth between the cortex and the limbic system, and the cortex contributes analysis, but decisions then arise from the emotional center. As Christian de Quincy summarizes:

> The limbic system enables us to non-rationally assess and evaluate incoming information at a rapid-fire rate of 400 hertz (cycles per second), and when the results of this process filter through to consciousness, we become aware of intuitive insights and hunches which may have no rational basis or explanation, but which nevertheless seem to be the primary guiding factors in our decisions and behavior.[28]

Cytowic goes on to say that we are not aware of much of this in our conscious mind, but this limbic process is always operating and involves much more information than we can maintain in the rational cortex.

Of course, everyone does not agree with this view, and I do not know if it is presents the whole picture, but it certainly helps explain several of the unknowns about our decision-making process. And it is reinforced by the work of Dean Shibata of the University of Washington.

He uses MRIs to scan brains during the decision-making process, and he has found that it is not possible to separate the "rational" from the "emotional" functions, for they are "integrated and overlapping." He found that the part of the frontal lobe often associated with emotions was very active when dealing with what would normally be considered rational issues and that "The circuits are very intertwined. There isn't just one separate part of the brain that drives emotional decisions and another part that drives rational thinking." He goes on to point out that "we are not aware of how we make decisions" and that, ultimately, "Our rational decisions are more biased than we may think."[29]

William James to the Rescue

One integrative picture of this process was given by William James, who highly valued the data given by our senses but did not believe it wise to discount intuitive and spiritual knowledge. His insight helped found Radical Empiricism, the gist of which is this: The experience of the five senses is clearly the basis for much of our knowledge; in the practical functioning of our lives, everything points to the assumption that there is material stuff out there to be dealt with, and this material stuff has a crucial role to play—so let's not get too caught up in discussions about whether we might be a "brain in a jar" (as postulated in one of Descartes's thought experiments).[k] In living our lives, said James, we can and should interact with the material world as we experience it and not worry too much about how our perceptions might be an illusion.

James went on to say, however, that we also have many experiences beyond those that come to us through the five senses, such as emotions, intuitions, and spiritual experiences. Further, these make up a major part of life, and although they are different from the experience of the senses, this does not mean they are less important, *nor less empirical*. In fact, if we are to be fully empirical (basing our

---

[k] Neither James nor Descartes used the exact phrase "brain in a jar," but it is the shorthand used to convey something they were talking about.

knowledge on experience), we must take *all* experience into account, including other ways of knowing.

In other words, in dealing with the material world, let's use the practical input from the senses because that works. At the same time, though, let us recognize that input from the senses does not explain all areas of life. To be truly empirical, we will need to use the most relevant data in other areas as well—including emotions, intuitions, and spiritual experiences. All these are direct experiences, provide information that works, and are subject to observation and study. These things are thus empirical, in a true understanding of that word.

In this light, James the empiricist provides a decidedly broad framework for understanding our lives and our decisions:

> Our normal waking consciousness, rational consciousness as we call it, is but one special type of consciousness, whilst all about it, parted from it by the filmiest of screens, there lie potential forms of consciousness entirely different. We may go through life without suspecting their existence, but apply the right stimulus, and at a touch they are there in all their completeness.
> No account of the universe in its totality can be final which leaves these other forms of consciousness…disregarded. How to regard them is the question, for they are so discontinuous with ordinary consciousness. At any rate, they forbid a premature closing of our accounts with reality.[30]

One fascinating result of this broad view of empiricism is that it is not in conflict with some streams of rationalism and certainly is not in conflict with intuition or an interest in things spiritual. As the modern philosopher Willard Van Orman Quine pointed out (one poll named him among the five most important western philosophers of the past two centuries), we think, live, and act within systems of understanding, and there is no way for one system to judge the truth of another.
Skeptico: That might be true of belief systems, but science can judge what is true.

Wisdom Seeker: Actually, Quine's point is that even science is a framework of understanding, and whatever knowledge we have within it is totally dependent on being in the structure. Any fact we report is embedded in a whole field of past understandings and ideas, and facts cannot be separated from the structure. Thus, science cannot judge the ideas of other frameworks. It is impossible to check the correspondence of sense data to a framework; we can only understand data within a framework.
Skeptico: Then how do we decide how to live?
Wisdom Seeker: Pragmatically, he says "We do what seems to work."
Skeptico: Then how do I know my system is the best?
Wisdom Seeker: Quine would say you can't.
Skeptico: I don't like that. What would James say?
Wisdom Seeker: James would say (although Quine probably wouldn't) that there are other worlds of consciousness to be explored, that true empiricism must include the emotional, spiritual, and even the nonordinary and mystical experiences we humans have, for they provide beneficial results that are unavailable in any other way. He might even say we can acquire a certainty about what we know through these arenas that can never be acquired through reason.

Climbing Mountains

Let me paint a picture: Imagine that you are part of a group that has decided to climb Mount Everest. Reason will play an important role in the venture, yet the ***motivation*** to climb Everest is not rational but falls into the category of whim. (Or maybe it is a calling, one of those deep urges that arises spontaneously from a place that one does not understand but feels too serious to be labeled whim.)

The fact is that few of the core motivations of our lives are rational. Reason, however, is valuable in sorting through our motivations, deciding which are most important, and especially helpful in determining which have the greatest possibility of success. Reason is also crucial in helping us figure out how our chosen goals can best be accomplished and organizing effective strategies to accomplish them.

So you have decided to climb Mount Everest. Having been moved by who knows what indecipherable reasons to make the climb, the next step is to join with others (no one has ever climbed Everest alone) who share your vision of enduring enormous pain and hardship to climb the highest mountain in the world simply "because it is there." Reason plays a role in assembling the group (who is a good climber, who has been there before, who has the various skills we will need), but intuition, friendship, and emotions also play a part.

Once the group is assembled, rational thinking is indispensable in the preparations: calculating the needed provisions, determining the schedule in relation to weather, coordinating travel plans, collecting maps and reports from previous climbers, researching the most useful gear, etc. One other action must be taken before the climb begins: roles must be assigned, an authority structure put in place. Everyone cannot do everything, and for a successful climb, each of us must accept and fulfill our roles, deferring to the leaders we have put in place when there is disagreement (guides decide about practical details, the climb leader decides about changes in route, the medical person decides what to do about illness or injury, etc.). And once again, in making decisions about authority, reason plays a role, but so do emotions, intuitions, and values.

The climb begins. What if one of those in charge seems to you to be making a mistake? You might question the decision, offer arguments for an alternate route—you might use reason to question or influence authority. But to remain a part of the group and fulfill the common goal, it will be necessary, in the end, to relinquish your individual "reason" and accept the decisions of the leader. This is reason operating as duty, or more broadly, as the belief that we are so deeply embedded with others that the most rational path is to modify, or even go against, personal "reason" in order to have a shared life.

This is one example of the complexity of reason—is it a personal thing or a communal thing? In most cases, for any shared venture to work, all must abide by the communal view of what is considered rational. Yet we do not always do this. Occasionally someone decides that the one in authority is mad, or evil, or is about to get everyone killed, and there is rebellion against authority. In our Everest climb, let's say the climb leader, with wildness in his eyes, proclaims that we will make the final ascent on the morrow, although a storm is brewing. You rebel and begin to talk to others, saying the climb leader is affected by the thin air, or has a death wish, or believes that this will be his last chance to climb Everest and doesn't care about the risk. Then a defender of the leader steps up and says no, the leader is the greatest mountain climber of all time and must know what he is doing.

So is it rational to obey the leader or rational to oppose him? Those who join the rebellion prepare their rational arguments for challenging the leader's authority—as did Thomas Jefferson in justifying rebellion by the American colonies against King George. The opposing side of every argument, however, always has its rational arguments as well, so supporters of the climb leader have no trouble mounting their defense, based on reason as they see it.[1]

As the Everest debate goes along, one climber says with great conviction: "We have to make the climb tomorrow. Honor demands it! I couldn't face my friends if we turned back." Let's assume this climber is from a culture that values honor over everything. Many do. Ancient Greeks fought wars over it, and early Americans fought duels. Although a duel might not seem rational to you, it seemed so to many early Americans. (A significant number of our forebears were willing to kill or be killed for honor's sake; a US president killed someone in a duel, and a leading founder of the country lost his life in another. It was "rational" to them, for it was upholding one of the ultimate values, which makes clear that reason is deeply entwined with cultural beliefs.)

---

[1] Edmund Burke, statesman and writer in England at the time of the American revolution, supported Jefferson's rationale for rebellion at the time. Burke changed positions a few years later, though, and used rational arguments to condemn the revolutionaries in France.

All this to say that being rational does not follow a fixed set of rules but involves a broad judgment including beliefs and values, culture and intuition. Mountain climbers will tell you there are moments when reason gives way to intuition—the best route to take, where to place the hand at a precarious moment, what to do in a sudden, life-threatening emergency. Reading the accounts of mountain climbers, I have been struck by how intuition is the constant handmaiden (and occasional dominant partner) in its marriage with reason. In extreme undertakings, as in any successful life, the two cannot be separated. (Much more in the next chapter.)

One further thought about climbing mountains: In extreme moments of any dangerous and challenging undertaking, the spiritual dimension of life is frequently the sudden guest at the banquet. In Maria Coffey's *Explorers of the Infinite: The Secret Spiritual Lives of Extreme Athletes,* case after case is presented of spiritual experiences springing unbidden from extreme physical circumstances. Further, in interviews with extreme athletes concerning why they undertook their adventures in the first place, a common motivation emerges that sounds remarkably like the motivations described by all spiritual seekers through the ages.

The Mystery of Reason

I have been pondering the meaning of reason and rationality for the better part of my adult life. If these words do not rest solely upon sense data and logic, how should we understand them? Equally important, how can we use what they point to in the living of our lives? Reflecting on these questions, reading the views of scholars through the centuries, and surveying many friends, the only thing that has become absolutely clear is the confusion that resides in these words. They have had many different meanings through history, and each meaning still has some purchase in the world today. Now, all these meanings are constantly mingling and overlapping with each other, creating the crazy quilt of incompatibly within which we live and within which we try to give order our lives. (There is a great deal of humor in discovering the degree of confusion and misunderstanding surrounding the words that are supposed to establish the very basis for clarity in human thought.)

Does this mean, then, that reason is actually some will-o'-the-wisp, a smokescreen we use to justify our personal preferences? Does where we "stand" always depend on where we "sit," on the preferences of our personal position? Is reason based solely on cultural conditioning? Is reason, in the end, completely arbitrary, a mind game we play to justify ourselves or use to persuade others to do what we want them to do? All these explanations have been offered.

And yet, and yet…. To me, the capacity to be rational seems more than these things, and has a solidity and rightness about it that goes beyond all such limited understandings. It is also important to note that we seem to be able to reason together—to be able to persuade each other at times with reason and reach understandings that go beyond culture and whim. All this is hard to pin down, and the fact that we have so little understanding of what these words mean after thousands of years of wrestling with them should temper all our definitions with humility.

Ultimately for me, reason does have a meaningful role to play; although mysterious, it is central to who and what we humans are. In its highest forms, rationality is not arbitrary and capricious but provides a standard by which we can evaluate our personal decisions and with which we can sometimes find common ground with others, transcending all enculturation. Perhaps much of the confusion lies in the fact that life, as Kierkegaard said, is lived forward but understood backward. It is easy to convince ourselves we understand the rationality of actions in the past, once choices have been made and consequences determined (although it is debatable whether our understandings are as accurate as we think they are). But living forward into the unknown is always shrouded in mystery, is always elusive of capture by rational thought.

An Attempt at Clarity

Let us be brave, however, and venture into this dense thicket of confusion with an attempt at clarity concerning how reason and rationality represent something at the very heart of being human, as well as offer help in living a fulfilled life. The first step is to acknowledge that there are no shared definitions for these words, nor a definition that can be demonstrated to be "right." At the same time, I can say with some certainty that if you wish to use these tools for decision making and living, it will be extremely valuable to have a clear understanding of what *you* mean when you use them. And if you wish to have a worthwhile interaction with others about the important questions of life, it will prove extremely valuable to find a common understanding with those with whom you are conversing.

Beyond those general provisos, here are ten aspects of reason and rationality that have been suggested by various thoughtful persons through the ages:

1. **Keeping an open mind:** Rather than being enslaved by whim or engulfed by authority, being rational is to step back and consider for oneself the consequences of actions from the broadest possible perspective and to step beyond the urge of the moment and consider how things fit into a broad vision, how your actions and decisions fit into the whole cloth of the life you are weaving.
2. **Collecting all relevant information:** Reason suggests gathering all the information possible in relation to a decision, then reflecting upon all the information, leaving nothing out, before a decision is made. It is to courageously weigh everything: logical arguments and sense data, yes, but also values, beliefs, the kind of person you wish to be, how the situation affects others, the cultural norms within which you are living—everything.
3. **Balancing community and freedom:** There is a constant tension between the urge for freedom and autonomy on the one hand and the need for relationships and community on the other. In this tug of war, reason is an essential tool in discovering a balance of

"rightness" between your own needs and desires and those of others and in considering the effects of your actions on friends, family, and community, without drowning in duty and responsibility toward others.

4. **Honoring tradition and authority: Irish philosopher** Edmund Burke made clear why it is important to respect authority and tradition; as he said, they have withstood the test of time. Since they have worked for a lot of people over long stretches of history, to honor existing authority is to be rational.
5. **Questioning tradition and authority:** On the other hand, reason must ask of authority: Do you still serve the highest good—or have you been taken over by those who are pursuing their own narrow purposes and goals? How do you fit with my personal beliefs and values? Reason provides a basis upon which to evaluate authority's effectiveness, suggesting we not follow religious, political, or cultural authority blindly but reserve the right to subject all authority to scrutiny, to examine its assertions in the light of the wisdom of our time and place.
6. **Recognizing a standard:** Being rational means accepting that there is some standard by which we can judge personal decisions, beyond personal prejudice, a standard that even provides a common ground with others in which we can mutually consider what is good and right in our shared life together.
7. **Proceeding with humility:** To be rational is to remember, as a fallible human being, that you could be wrong at this moment in what you think and believe. (It is humbling, but very valuable, for me to look back and see how many times I have been wrong in my life.)
8. **Including intuition:** Reason is in not opposed to intuition. On the contrary, they are the two legs upon which we walk toward wisdom: if one is missing, the walking is incredibly more difficult. (See Chapter 7.)
9. **Embracing the spirit:** Rationality does not conflict with mature spiritual insight and understanding. In fact, through most of

human history, reason and spiritual wisdom have been of mutual benefit and support. (See Chapter 12.)
10. **Refusing a narrow definition of reason:** Reason demands that we refuse a narrow definition of reason, for to do so severely limits its value.

Following these criteria, were our German Shepherds, Dante and Shakti, rational? Although I loved them dearly, and found them extraordinarily intelligent beings, I would have to say they were not rational by this definition, although Dante's commitment to duty did fit Kant's idea pretty well (and come to think of it, they were both of German stock). As for Shakti, one day when I was frustrated with trying to teach her a new trick, it struck me quite forcefully that she understood more than fifty words of the English language, and I did not understand one single word of hers! So although she might not fit my definition of rationality, the jury is still out as to which of us was smarter. (I also wonder if Shakti thought I was rational in trying to teach her what she clearly thought were stupid tricks.)

Applying Reason to Life

All ten of the preceding factors seem to me, to varying degrees, to be worthwhile as we employ reason in living a human life. Complicated? Yes! That is why simple definitions of reason have eluded us for thousands of years.

On a practical level, then, how might the use of reason be valuable in making decisions and living a full and complete life? An image: I am going along, minding my own business, when an urge to do something strikes me (a whim, or perhaps a calling?) I think, "Not supposed to do that!" (My cultural training.) Another thought immediately comes: "Yes, but several people have done something similar, and it turned out well for them." (Perhaps a rational thought, perhaps a rationalizing justification.)

Beginning to reflect on the urge, I realize that if I follow it, I will have to give up other things I want. I also consider the fact that my parents might not like it, but some close friends will be supportive. Continuing the inquiry, I think about how it fits with the kind of person I want to be and the kind of life I am trying to live. I try to be as logical as possible but quickly realize that it is more complicated than comparing apples to apples, or even apples to oranges; it is more like comparing blueberries to beefsteak, or apples to an orange dress. Leaving fruit analogies behind, how do I weigh the feelings of someone close to me against the importance of courage? There is no way to compare these things in a logical way, so all I can do is hold them inside myself, weigh them *subjectively* in relation to each other, and see what emerges.

Sometimes as I go through this process, from some mysterious place within that I do not understand, but think of as rational, a clear sense of what I should do arises. (This is related to intuition but different in that it grows more out of a *process* of thinking and considering.) It is characterized by an overall feeling of "rightness," a sense that I am on solid ground, that many different currents have been integrated—that the pieces of the puzzle I have been working through finally "fit." Further, there is a sense that I will be able to explain what I have decided, and some of the folks to whom I give the explanation will "get it." Those who have a vested interest in another outcome might not, but there is a feeling that I have gone through a process that can be shared with other rational beings, and that the conclusions I have reached will correspond to something in them and will call forth at least partial understanding from a common place we share.

Beyond Reason

We have come a long way from "reason as logic" if we can speak of reason as a "feeling" of rightness or a "sense" of how puzzle pieces fit together, but these words convey more accurately than others I can find what reason really is.

To climb Mount Everest, or to successfully climb the mountain of life, we must hold all the relevant information simultaneously, letting our actions and decisions flow from the sense of life that arises from a harmonious integration within. This is the ideal, and though seldom reached, this is the Reason of which Shakespeare speaks so grandly and the Rationality that is at the heart of being human. It is worthy of our best efforts.

Is this the end of the journey of decision making? Is the full use of reason the final step in making the best possible decisions for our lives? Perhaps, if reason is seen as starting with intuition, as Kant believed; as grounded in the spiritual domain, as Plato asserted and Thomas Jefferson implied; if it is broad enough to include the existence of the Divine as Descartes thought he had proved and the often skeptical Voltaire came to believe, and if it makes room for the extraordinary ways of knowing that William James felt were essential to a fulfilled life. The inclusion of all these aspects, however, is not the common way reason and rationality are seen today. This being the case, it is time to turn to the fourth way we humans go about making our decisions, a way that is sometimes seen as opposed, sometimes as partner to, reason: intuition.

CHAPTER 7

THE PLACE OF INTUITION

I seldom use an alarm these days, but I did for many years. The fascinating thing is that on days I planned to get up earlier than usual, I would wake before the alarm went off, usually just a minute or two before. The question is: What part of me was keeping up with the time while I slept? Since "I" was not conscious, where was this inner clock located?

In discovering guidance for living, Henry David Thoreau suggested we pay special attention to intuition, which he referred to as our "genius:" "If one listens to the faintest but constant suggestions of his genius, which are certainly true, he sees not to what extremes…it may lead him; and yet that way, as he grows more resolute and faithful, his road lies."[31]

Exploring Intuition

There have been a number of times in my life when I simply "felt" the right path to take, the right thing to do—without going through a process of reflection and consideration. Other times, this sense of knowing has come only after a period of reasoned reflection. In those cases, the sense is that the reasoning has been taken into account, but still the answer comes to me as a feeling of what is right to do and not as a calculation chart. With or without reflection, though, where do such answers come from?

The name most often given to this human faculty is *"intuition."* Many have praised its abilities and marveled at its capacities. Jean

Jacques Rousseau captured its highest possibility as "The sovereign intelligence which sees in a twinkle of an eye the truth of all things."[32] Plato, understanding that intuition takes us out of our everyday minds and reveals a higher perspective, called it "divine madness." Even Kant was forced by his intellectual honesty to admit, after saying that we must follow reason, that "imagination" (by which he meant something very close to intuition) is the energy that "drives our being" and that all of our "knowing" arises from this place.

At its best, intuition is *an instantaneous, direct grasping of the pattern of things, of how things fit together, bringing the many pieces of a puzzle into an ordered whole. It provides, in a flash of insight, an answer to a problem or a question, taking all the relevant factors into account.* It is as if the combination to a lock has been dialed, all the tumblers suddenly fall into place, and the mechanism moves. Intuition also arises as creative vision, as Mozart experienced when he saw in his mind's eye, in one instant, a whole work of music that was as yet unwritten. These powerful flashes, whether solving a problem or offering creative insight, bring a deep sense of "knowing," a profound sense that the right answer has been found, the right path has been discovered. The certainty of these moments makes intuition the source of our deepest truths, of our most important realizations. No wonder Kant had to bow to its importance.

Because intuition has been known from the earliest times, the ability to use it has been cultivated through much of history. Aristotle, St. Augustine, Descartes, Bergson, Spinoza, and Whitehead (to name but a few) are western philosophers who acknowledged its importance, with some seeing it as the very fountainhead of wisdom and others, like some spiritual traditions, as a "still small voice" providing insight. Even those who take a sense-based approach to knowledge, such as the staunch empiricist John Stuart Mill, must make room for it: In a statement contrary to his core beliefs (that all knowledge is derived from the senses), Mill admitted, "The truths known by intuition are the original premises from which all others are inferred."[33]

Intuition and Science

In the realm of science, intuition has been the ground from which most of the great breakthroughs have come, such as Descartes's dream-inspired vision for his lifework (which helped launch the scientific revolution) and Einstein's intuitive glimpse of relativity (he is quoted as saying, "The only real valuable thing is intuition"). Another example began with a vision in a streetcar in London and has been called "the most brilliant piece of prediction in the whole history of science"—August Kekule von Stradonitz's theory of molecular structure. Still another is the model of the structure of the atom which came to Niels Bohr in a dream and won for him the Nobel Prize in physics. (These and many other examples are presented in Willis Harmon's book *Higher Creativity*, which is a very good source for exploring science and intuition.)[34] Even Darwin's core idea did not develop over time, but on a day he was relaxed and away from his workplace, "the key elements of evolution fell into place in an instant."[35]

In *Quantum Questions: Mystical Writings of the World's Great Physicists*, American author Ken Wilber highlights the philosophical writings of the founders of modern physics, showing that, as they explored the mystery of the quantum world, they became self-avowed intuitionists and transcendentalists. The reason seems to be that this was the only path left open to them, as they came to see that time and space, the containers through which we experience life, are not hard and fast things, but deep intuitions.

Harvard professor Pitirim A. Sorokin, one of the twentieth century's greatest sociologists, was a life-long explorer of intuition. His studies led him to the conclusion that there are three forms of truth—sensory, rational, and intuitive—and that of these, "there is hardly any doubt that intuition is the source of real knowledge. It is especially indispensable in the apprehension of those aspects of true reality which are inaccessible to the senses and to reason."[36]

For Sorokin, intuition is "the source of true knowing," providing the possibility of knowledge that has an accuracy and appropriateness beyond any other. Intuition gives us a connection to "an awareness that flows through the underlying deep connectivity of things and events." In other words, it yields a glimpse into the underlying pattern of things.

Intuition and Living

All of this leads inexorably to the realization that in making important decisions, the development of intuition is crucial, for it is the only capacity we have that can take into account the whole picture, the whole gestalt of our lives. Because our conscious minds can focus on only a limited number of things at a time, intuition is the only faculty we have that can grasp the complete picture, can "see" how all the parts—unconscious as well as conscious—fit together.

Megan Rauscher gets to the heart of the intuitive process in her article, "Big Decision Time. Best To Sleep on It" in *Science magazine:*

> When faced with a major decision, such as buying a car or a house, it's best to do your homework, and *then forget about it for a while and let your unconscious churn through the options.* [Italics mine.]
> Unconscious deliberation may lead to a more satisfying choice than mere conscious deliberation alone, at least for major decisions.... Conscious deliberation is fine for the less important, more mundane everyday choices like deciding which shampoo or towels to buy, but not for bigger decisions.[37]

The author of the original study, Dr. Ap Dijksterhuis, concludes, "We can think unconsciously and that unconscious thought is actually superior to conscious thought for complex decisions."[38] Thus, in some mysterious way, our unconscious sorts through all the information we have collected about a subject, and at some point an answer or a glimpse of an answer appears. The name we most frequently give to the source of such answers is intuition.

It is important to note as well that this study is focused primarily on practical decisions, like buying a house or car. Imagine how much more, then, the conclusions of this study must apply to issues beyond the material realm—such as love, creative expression, hopes, dreams, and the values and beliefs we will use to guide our lives. For these things, the words of one of America's greatest philosophers, Ralph Waldo Emerson, ring clear: "Meantime, whilst the doors of the temple stand open, night and day, before every man, and the oracles of this truth cease never, it is guarded by one stern condition; this, namely, it is an intuition."[39]

To say this less poetically: *When dealing with the most important issues in life, after considering all the facts as thoroughly as possible, the highest likelihood of a good decision comes if we turn the decision-making process over to the mysterious "black box" of our inner sense of things.* And if Emerson is correct, this is the only door to the deepest knowledge about life and living.

Let's say, for instance, that I am considering something as simple as choosing a hobby. Most of us don't exactly choose a hobby, of course; it just seems to happen in a natural and unplanned way. But let's say I decide to do it in a conscious way. I might read books about various leisure activities, talk to friends about what they enjoy, reflect about what fits my nature.

All this is valuable, but when decision time comes, many questions remain: How important is the excitement I feel about one option as opposed to its monetary cost? How is anxiety to be factored in and what weight given to the negative counsel of a friend? Many questions cannot be answered in an objective way. Thus, after weighing all the options as thoroughly as I can, the best alternative seems to be to let the decision simmer for a time, to turn it over to that mysterious inner process and hope that an "Aha!" will arise—that a "felt sense" of what is best will spring up out of that inexplicable place called intuitive knowing.

Core Principles

Most people raised in countries with representative democracy believe that democracy is good. It seems "reasonable." But this idea did not seem reasonable to most inhabitants of the planet during much of the past. At the beginning of the American experiment in representative government, such an idea was not "reasonable" to most. Returning to the founding words in the Declaration of Independence (quoted in the last chapter): "We hold these truths to be self-evident, that all men are created equal." Thomas Jefferson, who penned these lines, was a child of the Enlightenment and was fiercely committed to the ideal that beliefs should be grounded in human reason. Yet his ultimate justification for the creation of the United States did not rest on reason.

Skeptico: Why do you say that?

Wisdom Seeker: Well, the core justification he gives is that the idea is "self-evident." But self-evident to whom? The British? Most people in the world at that time did not accept the idea he was proposing as "self-evident." Even most of his fellow colonists did not accept it. Further, most human beings in history before he wrote those words did not consider this idea to be self-evident. Jefferson's appeal certainly was not to logic, for asserting that something is self-evident is not a logical proposition. Rather, it seems clear that Jefferson knew that the best starting point for the core principle of the new nation was an appeal to an underlying value. Although this value was not held by most people at the time and could not be proven logically or demonstrated rationally, still, he felt deeply that it was true.

> **Thought Experiment—From What Source Do Basic Principles Arise?**
>
> Consider for a moment: How would you justify the principle of democracy?

If Sorokin is right about the three ways of knowing (sensing, reasoning, and intuiting), then the principle of democracy certainly does not come from sensing, and the rationalist Jefferson did not make a rational argument for it. Rather, Jefferson's appeal was, in essence, to ask everyone to look deeper, to use intuition to experience for themselves that we all have equal rights in some ultimate way in relation to government. Although few people held this view when he wrote, he was asserting that the idea was not simply being made up by the revolutionaries, but that it had an independent existence in some ground of truth, and that everyone who looked deeply enough would discover that truth for themselves. This is the only way I can understand what he meant by "self-evident."

If there is any doubt about this interpretation, the next lines from Jefferson's pen make clear that these "rights" did not come from reason but from a transcendent source, the "Creator." There can thus be little doubt that he is saying that there is a transcendent ground we all share, and that the "rights" of the citizens of the United States are justified there. Further, he is calling on everyone to use their intuition to understand that justification for themselves. In this way, Jefferson joins Emerson in affirming that the door to this knowledge is an intuitive awakening, beyond logical thought.

Another way intuitive knowing plays a central role in governmental functioning involves the US system of justice. Is it logical, based in law? In some ways it is. But at the heart of the system is trial by jury. Even with its flaws, this is a noble concept and an amazingly effective procedure compared with other alternatives. However, many studies have shown that when jurors reach the point of decision, most turn neither to logic nor to the law, but to a "gut sense" of guilt or innocence, to a feeling sense as to what is right and fair. In other words, they turn to intuitive knowing.

One further example: The core organizing principle of representative democracy is voting by the people. But on what basis do citizens make their decisions as to how they will vote? Study after study has shown that, after taking into consideration the facts and arguments, most arrive at a "feeling sense" with regard to the candidate who seems best.[40] They might give arguments to support their position, but the gut decision precedes the argument, rather than the other way around—arguments are marshaled to justify the decision after it has been made. How else can one explain the fact that thoughtful, intelligent people are continually coming to different decisions about whom to support in an election? Committed partisans are always able to give what they think are "rational" arguments as to why they are "right," but this does not persuade equally "rational" adversaries. How could it be otherwise? There is no way to quantify the hundreds of factors at play in an election. For good or ill, elections force us to fall back on our intuition about the candidates.

Problems with Intuition

There are, of course, problems with intuition, a significant one being: How do we know, at any given moment, whether what seems like a deep intuition is what it seems, as opposed to a desire or prejudice masquerading as an intuition? For example, in politics, how do we know when our intuition about a candidate is correct? Many politicians are masters of charade (as history has demonstrated countless times), so how do we know whether our sense of knowing has been hijacked by the charade? Concerning life issues, how do we know for certain if a decision has arisen from a true knowing versus a fear or fantasy?

Most of us have had the experience of thinking we had a clear "knowing" about something, only to discover later—to our chagrin—that things were not as we envisioned. The reason? It seems that in addition to our intuition, we have a strong tendency to rationalize the positions we want to take for very self-centered reasons. Then, if they prove to be in error, it is hard to admit this to others, sometimes even harder to admit it to ourselves. Centuries ago, Sir Francis Bacon observed this dilemma clearly:

The human understanding when it has once adopted an opinion… draws all things else to support and agree with it. And though there be a greater number and weight of instances to be found on the other side, yet these it either neglects and despises, or else by some distinction sets aside and rejects; in order that by this great and pernicious predetermination the authority of its former conclusions may remain inviolate.[41]

How then do we discern when we are lost in our prejudices, yet stubbornly calling them intuitions?

> **Thought Experiment—Discerning the Difference**
>
> How does one tell the difference between a true intuition and a whim, between a true knowing and a rationalization of a prejudice? In your own life, when an answer or a sense of direction arises, how do you know when to follow it versus when to question it further?

For me, the only answer is: This is difficult territory, requiring a lifetime's work. In doing this work, there are four different situations:

1. **Clear knowing:** I have had experiences that correspond closely to the profound knowing states described by Thoreau, Plato, Rousseau, Sorokin, William James, and so many others, states characterized by a clarity and sense of certainty that is unmistakable. This is what Thoreau meant by our "genius," and a few times this knowing has been so strong in me that there was no doubt about its validity. These insights have almost always proven true. However, for me such moments of clarity and conviction are rare.
2. **Clear knowing with resistance:** In a second category are moments when I have a sense of knowing, but some part of me does not like what I am hearing. (Sometimes a gut instinct can be "gut-wrenching.")

These moments seem to be times when my ego doesn't like what my deeper intuition is saying—my ego self would prefer a different conclusion, so it strongly resists the intuition. In these cases, in retrospect, my intuition was usually right, whether I followed its guidance or not. (As I get older, I make a greater effort to follow such guidance even if my ego self is not very happy about it.)

3. **Not knowing:** A third category concerns times when I feel no sense of "knowing," or, if such a feeling is present, the clarity and conviction are weak. At these times, it is usually best to wait for a clear conviction, to take time to walk in the mountains, meditate, talk to a friend, pray, take a trip, sing—things that have helped bring clarity in the past. (Always remembering, though, that the muse cannot be compelled.)

But sometimes waiting is not possible: Someone is in trouble right now; do I help or continue on with my own plans? Do I speak out on an issue that is being decided today, although speaking out will alienate friends and jeopardize my position in the community? Do I accept an invitation to speak, or meet, or let it pass? A job has been offered, and the deadline is today; should I take it? Do I begin a relationship with a person I just met or let that person pass on through and out of my life? In such moments, to wait is to freeze the flow of life. Much of life is to act, and refusal to act is itself a dramatic action. Normal human life is movement, and to break the flow can result in paralysis, where we find ourselves becalmed in brackish eddies.

Having spent much time in these waters, I have come to see that it is like being a riverboat pilot. (Mark Twain imprinted this image in my imagination many years ago.) A pilot begins to learn the "feel" of moving with the river, as shoals shift and new sandbars arise and dissipate overnight. The way forward is to trust the "feel," being careful, of course, but moving forward with confidence when the intuitive feel is right.

This is the best way I have found to move through uncertain terrain. As I do so, intuitions sometimes arise, and sometimes they do not, but the river of life keeps flowing. When I feel lost, I try to remember three things: (a) Perfection is not possible (so I cannot wait for the perfect answer); (b) inaction is a decision, and as dangerous as action; and (c) pausing to take a sounding, at least occasionally, is crucial. (Sometimes, in these moments of waiting, I bring to mind past experiences of intuitive knowing, which often helps me find the clear channel again—and to trust its whisperings when they arise.)

4. **Knowing that misleads:** A fourth category concerns moments in which I have a sense of "knowing" and follow it, only to discover that things are not working out. What went wrong? If I am really honest with myself, I can usually tell—in retrospect—that what I took for intuition was an aspect of myself wanting gratification or achievement or pleasure, a momentary emotion or desire carrying me along on a path that did not fit with the overall flow of my life. Looking back, I can see that I fooled myself, or a particular whim or desire "tricked me"—using my trust in intuition to get what it wanted. (Comedian Flip Wilson used to justify his questionable actions with "The devil made me do it.")

So, to return to this crucial question: How do we know when an inner voice is a deep knowing, the true whisper of intuition, versus a desire in masquerade, the devil in disguise? Long ago, the First Epistle of John warned: "Beloved, believe not every spirit, but try the spirits whether they are of God."[42] (A novel by James Hogg, *The Private Memoirs and Confessions of a Justified Sinner* published in 1824—long before Freud—develops this theme with amazing psychological insight; a man is being led down a path by the counsel of a "friend," advice that part of him wants to believe. Too late he discovers the real source of the advice and the disaster it brings to his life.)

A personal example: A strong sense arises that I need to tell someone "the truth" about something they have done. I tell them, a little righteously, what I think is wrong. At first I feel good, relieved, but gradually there comes the chilling sense that I was not following a deep intuition at all, but rather an urge to be "right," or maybe a wish to wound them for something I felt they had done. With enough such experiences, I begin to see that many of my urges and perceptions have arisen from a murkier place than intuition. Yet the feeling to act from this murky place has often been strong and seemed totally right in the moment.

This fourth category is the hardest to deal with, for when I think I know the right path, why would I pause and reflect? How do I find the patience to question my sense of knowing, and how do I discern when to wait rather than act?

There are no easy answers here. Painful honesty with myself helps, through which I gradually develop the ability—by trial and error, mistake after mistake—to distinguish the difference between a true knowing and a misleading one. (A Zen master was asked, "How did you become enlightened?" His reply: "One mistake at a time.") Perhaps a lot of mistakes, and a persistent reflection on those mistakes, is the only way to develop discrimination and self-knowledge—to finally develop wisdom. Perhaps recognizing and making peace with one's mistakes is the only path to self-acceptance and even to compassion—for oneself, as well as others. If we come to know ourselves well enough through this process, perhaps we will begin to catch the small clues that distinguish shallow whims and unfruitful fantasies from true knowing. If we can remember that intuitions are not always as they seem, then careful, honest attention will help us navigate these treacherous waters skillfully, like an experienced riverboat pilot.

Reason's Return

Kurt Gödel, mathematician extraordinaire and one the great logicians of all time, suggested that there is a realm of mathematical law that can be accessed only by a combination of intuition and reason.[43] Thus we come full circle, back to the importance of reason, but now as a partner to intuition. Not reason in the narrow sense, but reason in its role of consciously considering everything from the broadest perspective, of weighing all the factors as carefully and fully as possible. Those who use broad definitions of either reason or intuition will often include the other in their understanding. Many of the definitions of reason given earlier include intuition within reason's purview, and those who focus more on the intuitive side characterize reason as the fact-gathering and organizing aspects of intuition.

However you wish to approach them, the important point is that both reason and intuition are used to suggest things that go on in the human psyche that we do not understand. We certainly do not know how to separate them as they function (can you find your intuition switch or your reason switch; do you know how to turn either on or off?) Yet we are prone to put labels on them, as if it is possible to draw sharp lines between them. Ultimately, perhaps they are not separate at all but part of one process. However, for me there is a difference in feel and flavor for what each word suggests, so I do find it helpful to think of them as separate—but complementary.

Thinking about them separately for a moment, then, the first thing I notice is that it is easy to see them as complementary. Reason lends itself to an organized effort, a process of working toward an answer or a decision. On the other side, the very nature of intuition usually involves a sudden flash, and its source is quite mysterious. We do not even know the perspective from which intuition speaks, the point of view that it serves.

Does it serve a particular desire, helping a person fulfill that desire (I want more money); or does it serve a broader personal goal (a full and rich life); or does it lead to fulfilling the needs of those with whom we are close (to sacrifice our own goals for friends and family); or does it spur us to serve the broader communal good (risking life and limb for the tribe or nation); or does it call us to a higher cause beyond even the community (service to humanity or spiritual realization)? Does intuition take into account the dangers of life, or does it serve some purpose in which one's physical comfort, or even survival, is of little concern?

> **Thought Experiment—Intuition's Perspective**
>
> If an intuition arises in you, do you always follow it? Should you? Many people through the ages have followed an inner sense that led to great sacrifice—for another, for others, or for something they believed in. Would you follow it there? Should you?

This question of *perspective* brings us back to the importance of reason. We are not sentenced to follow our intuition. We have a choice as to the perspective we will follow, and I cannot find a way to definitively discern the perspective from which intuition speaks. (Too many times I have deluded myself into thinking I knew, only to reap unpleasant consequences.) This frequent lack of certainty provides a powerful motivation to include reason in my decision-making process. After the intuitive flash, it is valuable to consider everything from the broadest conscious perspective, which is, in a way, the essence of being human. In this process, reason brings to the table a consideration of values, of others, of life plans, and of one's relationship to culture and community. Intuition might honor these things, but we cannot know this for sure, for we do not know the ultimate goal of our intuitions.

The Dance of Reason and Intuition

Kant was trying to get at the relationship between intuition and reason in *The Critique of Pure Reason* when he said: "Thoughts without content are empty; intuitions without concepts, blind." I think he meant that the original material for our thinking must come from intuition; it is in that fuzzy terrain that everything begins. Something must focus our thoughts in a particular direction and provide the original content, and thinking itself cannot do this. At the same time, intuitions must be processed by thinking if they are to be of value, for content comes forth all the time that will confuse and mislead until we think through the consequences and use our reason to relate the raw material of our intuitions to a coherent life.

One way I have tried to understand the interaction between the two is by carefully examining my own decision-making process. Beginning with a question, I notice that many thoughts and feelings at first parade through my mind with a certain amount of randomness; thoughts frequently jump from one topic to another. Furthermore, all these cascading images and feelings are mostly beyond my conscious control. If I begin to concentrate on the question, however, if I begin to focus more intently, the process settles down, does not feel quite so random. Although "I" cannot completely control it, this conscious "I" learns to participate in the process. It can decide to focus on a topic, and this decision makes it more likely that the process will stay focused. Then, if I exercise the discipline to return over and over to the problem, I am more likely to have an intuitive flash concerning it.

In this process, there is some mysterious way that reason interacts with intuition in my consciousness. As I stay with a topic, patterns emerge, and currents begin to cohere into functional harmonies. Some of these patterns persist over time and become integral to who I am. This process is not subject to my conscious control, yet it is not separate from conscious input, either. In the best case, it is a dance, with the partners moving in harmony, one taking the lead for a moment, and then the other, neither knowing when the last transition occurred nor when the lead will shift again. This is the dance of reason and intuition as it moves and guides my inner being.

Thus for me, the ultimate human act is to listen to my intuition as best I can and then to engage my reason in making a conscious choice as to who I will be and how my life will be lived, from the wisest "feeling sense" I can find. Is this reason or intuition? It is both working together—intuition acting as a flash of insight and reason providing a conscious process to bring the insight into relation to the other currents of my life.

But this chapter is on intuition, so let me close with a paean to the beauty and importance of this marvelous faculty. In many ways, Friedrich Nietzsche ushered in the modern philosophical era (which is less favorable to intuition than most) with his critique of the "weak-minded" spiritual systems that held sway before his time. Yet even this apostle of the end of transcendence, this bringer of the materialist age, waxed eloquent in his famous work, *Ecce Homo*, glorifying the realm of knowing I am calling intuition (and he, inspiration):

> One hears, one does not seek; one takes, one does not ask who it is that gives; a thought flashes up like lightning, with necessity, unfalteringly formed....
> It is a rapture, the enormous excitement of which sometimes finds relief in a storm of tears; a state of being entirely outside oneself with the clearest consciousness of fine shivering and a rustling through one's being right down to the tips of one's toes; a depth of joy in which all that is most painful and gloomy does not act as a contrast but as a condition for it, as though demanded, as a necessary colour in such a flood of light....
> Everything is in the highest degree involuntary but takes place as in a tempest of a feeling of freedom, of absoluteness, of power, of divinity.[m] [44]

If there is even a small chance that what Nietzsche describes here is true—that each of us can touch, for an instant, a clear state of knowing (which many wise teachers throughout history have suggested and urged us to discover for ourselves), then the potential reward is great. If it is possible, this becomes one of the crucial tasks of life: to access this "freedom," this "power," this connection to "divinity" for ourselves. To do so, however, it is essential to develop a better understanding of the nature of the reality in which we live. Let us turn, then, to the question: What is reality?

---

[m] I should emphasize once more the necessity of discernment between deep intuitions and the promptings of less profound urges and desires, for it was Nietzsche's failure to make this distinction that led to the misuse of his ideas in terrible ways (i.e., by the Nazis). Still, the above words capture the sheer beauty and wonder of deep intuition as well as any I know. (How would his legacy, as well as his own life, been different, if he could have understood this distinction more clearly?)

CHAPTER 8

WHAT IS REALITY?

I have been fortunate to travel the world, visiting cultures quite different from my own. In each new place, I discovered things that seemed natural enough there that I knew would be considered crazy back home.

It seemed at first normal to judge things by my reality, the one all my friends thought was right. But gradually came the view that the number of those who differed was quite large and our number, when compared to the whole, quite small.

I looked for support to the great figures of history but found that each had some beliefs that differed drastically from my own. Perplexed, I turned to the most solid citizens I knew, but found radical disagreements there, too: Fine scientists had extreme political views (at least they seemed extreme to me), and teachers I respected had wild notions of economics and sex.

Then I began to notice that even among my friends, there was a variety of views, and those who seemed to have valid answers in one realm would be clueless in the next (for instance, great at business but making a total mess of their emotional lives).

So what was I to do: Double down on my claims, circle the wagons with a dwindling core of believers who supported my views? Or could it be that every take on reality is but a glimpse, an attempt to organize the world in a manageable way, always incomplete? What if every view is partial, no matter the conviction of those who claim it to be true?

Panic! What is real? How do I know what is true?

But then, a sense of relief as a way forward appears: Admit that you do not know all (perhaps no one does), so seek to accommodate and integrate everything that is real. By this means, the more you will grow and gradually move from that which is partial toward what is whole.

Questioning "Reality"

It has been reported that monks in Tibet, sitting in cold caves in deep meditation, can rapidly dry wet blankets wrapped around their bodies; that in Sri Lanka ordinary folks in deep trance can walk on red-hot coals without injury; that yogis in India can go without air for thirty minutes; and numerous accounts from all over the world report that prayer has healed the sick. Do you believe all these things have happened? If not, why not? If so, why?

Unless you have gone to Tibet or India or Sri Lanka to study these phenomena or have studied the effects of prayer on illness, you cannot know whether these things have occurred—or whether they are occurring now. Therefore, if you disbelieve them, why are you choosing to do so? In disbelieving, you are not being scientific, nor rational. To be scientific about them, you would study these phenomena with an open mind. After much study, you might form a tentative hypothesis about the truth or falsity of a particular report, but this hypothesis would remain open to new data. Being scientific, you would not make a generalized act of faith that all such reports were true or untrue.

To be rational about such things, you would withhold judgment until you needed to make a specific decision. As a rational being, why would you need to make an abstract decision about whether unusual events were possible or not? If you needed to make a specific decision about a specific course of action in your own life, you would take into account everything you knew up to the moment of decision and then make the best choice possible.

Being rational, you would act or not act in a specific way in a specific circumstance based on your best judgment—but you would not need to "believe" one way or the other in a generalized way about the ultimate truth or falsity of *all* such phenomena. At the other end of the spectrum, if you have not investigated or experienced these things yourself, and yet believe that they have occurred, why do you make that choice?

We humans seem to have a tendency to make broad generalizations of belief or disbelief concerning things we know little about. This tendency starts with enculturation: When children come into the world, it is always within a specific cultural system. These systems provide invaluable guidance about how to navigate the activities of daily life within a particular culture: what to eat, how to protect oneself, how to get along with others, and much more. This set of "givens" is a *consensual reality*. Without such answer systems, every child would have to create a complete reality for itself—an impossible task. However, being enculturated into a consensual reality also involves being indoctrinated into rules about "the right way to do things," as well as about what is "wrong." Further, it includes strong assertions about how to see and understand the world, about what exists and what does not exist.

As we go out into life, we think we know, based on our consensual reality, what "reality" is. But what we know is not "reality," just what we see from within our particular conditioned framework. For this reason, it is often a shock to discover that other cultures believe—and even see—quite different things from what we believe and see. It is not surprising, then, that when we encounter radically different views, most of us have a tendency to dismiss or denigrate the views of "the other" without investigating the evidence; we simply jump to disbelief about things that do not fit our enculturated view.

> **Thought Experiment—Travel the World in Your Mind**
>
> To get a sense of how we tend to see the world through an enculturated lens, imagine for a moment how different the world would look if you had grown up in a rural village in China or as a member of a remote tribe in New Guinea or in a family of devout Hindus in India. In your mind's eye, put yourself in each of these situations for a moment. What would you believe about how to live, about what was possible and impossible? What would you believe about "reality?"

Although we in the modern world have been conditioned to see what we see just like everyone else, there is a tendency to believe that, to a great extent, we have personally developed our own point of view—without noticing that to think we have done this is an enculturated belief in itself. Looking carefully at my own experience, I see how much my worldview derives from the people with whom I grew up, as well as the people, books, movies, magazines, and Internet sites I have spent time with through the years.

The wide range of beliefs in modern cultures does provide the opportunity for a certain degree of choice, but there is a deep urge in the very fabric of our being to find support for whatever beliefs we already hold. Thus, when one of us, through choice or necessity, leaves our birth culture, we almost always join another consensual reality or create a new belief community with like-minded souls. Then, once in the new consensual reality, we tend to become as rigid with regard to its beliefs as we were with the old. (Not everyone does this, of course, but it is a strong tendency that only active work can overcome.)

Because of this tendency, most of us do not give much credence to the views of people with whom we disagree or those who see the world differently from our group. On the contrary, we look for people who agree with us and tend to listen to them and spend time in their company, to look for and hang out with those who reinforce our worldview, those who confirm for us what we already believe.

One consequence of this tendency is that most of the feedback we get from others for what is "real" comes from those who have been enculturated in the same way as have we have; thus most gang members check with fellow gang members; liberals check with others of a similar belief, as do conservatives; scientists check with other scientists or those who share their assumptions; Tibetan lamas check with other lamas; and so on. How, then, do we know that the reinforcement we are receiving from others is anything other than the ongoing enculturation process of our "tribe"? (Maybe the comedian Lily Tomlin got it about right: "I refuse to be intimidated by reality anymore. What is reality? Nothing but a collective hunch.")[45]

Having a consensual reality is not a bad thing; in fact, it is quite necessary. When growing up, we need established patterns within which to function—answers to questions about how to act, how to live, what is important. As adults, we need to know the rules of the culture in which we live, even if—especially if—we decide to break those rules. (One definition of insanity is being oblivious to the rules of the society in which one lives.) One aspect of wisdom, however, is to understand not only the value and necessity of a consensual reality, but its limitations as well.

Who Will You Believe?

With so many cultures in the world, does any one of them have an objective claim on "reality?" It can be clearly demonstrated that some cultures are better at certain things than others, and we can, to a certain extent, study the strengths and weaknesses of each. However, any such study will be organized from a cultural perspective, and most of us begin with the view that "our" consensual reality is the most accurate, the most true. (Or we have become disgusted with our own and tend to glamorize another.) Either way, anyone starting such a study starts with a bias in place.

As discussed in Chapter 5, cultures tend to indoctrinate their members into a sense of their own superiority. But objectively speaking, because we each look through our enculturated eyes, which of us has a standpoint from which to judge another? Would a lifelong soccer aficionado be the person to ask if soccer is a better sport than basketball? Does it even make sense to ask whether one sport is better than another? Perhaps it is valuable to consider what each sport has to offer its participants, but in an overall way, "better" is probably not a useful question. The same is true of cultures, yet we have a strong urge to judge, probably because we are hungry for reinforcement that our way of living is "the best," that we have found "the right way" to live.

This makes it especially important to recognize that how we perceive the world is highly malleable. An experiment done with two groups of kittens, each placed in a controlled environment before their eyes were open, will illustrate the point. One of the environments was a horizontal world made up of horizontal lines and shapes; the other was a vertical world, with vertical shapes and lines and minimal horizontal ones. After being raised in these separate worlds (with nothing to focus on during a critical window for perceptual development except either vertical or horizontal realities), the kittens were then put in a "normal" environment. In that world, to an extraordinary degree, it was discovered that past experience determined perception: The "horizontal world" cats could not see vertical shapes—they would literally bump into them. And the cats from the "vertical world" did not perceive horizontal shapes and lines, could not function effectively in relation to them.[46]

Hypnosis is another fertile field providing fascinating hints as to what is "real." In one experiment, hypnotized subjects were told that they would be taken into a room where they would see two boxes on a table. Once in the room, the hypnotized subjects did, *in fact*, see two boxes. The startling aspect is that those conducting the experiment had placed *three* boxes on the table. Thus, the people conducting the experiment continued to see three boxes, while those under hypnotic suggestion saw only two.[47]

Our early conditioning as children parallels this experiment—we are conditioned to see the world the way the people around us see it, our minds being molded and shaped to participate in the shared reality. So we see "two boxes" in the world, like everybody around us, because we have been conditioned to see two boxes, whatever the "reality" might be. Because our perception is shaped in this way, how do we get outside the conditioning to see what is "really real"?

Another fascinating experiment: Subjects were given the hypnotic suggestion that they would open a door during their normal day when they heard a specific trigger word. The people conducting the experiment then interacted with the subjects in their daily lives, casually saying the trigger word in conversation. The responsive subjects invariably followed through with the hypnotic suggestion, opening a door repeatedly with each new mention of the trigger word—even though the action was completely out of place in most situations they were in. Up to this point, the experiment is a fairly straightforward example of the power of hypnosis.

But there is more, much more: When the subjects were asked *why* they kept opening the door, they gave "rational" explanations for their actions, at least explanations that **sounded rational to them!** That is, their thinking minds came up with the most reasonable-sounding explanations they could latch onto when asked for an explanation for their behavior. However, these explanations were not based in reality but were fictions created to make what they had done seem rational to the questioner, as well as to themselves. Not being conscious of the real reason (the hypnotic suggestion), they couldn't give that explanation, so their minds "created" a justification on the spur of the moment. And crucially, the subjects believed their explanations, thought they were rational: their explanations made sense to them. Of course they did: their own minds had created them. They just weren't based in a shared reality.[48]

This experiment seems amusing until one has the courage to ask: How much do I operate in this way every day, giving the people with whom I interact—and myself—the best "rational" explanations I can think of to explain my actions, whilst in the background lie other motives, hidden behind veils of enculturated belief, or perhaps even guided by my fears, ambitions, and expectations?

What's Really Out There?

When you look out at the world and "see" a tree, you think that the tree is "out there." But is it? Charles Darwin reported in his diaries that when the *Beagle* sailed into a harbor in Patagonia, the natives on the shore **could not see the ship.** Their past experiences did not include sailing ships, so their minds could not take in this new phenomenon. Fortunately, the local shaman was less culturally bound and could "see" things outside of his enculturation. With his help, over several days, the rest of the natives were gradually able to "see" the *Beagle*.

A more prosaic example: If a fly is sitting on your forehead, looking in the same direction you are looking, will it see the same thing you see? Because a fly's perceptual system is quite different from yours, whatever the fly is seeing will be very different. Which image, then, captures what is really "out there"? Surely the answer is "Neither." Each image is created by the perceptual system of the viewer.

The Magician in the Brain—Turning neural stimuli into thoughts

When I "see" a tree, what am I "seeing"? An image in **my mind.** Where does that image come from? Perhaps it starts with stimuli from the world, but it is built of images and expectations already present in my mind. In my early years, an image was created that I now associate with "tree" through many instances of someone pointing to an object and saying, "Tree" or pointing to a picture and saying, "Tree." Gradually, an image formed. But what if, through those early years, everyone had pointed to the same objects and said, "Those are the spirits of your ancestors"? Or what if I had lived in a desert without trees and had never been shown a picture of a tree? Or what if, through the eons, my ancestors had focused only on the forest in the distance, and through my early years they had continually directed my attention to the forest at the far horizon without mentioning individual trees? What, then, would I see? (Would I be unable to see the trees for the forest?)

Stepping back another level, one can even question whether real things are "out there" to which we are responding, for what I perceive as "out there" might be nothing more than imaginings in my mind. Dreams are like that, yet they seem real enough, while in the dream. This is problematic, for if this can happen in a dream-state, without any stimuli from outside, how do I know that what I perceive as "out there," right now, is not being created in the same way? Well, I can check it out with other people. However, I can do this in a dream as well and get perfect confirmation in the dream that others are experiencing the same thing as am I.

But let's not get stuck in this ages-old philosophical quandary as to whether everything is a dream or perhaps an illusion of the mind. Assume that problem away by adopting with me for a moment the position that light rays are really striking something "out there," bouncing off something that really exists, which then sets in motion neural impulses that travel along optic nerves to the brain. Assume further that in the brain, these neural impulses cause an excitation, which is not so hard to imagine. But here we are stuck. How, at this point, do neural impulses that in no way resemble a tree become the thought, "Tree?" This is quite a magical leap, and for which no one has been able to supply a very good explanation.

There is little doubt that when neural impulses arrive in the brain, physiological changes occur there. We can measure these physical changes, detecting various physical things like heat and motion, but this does not give us a clue as how this physical activity makes the leap to becoming a conscious thought. Here is the "big question" in consciousness research, for no one knows how this happens. After all the time and money spent on brain research, there are not even any widely accepted theories as to how this happens. As British philosopher, mathematician, and astronomer A. S. Eddington put it, a neural impulse and a conscious thought resemble each other about as much as a telephone number resembles the owner of a telephone. He goes on to say that something "plays on the extremity of a nerve, starting a series of physical and chemical changes that are propagated along the nerve of a brain-cell; there a mystery happens, and an image or sensation arises in the mind which cannot purport to resemble the stimulus which excited it."[49]

In other words, what you perceive as a tree "out there" arises from neural impulses that bear no resemblance to the thought being generated. Neuroscience cannot distinguish a neural impulse that becomes "tree" from one that becomes "frog." The leap from neural impulse to thought is a truly great mystery and calls into question any fixed view of "reality."[n]

I emphasize this mystery because, in spite of much progress in brain research, the leap from neural impulse to conscious thought continues to defy all our efforts of understanding, although it happens thousands of times a day in every one of the billions of inhabitants of our globe. Not only this, but we do not even understand where in the brain a thought is created.

To grasp the full force of this, imagine that the greatest scientists, neurosurgeons, neurologists, and researchers in the world come together for the sole purpose of constructing a human brain. Imagine further that science has progressed to the point that every physical component in the human brain is available to them. The group works on this task for months, putting all the physical components of a brain together exactly as it has come to be understood during hundreds of years of research. Finally, the work is done, and neuronal signals are sent through the constructed brain, just as happens in a living human being. The signals fire

---

[n] A few studies have been conducted suggesting that once an image or word has been formed in the mind, it might be possible to "read" it through brain scans without the person in whose mind it exists communicating in any way. I am not aware of any studies, however, that suggest how a neural impulse becomes an image or a word, or any means of determining what word or image a neural impulse will become, out of millions of possibilities, until that mysterious transformation has been accomplished by human consciousness.

and buzz, but what now? Do any of the scientists or researchers have any idea how to turn those neuronal signals into a thought? Where in this brain would they locate the mechanism to do this? What would it look like? No one has a clue. Even more complicated, where and how would they store memories? All this is simply unknown.

The Judge in the Mind—What to let in

One way to think about this gap is the difference between the brain and the mind. The brain is the physical thing, but the mind is where thoughts are somehow created and stored. Neuroscience knows a lot about the brain but surprisingly little about the mind, mostly because the focus of research has been on the physical instrument, with the hope that all questions could be answered in that domain. It becomes less likely every day that this will be the case.

Exploring the difference between brain and mind, Dr. William Tiller, retired professor and department chairman of Materials Science and Engineering at Stanford University, points out that "we perceive with our eyes only a very small band of the entire electromagnetic spectrum. We also sense only a very small band of the auditory spectrum. It cannot be a stretch to realize that we perceive only a very small band of our entire 'reality.'"[50]

Thus, we start with being able to perceive only a very limited amount of the available information. Next, at any given moment, thousands of sights, sounds, smells, tastes, and sensations are available to the senses, but only a small percentage of those ever become relevant to the mind. How does the mind make all the decisions it has to make as to what will be considered significant? It is certainly not a conscious process: We are not aware that these decisions are being made. Further, to do it consciously would be impossible, requiring millions of decisions every day. But this unconscious process, this sorting of relevant and irrelevant, dramatically determines our experience of life.

Aristotle believed that the "eye" went out to find the images it deemed relevant. There may be some truth to this, for as mentioned earlier, conditioning significantly determines what we see: Two people from totally different cultures will take in quite different information when placed in the same environment. In the woods, one might see the track of a deer, while another focuses on the danger of mosquitoes. Viewing a serene landscape, one might become absorbed in the beauty, while another contemplates the financial opportunity.

The broad culture in which we have been raised is one significant factor with regard to what we will take in, but great differences also occur between two people from the same culture with different early experiences. For instance, someone who grew up in a dangerous neighborhood with dangerous parents would register different data than someone who grew up in a safe home and community. In a room full of people, one might notice the loving gesture, another the hostile look. Or to consider another example, someone who is brave will see a different pattern from one who is fearful. But whatever one is registering, it is only a small part of the data available, and others are organizing around different information. Because this is happening mostly at the unconscious level, our world is therefore given to us by means we do not understand.

For example, remember a time you were deep in thought—absorbed in a book or a math problem—and someone tapped you on the shoulder, saying, "Why didn't you answer when I called you?" You realize that you were so absorbed in what you were doing that you didn't hear them, even though *the sound waves from the voice must have hit your ears a few moments ago in the same way they hit your ears after the tap on the shoulder*. Before the tap, though, you did not register the sound waves in your consciousness. How did it happen that sound waves of significant volume did not make it to your consciousness? How was the decision made to exclude those sound waves from awareness?

Or consider the oft-reported phenomenon of a mother hearing the soft cry of her child several rooms away in spite of the loud din of a party. No one else hears the cry, yet the mother does. How do those sound waves make it to her awareness, but not to someone else's, even those closer to the child?

These examples can be seen as confirming Aristotle's view that our minds go out in search of the information we want, but one last example is especially confirming: Many nerve fibers run between the sense organs and the brain. However, neuroscientists have discovered that for every nerve that carries information *to* the brain, there are as many others carrying messages *from* the brain toward the sense organs! Why do they run in that direction? The best current explanation is that the whole human system is sending signals out to the senses, giving instructions as to what to let in. But since this is happening at the unconscious level, a process outside the conscious mind is determining what we will register in awareness.

The Wizard of Oz—Organizing meaningful patterns

The final step in "seeing" the world is that the limited amount of data (limited in relation to all that is available) that reaches the mind must be organized into meaningful patterns. William James called the raw data available from the world a "blooming, buzzing confusion." He was following the thought of Immanuel Kant, who said it was a "rhapsody of sensation." Kant went on to argue that this cacophony **does not** give us the world we experience and that to make sense of the sensations, we must use concepts already in the mind to organize that data into meaningful patterns—into thoughts, ideas, and images. Crucially, these concepts are not "out there" in the world, but inside of us—in our minds.

> **Thought Experiment—Where Do Organizing Concepts Come From?**
>
> Can you remember consciously creating a conceptual framework, then putting it into your mind to organize the data of your experience? If not, how did this happen, and are you sure you agree with all the organizing concepts that somehow, unconsciously, appeared in your mind?

I have actually considered this at some length, and I can remember consciously working to *change* a conceptual framework, to change the lens through which I was trying to make sense of the information coming in—but I was always working with a framework already in place, prior to my awareness of it. For example, the lens I was given with which to see other cultures had a strong bias toward seeing them as inferior to my own. Gradually I began to notice that much of what was making its way into my awareness as I traveled to foreign lands was information that confirmed that assumption. With this realization, I began to actively attempt a more balanced view, but at first it was not easy—the conditioning was subtle and strong. Slowly, however, my conceptual framework for seeing other cultures changed— but bringing about the change required much effort.

To put all this succinctly, reality does not arise from outside and strike an unbiased eye. We are conditioned from birth to organize the information that comes to us in a particular way. Our minds are geared to fit new information into patterns that we expect. A dramatic example: Several studies were conducted at Innsbruck University in Austria in which subjects were asked to wear special glasses that had the effect of making the world appear upside down—anyone wearing the glasses saw an inverted world. The volunteers were asked to wear these glasses every waking moment for several weeks. At first, as you might expect, the experience was disorienting and caused lots of problems in doing even the most basic things. But then an amazing thing happened: After the glasses had been worn for a few days, **the world no longer appeared upside down!**[51]

How could this be? The glasses were still inverting the world! The explanation seems to be that the mind *wanted* to see the world the way it had been trained to see it, so it adjusted the images coming in to fit what was expected—it organized the information into patterns it had been conditioned to see rather than how the information arrived in the brain. But if our minds can do this on their own, without a conscious choice, how do we know what is really out there? Further, if the mind does this with physical reality, isn't it more likely to be doing the same with regard to information concerning subjective feelings, values, and beliefs? What, then, is "reality?"

Evaluating the Extraordinary

Given all these difficulties with knowing what is real, what if you would like to determine once and for all whether Tibetans in deep meditation could actually dry wet blankets with their bodies? To pursue a scientific answer, you would go to Tibet and investigate. You would interview those who had seen it as well as those who claimed to have accomplished the feat, and you would begin to draw tentative conclusions. But no matter the number of positive reports, you still could not be sure; it might simply be a story everyone there had been enculturated to believe.

Being persistent, the next step would be to find someone who said they could do this amazing thing and set up a scientific experiment with that person using the strictest objective standards. Consider, though: If you conducted such an experiment, and the person failed, what would this mean? Only that this one person did not succeed in this one instance, nothing more. Maybe your subject was an imposter, whereas the real adepts never demonstrated the ability to outsiders. Perhaps your subject was just having a bad day. This is the sticky wicket that is too often overlooked in attempts to disprove extraordinary phenomena: If a test fails, no broader conclusion can be drawn other than that one experiment failed.

Good analogies come from science. When scientists are trying to discover something new, test after test might fail; it might be years before one positive result is achieved, but it is that one success that is important, not all the failures that came before. When medical researchers are trying to find a drug to help with an ailment, they might try many that fail before one finally works. Or when physicists were trying to demonstrate that an atom could be split, many attempts were made, and each failed. That did not prove that an atom could not be divided (although some argued for this point of view), but it only proved that the attempts to that point had not been successful. But they kept trying, and after many years and many attempts, the atom's integrity was breached.

The crucial point: If you are trying to prove scientifically that something is possible, you might have to push through hundreds or even thousands of failed experiments before one comes along to provide confirmation. And conversely, if you are trying to prove that something *cannot* happen, you must refute every single instance of its occurrence, as well as prove conclusively that it can never, ever happen in the future (and proof is ***not*** simply a theory that the occurrence is impossible).

Thus, to know for sure that something considered "impossible" is really impossible, every single claim made for its occurrence would have to be evaluated. Even after this, there would remain the problem that all evaluations are conducted from within a belief system, all perceptions occur within a framework, so you cannot be sure that the belief "glasses" through which you look are not making what you see fit your prior beliefs. In other words, how could you be sure you were not in the same situation as the natives who were unable to see Darwin's ship? If you started with a belief that something was impossible, perhaps your mind, prior to consciousness, organized the data to create the reality you wanted to see, rather than what was really there.

In my view, many claims about extraordinary occurrences arise out of wishful thinking, exaggeration, trickery, and delusion. But the sheer volume of smoke suggests that, in some areas, there might well be fire in there somewhere. It is useful to try to sort out false claims, provided that one maintains the recognition that disproving individual claims does not lead to sweeping assumptions about what is possible or impossible. As William James so elegantly put it, if you want to prove that all crows are black, it is not enough to show that many crows are black; what you must show is that there is not one white crow anywhere, has never been, anytime, anywhere, or your proof fails.

What if an experiment concerning an extraordinary phenomenon succeeds? You are faced with a different problem, but a problem nonetheless. Seeing what looks to be proof for something extraordinary, there is the danger that it was a trick or that the performer, the crowd, or the circumstances hypnotized you. Perhaps the result grows out of your wish to believe. Of course, this problem extends to all "proofs" about reality, including science. Many theories at one time accepted as having been demonstrated by the scientific method have turned out to be false, either because of fakery, mistaken assumptions, or overzealous researchers accepting proofs because of a wish to believe.

One especially interesting example: Experiments conducted in classical physics under the assumption that light is wave-like "proved" that to be so. This conclusion seemed settled until it was discovered, as quantum mechanics developed further, that if you set up an experiment under the assumption that light behaves as if it were made up of particles, the "evidence" switches sides and confirms the new assumption. So which is it: wave or particle? Well, apparently the answer is either/or, depending on how the experiment is conducted. And it is not merely an issue of light having the properties of both. In later experiments, set up to force light to behave as one or the other, it was determined that light could be either, depending on whether it was being observed. Going a step further, Anton Zeilinger of the University of Vienna set up an experiment in which someone would decide whether or not to place a beam splitter in the path of a narrow beam of light. That decision seemed to determine which form the light would take and most amazingly, the light seemed to take on the appropriate form **before** it reached the place the beam splitter was, or wasn't—a dramatic example of the observer effect.

A similar experiment has been conducted many times with electrons, and the repeated conclusion is that electrons act as if they are particles in a definite location when observed but seem to be waves when they are not being observed. All this has led to several staggering implications of quantum mechanics for understanding reality, of which Heisenberg declared in *Across the Frontiers*: "Not only is the Universe stranger than we think, it is stranger than we can think."[52]

To say this is a slightly different way, one prominent interpretation of the light experiments is that light is neither wave nor particle until it is measured, until it is registered in human consciousness. And this is the case with all subatomic particles as well: They do not exist except as probabilities until they are measured. They do not even have a position until measured. I think this is what one of the greatest physicists, Werner Heisenberg, was getting at when he declared *in Physics and Philosophy*: "What we observe is not nature itself, but nature exposed to our method of questioning."[53] An even broader issue brought up by Heisenberg and others in the development of quantum mechanics is that the material underpinnings of the world seem to exist only as probabilities until consciousness "collapses the wave function" and creates a measurement, fixing the reality of that moment, which suggests that consciousness itself is intimately involved in creating what we think of as reality.

Skeptico: Surely you aren't suggesting that this consciousness is outside the material realm.

Wisdom Seeker: That seems to be the conclusion of several imminent intellectual figures. In grappling with one fundamental problem raised by quantum mechanics, that something outside a material system has to become aware of it in order to turn the probability into an actual state, one of the greatest mathematicians of all time, John von Neumann, said the only candidate he could find for this was consciousness.

Skeptico: Oh, I have heard something like that, but that only has to do with events at the quantum level, not in the everyday world I live in.

Wisdom Seeker: Some people take that point of view, saying that there are separate laws that govern the quantum world, separate from the everyday world. However, this is precisely what von Neumann was rejecting. His view was that there is no place you can draw a line between the quantum world and the everyday world, that everyday reality is constituted from the quantum level, so how could there be a separate "real" world? His view is that the entire physical world must be thought of in quantum mechanical terms so that everything is subject to those laws—which means that measuring instruments are in an indeterminate state until an observer has a conscious experience of a measurement. This, in turn, means that something outside of the material world is necessary to collapse the many wave-function possibilities into actualities. The only candidate he could find for this? Consciousness.

Skeptico: What do you believe?

Wisdom Seeker: I don't know what is true concerning all this. There is much disagreement among the experts with regard to how the ideas of quantum mechanics affect the reality we experience. I just bring this up as another example of how mysterious "reality" is.

Skeptico: Do you think thoughts can affect the material world?

Wisdom Seeker: It's hard to know how to understand this, but many years of experiments led to a remarkable assertion by the Dean of Engineering at Princeton University, Robert Jahn. He extensively studied the ability of the mind to affect the physical world without any direct physical contact, and he reported his finding in the book *Margins of Reality*. His conclusion, backed by an enormous amount of data, shows that our minds can, in fact, do that. Many other reports present evidence of an "experimenter effect" that colors every attempt we make to determine what "reality" really is. And in medicine, countless studies show that what a patient believes, as well as what the medical researcher believes, affects the outcome. This is the reason experimenters must go to so much trouble to make experiments "double-blind."

Skeptico: Can you explain that in a different way?

Wisdom Seeker: This takes us back to the issue of enculturation. Philosopher Richard Rorty came to the conclusion that all knowledge, even scientific knowledge, can be thought about only within a framework, and that framework cannot tell us what is objectively real. The simplest piece of information in a scientific experiment is already embedded in the framework in which the experiment was created.

Skeptico: But that's just philosophy. Is there any practical effect to this?

Wisdom Seeker: Well, a number of biologists, such as Bruce Lipton, say the implication is that our minds can directly affect the health of our bodies. Benedictine monk David Steindl-Rast has written extensively about how cultivating an attitude of gratitude affects our experience of life and our health. Several new studies show that positive feelings spread through a network of people (as do negative feelings, unfortunately). Many people, like physician Larry Dossey, have explored how prayer can affect the health of another person. Philosopher Martin Heidegger, in his later works, went so far as to say that we find ourselves in a box of our own making, that the whole framework of Western thought is to try to force reality into our thinking process, but that reality is beyond that and can be known only if we stop trying to force it into our concepts.

Skeptico: Whoa, that's enough! My head is spinning.

Wisdom Seeker: I sympathize. That happens to me when I try to understand these things. The complexity is probably why so many people rush to embrace simplistic answers of all kinds. But there is danger there: Through the need for simple answers we encase ourselves in concepts that hinder finding and living a fulfilled life. Peggy La Cerra, co-author of *The Origin of Minds: Evolution, Uniqueness and the New Science of the Self*, says that "our intelligence system is completely self-centeredly organized, and we are strongly biased to think and behave in ways that promote our own agenda." She goes on to list ways recent scientific research has discovered that we distort reality: "We think that our ideas are better than those of others…; we assess the logical strength of arguments on the basis of our beliefs, regardless of their objective strength…; we believe information that agrees with our expectations…; we reject new information that contradicts our beliefs…; we perceive our knowledge of others to be greater than their knowledge of us…; and we attribute our successes to our personal traits and characteristics and our failures to situational factors." The one she likes best, however, is this: "We assume that these biases characterize other people's minds but not our own."[54]

Skeptico: It is hopeless!

Wisdom Seeker: No, not really. My own experience suggests that I do not need absolute and final answers about the questions we've been discussing to move toward a fulfilled life. Even more, acknowledging how little I understand actually frees me from the snare of narrow and partial concepts, and this in turn allows me to continue to learn and grow. I have found that, for myself, being open-minded is an essential element in discovering the most fulfilling way to live.

Living with the Mystery

Most of what we have been considering so far has to do with the perception of material reality and how that is affected dramatically by our mental constructs and assumptions, even by consciousness itself. But if material reality is affected in this way, it seems likely that our perceptions about things that are harder to measure are affected even more, things such as feelings, what we perceive as dangers, the opportunities for our lives, and what others are thinking and feeling. In other words, it is likely that if we are fearful, we are likely to encounter a lot of situations that seem dangerous. Or we will project onto others what is going on inside us, so that if we are angry, we are very likely to perceive a lot of the people we meet as angry. On the other hand, if we are optimistic, we will see opportunity on every hand, even in the most difficult circumstance, and if we are kind and compassionate, we will frequently experience tender feelings toward others. As the wisdom of the Talmud captured it a very long time ago: "We do not see things as they are; we see things as we are."[55]

How do we come to grips with this mysterious world in which we find ourselves, feeling a need for something solid to believe in, yet continually discovering that a great deal is unknowable within the finite human perspective we inhabit? What do we do with the urge to know (about what to expect, about what is real and true) when the most intelligent response to understanding "reality" is to accept how much we do not know? To do this is hard. There is a saving grace, however: We do not, in fact, need to know "the ultimate truth about reality" in order to have a fulfilled and meaningful life. We need only to keep opening into the largest truth we can find, continually making the best decisions we can make on the basis of our current knowledge—then living as faithfully as possible with those decisions, while at the same time allowing what we know and believe to change and grow. Being open to change in our core beliefs is scary. It is much more palatable, however, when we realize that rigid, fixed beliefs usually grow out of a wish for certainty rather than great knowledge, and rigidity leads to imprisonment rather than liberation. To remember this, keep in mind this insight from Niels Bohr: "Profound truths" can be "recognized by the fact that the opposite is also a profound truth, in contrast to trivialities where opposites are obviously absurd."[56]

How best to function in such a framework? Stay open-minded about things until you have to make a specific decision. When a decision is needed, take everything you know into consideration and make the best decision possible, based on your knowledge up to that moment. Simultaneously, hold open the possibility that you might not have understood the whole picture and leave room, as time goes by, for growth and change in relation to what you decided.

To say this in a slightly different way, when you need to decide, do so with courage, and then act with confidence that you have done the best you can. Also, however, be willing to acknowledge that there is much you do not know and that your decision might have been wrong. This gives you greater freedom to adapt as you move forward, as opposed to a path of endlessly trying to convince yourself that you were right from the start—which only leads to compounding the initial mistake as you stick with a failing course of action. By staying open to change and correction, while at the same time remaining responsible for the decisions you have made, you become a master sailor, constantly correcting course as the winds and the seas around you change. On such a course, with humility as rudder and courage as sail, you can live fully, even in the absence of certainty.

Holding It Lightly

Skeptico: What about the firewalkers and breath-holding yogis you mentioned? What do you think about them?

Wisdom Seeker: Many people tend to disbelieve such phenomena simply because their consensual realities do not acknowledge such things are possible. Yet some cultures include these as possibilities, and no consensual reality is the final arbiter of another's truth. Every consensual reality includes some possibilities that are excluded by others. Millions of Chinese see realities that most Americans do not see, and millions of Americans believe in events that most Chinese would consider ridiculous. Millions of tribal people have had experiences that skeptical scientists do not acknowledge, and many scientists believe in "laws" that tribal peoples find laughable.

This became especially vivid for me when I came across a couple of articles about firewalking in old periodicals. In the May 1959 *Atlantic Monthly*, Leonard Feinberg, PhD, from the University of Illinois, described his experiences as a Fulbright Professor in Ceylon (now Sri Lanka), where he witnessed it.[57] In the April 1966 *National Geographic*, Gilbert Grosvenor, who had a sterling editorial reputation, and who was the recipient of several scientific writing awards, also reported his firewalking experiences.[58] Both articles strongly suggested that firewalking was sometimes real and that, in some cases, it was neither faked nor mitigated by "cool fires." The reports of both men are highly credible, yet this is something I have never experienced myself, so I don't have a strong opinion, and I find no reason to rush to judgment about it—either pro or con.

As for whether Tibetans can really dry wet blankets with their bodies, the best evidence I know comes from Harvard Assistant Professor of Medicine Herbert Benson, who went to Tibet four times and studied this phenomenon. His report:

> Our teams documented that monks could indeed dry icy, wet sheets on their naked bodies in temperatures of 40 degrees Fahrenheit. Within three to five minutes of applying the dripping

three-by-six-foot sheets to their skin, the sheets began to steam! Within thirty to forty minutes, the sheets were completely dry, and they were able to repeat this process two more times.[59]

In coming to terms with reality, the crucial point is that our cultural conditioning is necessary and important, but it does not provide "the truth" about what reality really is. In fact, consensual realities probably hide as much as they reveal. The challenge is to use a consensual reality as a tool for living and to relate to the people around us while coming to understand what it hides from us as well.

Yet this does not require a fall into complete relativism. Because of the problem of knowing what is really real, some influential postmodern thinkers, such as Michel Foucault, have held that all truth is relative and everything is an issue of power. However, just because something is unknown does not mean it is unknowable, and the absence of certainty does not suggest the absence of truth.

Some of what each of us takes for truth is very likely relative—that is, it arises from our consensual realities and is not true beyond our cultural conditioning. This is the case no matter the view around which we are organized, whether Hindu, scientific, Christian, skeptical, Buddhist, or points in between. But nothing in this chapter proves, or even suggests, that all truth is relative. This is the fallacy of "some" versus "all." Much is probably relative concerning what we take for truth, but there is no reason to believe that "some" should be expanded to "all." The only thing that is clear is that truth is difficult to know. Accepting this, and recognizing the limits of our own point of view, we can begin to open ourselves to deeper and deeper truths, the truths that lie hidden behind the veil of the way we have been conditioned to "see."

As this relates to the spiritual dimension of life, what we can conclude is that those who argue that spiritual realities are an illusion make the argument from within their particular consensual reality, and those who approach the spiritual from a faith system formulate their arguments from within that reality. All sides are subject to Einstein's observation that "it is the theory that decides what we can observe." This suggests that if there is a "real truth" out there, it is mediated by motive and assumption, and we will only discover "true reality" when completely free of enculturated views, as well as personal expectations, fears, agendas, and beliefs. Another wise saying suggested by the Tao Te Ching captures this essence: Truth waits for eyes unclouded by longing.

Let us turn, then, to an examination of how our views about the world arise and how they hold us in their sway.

CHAPTER 9

Worldviews—Path or Prison?

Often I walk in the mountains, following trails that were laid down by wolves, or elk, or animals so far in the distant past that there is no record of them now. Humans have assumed maintenance of these trails in recent times, improving them for the benefit of all, be it bear, tourist, or chipmunk. Occasionally, on an old trail seldom used by humankind, I see fresh signs of a large bear, and after a brief shudder, a smile crosses my face as I feel the presence of the wildness that once ruled these lands.

In the mountains, it is much easier to travel if someone blazed a trail and still others have maintained it through the years, through the millennia. It is not necessary for this to be done intentionally, for simply walking a path maintains and preserves it for the next traveler. (Much gratitude, though, to all those who preceded me on the trails I walk, inner as well as outer, especially those who set out intentionally to maintain and enhance the life trails I travel.)

Trails are essential in life, whether walking in the mountains or becoming a doctor, lawyer, or Cherokee chief. Cultural trails create pathways for living, channels through which knowledge flows, guiding each new traveler toward a delineated destination. When laid out wisely and well, trails make the journey smoother and safer for those headed in a shared direction.

Yet trails also bring limitations—limiting where one can travel and what one will see along the way. Trails define where to look, how to look, and what to look for. Outward trails are visible to the naked eye; inner trails are less visible, but no less real, for they are the beliefs, values, expectations, and assumptions in which we are embedded. Inner trails are the worldviews by which we live.

Where We Are

Summarizing the journey we have taken together so far: We each find ourselves *here*, in this moment, having an established pattern for living, put together mostly from the stories we were given as we grew up. Poised on this living edge, we have many decisions to make concerning how to move forward. Occasionally we might have extraordinary experiences that seem out of time, but soon most of us are back in our everyday worlds, with many decisions to make about how to spend the moments of our days.

The raw materials and tools we work with in making these decisions are: (1) urges and desires that arise continually (many as whims, but perhaps some as deep callings, though it is hard to know for sure which is which); (2) the guidance of culture and community (that came to us as stories in our early years and now is joined by new stories from other cultures and communities that we have encountered and from which we have incorporated new ways of understanding); (3) the marvelous tool of reason (whatever it is, for there are many different ways to understand it); and (4) the mysterious faculty of intuition (when we just seem to know something but without knowing where that awareness came from or what ultimate purpose it is guiding us toward).

This, then, is where you are right now (and where I am as well), with one additional, complicating factor. We are in a world about which our knowledge is limited; we exist in a "reality" that can be understood in different ways, to which our personal worldview gives some order and definition. However, every worldview is limited, so my worldview, as well as yours, is partial and incomplete, although it would be impossible to function without one.

Thus we understand ourselves, as well as "reality," through a worldview embedded in us as we were growing up, then modified by decisions we make: where we will focus our attention, the people with whom we will interact, what we will believe, and what we will refuse to believe. Changes in our views keep being made, but even so, we continue to live within a worldview, a framework of assumptions by which we understand who we are and what life is about.

The bottom line: Worldviews are both path and prison—path because they organize thoughts and understandings into manageable channels and prison because they predispose us to see things in certain ways while blinding us to knowing ourselves and our world more completely. In India, a trainer ties a young elephant to a large tree with a strong rope. The rope holds tight against all pulling and tugging by the young elephant, creating the belief that it is useless to try to escape. When this belief is thoroughly embedded, the trainer can use a flimsy rope and a small tree—even with a grown elephant—and it will not try to escape, for it assumes the rope is unbreakable still.

Like the elephant, many of us function within our worldviews without recognizing this to be the case. The assumptions by which we live simply seem like "the truth," incontrovertible and unassailable, given by the Laws of Nature or by God. Yet here, in this embedded place, there is no position from which to question our worldviews, even those filled with contradictions and generating unhealthy actions. A good friend[60] describes the situation this way: Imagine a child who, when growing up, was given a set of rules for living, along with a brown paper bag containing the full explanation for why those rules had to be followed. There is one condition, however: The child is forbidden to look inside the bag and examine the explanations. Many of us, for ten or twenty years, or even a lifetime, carry our bag around, never looking inside. If someone asks what we believe, we repeat the answers we were given. If a questioner probes deeper, challenging the validity of our answers, we respond by pointing to the bag and saying (often with great confidence), "The explanations are all in there."

The Problem with Trails

Having our assumptions embedded in this manner can lead to rich and fulfilled lives. Many people throughout history have lived in this way, sharing assumptions with the people around them and avoiding much of the angst present in the world today. However, many have also given their allegiance to unhealthy, even dysfunctional worldviews. For example, many have accepted systems that were advantageous to those in power but cruel to those at the bottom of the social scale, sometimes even if they were the ones at the bottom of the pile.

Even healthy cultural systems at times curb individual urges, restrain impulses that might, if fully expressed, cause harm to others, or create conflict within the community. This makes it inevitable that there will be tension between inner urge and outer rule, giving rise to moral dilemmas and difficult choices. For instance, we might "know" what we are "supposed" to do, but strong urges lead in a different direction. Which will we choose—the worldview we were given or the inner urge that seems to carry life's energy and vitality? And how can we tell whether an inner urge that seems strong is a passing whim, best relinquished, or a call to a fuller and more complete life?

Much of literature revolves around these conflicts between inner urge and societal rule; for instance, what to do when one falls in love with someone outside the accepted group? (The story of Romeo and Juliet provides a striking example.) In real life, countless conflicts have arisen between those who were previously in relationship but clashed over competing worldviews, leading to pain and misery all around. (Think of the many stories of young people estranged from parents in this way, or the many tales, in literature as well as real life, of those drawn to a path that parents and/or community did not approve, leading to anger, resentment, and loss.)

Sometimes the conflict is not with others but within oneself. Many are the novels, as well as real-life examples, of those who have directed fierce condemnation at themselves, have felt racked by guilt and shame, for having done things their upbringing defined as "wrong"—even though the same actions would have been acceptable in an adjoining country, or community, or even in the family next door.

Skeptico: Well, maybe we should just follow the rules.

Wisdom Seeker: It is not so simple, for doing so can be a great danger as well. Many biographies and novels describe the sadness and grief over paths *not taken* when choices were made to follow cultural rules rather than one's heart, choices that later in life caused great despair (Tolstoy's *The Death of Ivan Ilyich* is a powerful example).[61]

Unfortunately, this conflict between the call of the heart and the teaching of culture is not limited to literature or to those with broken lives, not by a long shot. Who, in fact, is free of such conflict? Many of the most revered among us have had to go through these struggles, including artists, adventurers, and even spiritual luminaries such as St. Francis of Assisi, the Buddha, Mohammed, and in recent times, Ramana Maharshi. Each of these and many more faced painful conflicts with family, the culture of their birth, or both.

All these struggles are made especially poignant when one realizes just how hard it is to know with certainty which actions are really "good" and which are "bad." How can we know for sure that the rules we were given, or even the ones we have adopted, are right and good when we discover that many fine people in the past, even those who seem blameless in their personal lives, accepted societal rules that justified slavery, torture, abuse, blood-thirsty revenge, cruelty toward children, mutilation, and sexual practices that caused great harm to the victims?

Over and over, the dilemma comes back to this: When do we follow the rules we were given (or that we have adopted in our current worldview), and when do we follow our own inner compass? There is no escape from this dilemma, for our inner compasses inevitably include urges and desires that, although bringing vitality and energy, can also lead to actions that harm others, elevate a moment's pleasure over long-term goals, and can even lead to being cast out of society's embrace.

To make it even more complicated, many of the great moral and spiritual leaders of human history, those who we think of having put in place the "rules," often have been those who broke the rules they had been given in favor of a higher calling, the ones who proclaimed that what was truly "right and good" was in conflict with the established order of their time and place. For instance, the great prophets of Israel called on kings and commoners alike to abandon cultural norms in favor of a higher justice and devotion. Jesus repeatedly stepped outside the boundaries of his society to proclaim a new vision—as did Confucius, Mohammed, the Buddha, Gandhi, and many more. In recent times, Martin Luther King, Jr., captured the dilemma succinctly in his letter from the Birmingham jail: "There are two kinds of laws: just laws…and unjust laws. One has not only a legal but a moral responsibility to obey just laws, but…one has a moral responsibility to disobey unjust laws."

Yet how do we know which laws are just and which unjust? Who decides, for societies ask their members to follow **all** the laws? How, from within a culture that asks us to follow all the rules, do we come to terms with the realization that some rules are flawed, perhaps even corrupt, and that the good life will be achieved only by challenging those that undermine our fulfillment?

Can we simply follow our inner compass? No, for it shifts between deep conscience and flighty whim, changes from moment to moment, so that at any given time it is very hard to tell where the urges of the inner compass are coming from. Further, sometimes the best path is to follow society's rules even though we think they are flawed, for we might be wrong, and those injunctions are what keep us from harm, and perhaps even lead to a fulfillment we would not have found otherwise.

There are simply no black and white choices in this rocky terrain. Even when the rules are more or less right, one's unique path can be discovered only by breaking the rules in order to get in touch with a deeper current of individual meaning. This is the hero's journey, the central myth of history according to Joseph Campbell in *The Hero with a Thousand Faces*. Within this framework, those who are not able to break free will find their life energies frozen, full expression blocked, and life will be barren. They will dwell in the "wasteland" until they discover the courage to forge their own way. This means that in spite of the danger, there are powerful reasons to step outside one's worldview, at least for a time, to catch a glimpse of whether one is truly headed in a fulfilling direction, to get far enough outside the "givens" to be able to see alternatives for oneself as well as one's community.

> **Thought Experiment—Recognizing "Ropes"**
>
> To catch a glimpse of your worldview (the "ropes" that bind you in the way that our friend the elephant was bound), think of a point of view you strongly disagree with, held by someone in a different social group, religion, or political party, one that seems wrong to you—perhaps unhealthy or dangerous. Why do you think those who hold this view do not see what you see? It must be that they are looking through a different lens than the one through which you look. Can you, then, for just a moment, step into their point of view?

What, Me Rationalize?

Skeptico: Sure, many cultural systems are flawed, but I have strong, rational arguments for mine.
Wisdom Seeker: Perhaps, but part of your conditioning consisted of ideas that defined your worldview as rational, as well as the rules by which rational would be understood.
Skeptico: I know that, but everyone I talk to agrees with me!
Wisdom Seeker: Most everyone you talk to has been enculturated in the same way; you constantly reinforce each other in your shared beliefs, marveling at their strength and beauty.
Skeptico: I am more than willing to debate my point of view. Anyone will be able to see that my arguments are rational and right.
Wisdom Seeker: Who will judge the debate?
Skeptico: Well, clear-thinking people.

Wisdom Seeker: Clear-thinking by whose standards? Can the judges of your debate be from another worldview? If you want a real test of your ideas, try making your "rational" arguments to someone from a completely different system of thought, and see if you persuade them.

Why So Little Agreement?

There are hundreds, perhaps thousands, of dramatically different belief systems in the world today, each thinking its arguments are persuasive. How can such divergent points of view all believe they are right? The best explanation I can find is that most of us go about collecting arguments in favor of our point of view while ignoring everything else. Some of us go a step further: In trying to protect and project our views, we get into verbal battles, and sometimes even armed conflict, so we won't have to truly listen to the ideas of others.

The mind is an amazing instrument and, if used to buttress one's beliefs, capable of developing endless arguments as to why one is "right." A Yale graduate student provided a nice demonstration of this back in 1956. He asked a group of people to rate the desirability of a number of items, then let each person keep one item from the group rated highly desirable (all the items in this group seemed to be equally desirable to the person at the time). After choosing which to keep, all were asked to rate the items again, and "suddenly they had a new perspective. If they had chosen the electric sandwich press over the toaster, they raised its rating and downgraded the toaster."[62]

Uniformly, the participants quickly convinced themselves they had made the right choice, rationalizing the choice to themselves. As summarized by columnist John Tierney: "In general, people deal with cognitive dissonance—the clashing of conflicting thoughts—by eliminating one of the thoughts. The notion that the toaster is desirable conflicts with the knowledge that you just passed it up, so you banish the notion. The cognitive dissonance is gone." It seems our minds are organized to constantly rationalize our views and can quickly change both the facts we see as well as our perspective on those facts to defend a point of view in which we are invested.

Living in this way has its benefits: When presented with a question, we have a ready answer about what is good and bad, right and wrong. But this leaves us trapped, with no way to judge what is truly healthy versus unhealthy, no way to see the dysfunction within our own worldview.

How to escape this prison? Respectful encounter with other views—this is how we are most likely to learn and grow. I have heard it said we could never understand our own belief systems until we have understood the basic tenets of another. Or to put it more bluntly, without being able to see the perspective of another, there is no way to know whether you have been brainwashed.

Common Strategies

Each of us searches for a solid place to stand, wants to believe that our views and assumptions give us valid guidance for how to live a fulfilled life. We cling to our beliefs, asserting their validity, even though feelings of confusion, sadness, anger, and depression creep in. Looking around, we discover that a large number of people in the modern world, following their given worldviews, are alienated and struggling, spending time on things that are shallow and meaningless, finding no greater fulfillment than we ourselves have found.

We try various escapes from this dilemma. Perhaps we try to force the world to be as we think it should be, or we distort our vision and see it as we want it to be. We might try to persuade others to agree with us, thinking that if only enough people would accept our views, we could be sure we were right. Perhaps we join a group that directs its convictions outward, finding enemies "out there" to avoid inner doubt. Or we might be among those who are so loosely attached to our worldviews that we have a hard time making decisions or knowing what is right and wrong, deciding only with difficulty what is worthy of effort and decision.

Another strategy involves putting on a mantle of happiness, trying hard to convince ourselves that we feel good. With this strategy, however, a wave soon comes along, rocking the boat, and we glimpse the turbulent waters underneath. (When I have tried this strategy, the feeling was one of bravado, of being a salesman who was trying to sell an overvalued product to myself, as well as others. It worked for a time, but seldom for long.)

Perhaps we find ourselves amongst the goodly number of those who have concluded that although many people are doing well, we ourselves are not—giving rise to the feeling that "there is something wrong with me." This tendency, to see others as doing well while you are not, is common, reinforced by the propensity by many of us to present to the world a positive image, even though, inside, that is not how we really feel, at least a lot of the time. (This is where the self-help industry comes in, with entrepreneurs claiming to have found the key to happiness and success. Hard to discern, however, the few who have truly attained fulfillment from those who are using others' dissatisfaction to make a buck.)

I know both sides of this pattern from my own experience, having at times thought, "There is something wrong with me" and at other times putting on a very positive image when interacting with others. I have also talked with a significant number of folks who felt that most everyone else was doing well, while they themselves were not. When asked for an example of someone we both knew who was doing well, though, they often named someone I knew to be struggling (but talented at putting on a "doing well" persona).

> **Thought Experiment—The Charade**
>
> Think of a time you went to a reunion or a party and put on a cheerful demeanor, while inside you felt your life was a mess. Or think of a time you ran into someone you hadn't seen for a while, and although you weren't feeling good about yourself, you gave a positive response when asked how you were doing. Is it possible that those who seem to be doing well are doing the same when they talk to you? How many of us are simply playing a game of charades with each other?

At this juncture, two powerful currents collide: We want to believe, are desperately trying to convince ourselves that our worldviews are right and true, yet the feeling persists that all is not well, giving rise to sadness, alienation, anger, and/or depression. A common response to this swirling vortex of confusion is to redouble one's commitment to current beliefs, but this always brings conflict: conflict within, as one tries to suppress challenging feelings and thoughts; and conflict without, as efforts are made to get others to go along with one's views, leading to battles between "worldview teams."

Skeptico: So what do I do?

Wisdom Seeker: Maybe it is time for radical measures! I cannot know if my worldview is serving my life if it is all I know. Maybe a cure lies in daring to question the underlying assumptions from which I live.

> **Thought Experiment—Questioning Your Worldview**
>
> Think of someone you know who is struggling right now. If you look carefully, you might be able to identify some of the assumptions that person holds that contribute to the difficulty: perhaps a fantasy, an expectation about how the world is supposed to be, a stubbornly held belief, a "moral" position that does not seem to be moral to you. Now consider: Is there some way you might be as enmeshed as is your friend in a framework of assumptions that is not working? Could this be the cause of some of your problems? Can you think of an example?

Challenging one's worldview is hard, sometimes frightening, and leads to further questions, one of the most difficult being: Is there a place to stand that is solid, that will hold firm after all the questioning is done? I believe there is, but to arrive at that ground, each of us must first experience the queasy unsteadiness of the shifting sands on which our castles of belief have been built.

Clashing Worldviews

Moving from individual experience to that of our societies, it seems clear that clashing worldviews have created many of the problems of history, causing enormous pain and strife, for when worldviews collide, the reaction most of us have is to "support the home team." In recent times, as the world has become more crowded and the number of different identity groups has increased, conflicts have become ever more numerous.

An analogy: I love sports, and have been an avid fan of my university's teams for many years. At times I have had a deep sense of identity with a particular team, even though I didn't personally know anyone on the team and probably had little in common with either players or coaches. In spite of this, when a team I had identified with did well, I felt better about myself—momentarily felt more capable, more likely to succeed. Conversely, when "my" team failed, I felt I had been personally defeated.

The result of this kind of identification can be powerful. At times I have been absolutely convinced that "we" deserved to win; that "we" had worked harder, had the best players, and played with greater determination, though the only evidence for this rested on my team's press releases and the report of fans who shared my views (and I don't remember consulting similar reports from other teams.)

Incredibly, the supporters of other teams seem just as fervent as I! How can this be? How can another team deserve to win when they are playing "my team?" This is hard to take in when one is a fan, yet there it is: When two teams collide, the fans of both sides are equally convinced of their side's virtues, their right to win.

Because this tendency seems to be a strong aspect of human nature, how much more intense must be the feelings we have when worldviews collide? If we can quickly and easily convince ourselves about a sports team's right to victory, how much more will this be the case with regard to core beliefs, to the ideas around which we make the important decisions of life? Thus, when worldviews collide, as they often do in the modern world, it becomes a dangerous planet.

Of course, worldview clashes have been going on for thousands of years, and many solutions have been tried to lessen the frequency and intensity. One method has been efforts by various groups to persuade those with differing views to convert to their point of view. When persuasion hasn't worked, the strongest groups have sometimes used force to insist that everyone comply with their opinions. When this has failed, attempts have sometimes been made to expel or even eliminate those with different views, and the atrocities that have resulted from these efforts have at times been unimaginable.

Religions have been castigated because some members have committed atrocities, but this is to miss the tendency we humans have always had to, at times, do horrible things, whether as part of a religion or not. This tendency seems to be part of human nature, as evidenced by the bloody conflicts that have occurred between all kinds of groups over territory, water rights, land ownership, pride, money, oil, who gets to govern, sports, relationship questions, and on and on. Religions sometimes get involved in these conflicts, and religious leaders sometimes take the lead, but no more so than other leaders. And to their credit, many religious leaders have opposed such violence and spoken out against scapegoating the "other," even when it was not in the short-term interest of their group. Many religious leaders have done this, sometimes at great risk to themselves, while few people through history without a religious point of view have done so.

The amazing and sad thing about all this is that coercion and violence are still being tried as a solution all over the world today. That's amazing, because such attempts have never been successful: After thousands years of coercion and violence, the world has more competing worldviews than ever, making vivid the fact that all such efforts have failed. Sadness comes from the realization that, after so many failures, we as a species have not learned that these methods do not work. At times we are like those in a sinking rowboat, furiously bailing water but emptying our buckets into the back of the very boat we are in.

Our Basic Nature?

One of the reasons we humans keep trying to suppress or get rid of those who don't agree with us is that there seem at first glance to have been "successes" with this strategy. But such success is mostly illusory. One powerful group might subdue another, even eliminate it entirely, but over time, such actions almost always beget difficulty for the victors. The negative consequences are sometimes subtle but real nonetheless:

- For generations to come, there are revenge attacks from the vanquished and those sympathetic to them, leading to vast and unproductive expenditure on protection and security.
- In the long run, rulers groups that organize around suppression, imprisoning large numbers of opponents, and frequent wars squander and exhaust their wealth.
- The military might of victors in war is often exhausted by their efforts, inviting attacks by new enemies. (Many are the nations brought low by an opponent that waited for ill-conceived actions against another to weaken their potential foe).
- A process is set in motion within the culture that continually narrows who is "acceptable," leading to internal fights between smaller and smaller factions and eventually to chaos (the French Revolution is a good example).
- A backlash of emotions arises within the community of victors because of decisions made to achieve victory (as portrayed in many ancient Greek stories, such as the terrible fate of most of the victors in Homer's *Odyssey).*
- An atmosphere of fear is provoked among those who have attained power through force, for if this is the accepted road to power, those at the top must constantly be on guard against the next claimant to the throne. (History is full of betrayal, suspicion, and murder within royal courts and dictatorships established through this kind of power.)

- At the moral level, there is an undermining of the value of human decency in the aggressors, which corrupts their lives and those of their offspring for generations to come.

Skeptico: Isn't violence and conflict simply the way the world is?
Wisdom Seeker: In a word: No. One of the most destructive ideas ever perpetuated is that life is primarily about conflict, competition, and the survival of the fittest—that we live in a "dog-eat-dog" world. The tendency toward asserting power and control over others is one aspect of human nature, but not the only one, not by a long shot. As biologist Elisabet Sahtouris documents extensively in her book *EarthDance*, a flourishing life is much more about cooperation and creative symbiosis.

Over time, it is not domination that succeeds, but cooperation. Bacteria learned to cooperate with each other to create vast colonies. Each living cell is a complex interaction of parts that have come together and learned to cooperate in exquisite ways. Ant colonies are successful because of an amazing level of cooperation. Flocks of birds have astonishing levels of cooperation, as do some herds of animals. Or consider the human body: It is made up of trillions of individual cells that perform a dance of cooperation defying description.

On a larger scale, oceans are vast, cooperative ecosystems made up of trillions of organisms, as are rain forests and prairies. Looking at what really works, over time, at every level, it is when the urge to dominate gives way to cooperation that systems succeed. The great civilizations of humankind are those that developed a high level of cooperation among many people.

Skeptico: But didn't some of those civilizations treat some people very badly?
Wisdom Seeker: Yes. Although many people had to cooperate for a civilization to be successful, everyone was not always included cooperatively; at times some were coerced. But if a large number did not buy into a civilization, it did not last very long.

Successful societal systems, in fact, must have ways to encourage, educate members toward, and sometimes enforce the alignment of the various parts with the whole; this is the issue in the first part of this chapter concerning the balance between individuality and cooperation. A number of ancient societies seem to me to have erred in the direction of enforcement and control. However, many societies today err on the opposite side, emphasizing competition and individual aggrandizement in ways that undermine the possibility of fulfilled lives because the central importance of cooperation and community is not recognized or supported.

Finding a Balance

Those who initiate harm toward others seldom escape the consequences themselves—at either the personal or the cultural level. At the personal level, this is because one's actions determine the kind of person one will become, the kind of person one will live **as**. If you have created a negative energy field, you have to live in it all the time. (We can get away from others, at least for a time, but not from ourselves: We cannot escape the energy fields we have chosen, consciously or unconsciously, to create and within which we live.)

At the cultural level, the cumulative balance between aggressive and cooperative actions will decide the kind of society created, the kind of society that each member will, therefore, live within. The example of systems that have succeeded over time suggests that we are far better off to direct our actions toward cooperation, respect for others, and compassion rather than violence, control of others, and domination. We seem to be free, both individually and collectively, to choose, and each of us is continually making a lived response as our choice. As I consider the path I will take, Gandhi's words ring in my heart and mind: "I infer that it is the law of love that rules mankind. It gives me ineffable joy to go on trying to prove that."[63]

Gandhi was a skilled lawyer, and he knew he could not prove in a legal or logical way what he was saying. However, he also recognized that anyone who wished to disagree with him could not prove an alternative, either. Thus, in the absence of proof, he had a choice, and he chose the most positive possibility he could find for his life. The consequence was that he, and those around him, got to live in the feelings generated by someone committed to love. In the absence of proof, what better choice could one make?

Skeptico: That sounds nice, but some people can behave very badly. What of self-defense, protecting one's group from aggressors, acting to defend the oppressed?

Wisdom Seeker: Your questions bring to the fore one of the thorniest moral questions we humans face. Gandhi was willing to suffer physical punishment rather than harm another, but few of us are capable of such sacrifice, and perhaps few of us are called to it. For many, the use of force seems legitimate to protect oneself, one's loved ones, and one's culture. Further, force is sometimes essential for maintaining order and providing safety. At the same time, the cry of "self-protection" is frequently used to justify aggression and oppression, so to build healthy societies we must be constantly vigilant about using "self-protection" as an excuse to justify our wish to dominate and control.

Skeptico: Is there a way around this?

Wisdom Seeker: A leader who agonized over these questions with immense and terrible sincerity was Abraham Lincoln. One of his conclusions: "In great contests each party claims to act in accordance with the will of God. *Both may be, and one must be wrong.*" [italics mine][64]

Skeptico: What does that mean?

Wisdom Seeker: I think he meant that because the two sides were fighting, they obviously had different views, so one had to be wrong, and if so, each side should constantly be questioning its own views—rather than arrogantly claiming to speak for God—for it might be the side that was mistaken. What a difference it would make if we humans could hold the thought that in intense conflicts, our side might be wrong. Lincoln's advice for handling this dilemma is profoundly wise. To paraphrase: Spend less time claiming that God is on your side and more time humbly examining your own motives in the hope that you will be able to truly serve the highest good.

Another wise counsel comes from Rabbi Abraham Heschel in an article entitled *"No Religion Is an Island,"* in which he speaks about the conflict between religions (but the thought is just as apt for competing worldviews): "Should we refuse to be on speaking terms with one another and hope for each other's failure? Or should we pray for each other's health and help one another in preserving one's respective legacy, in preserving a common legacy?" Needless to say, Rabbi Heschel recommends praying for each other's health and helping sustain one another's traditions.

One more quote, a poem from the twelfth-century Spanish Sufi, Ibn Arabi:

> Before, I used to reject my fellow beings if they did not profess the same religion as I.
> Now, my heart has become receptive to every image.
> It is a meadow for the grazing deer,
> a monastery for the monk, a temple for idols,
> a Ka'ba for the pilgrim,
> - Torah scrolls and a copy of the Qur'an.
> I profess the religion of love,
> wherever its caravan may turn.
> Love is my law and my faith.[65]

Individuality Within Worldviews

We have traveled a long road from making individual decisions to the functioning of large systems and cultures. Yet our personal decisions cannot be separated from the systems within which we live or the worldviews adopted and enforced by the cultures and communities around us. It is impossible to live a human life without some relation to the patterns instilled in us when young or incorporated later through choices made as we grew and developed. Whether we willingly submit, rebel, work to change, or simply endure, we are always in relation to patterns, systems, and people. The lone rebel is escaping patterns, and the monk in the cave arrived there through ideas acquired from people who went before.

However, the world around does not have to be going well for us to have a fulfilled and meaningful life. We simply have to develop the right relationship to what is going on. We have to find a way to be with the wrongs, the difficulties, and the challenges around without being overcome by them. And in fact, many have had meaningful and fulfilled lives in difficult times: Nelson Mandela, Lincoln, Gandhi, the Dalai Lama, Confucius, Jesus, Viktor Frankl, and many others come to mind.

Nor can systems be free from individuals; systems and communities are made up of "us." (Many problems are caused by treating systems as if they are things in themselves, rather than made up of individuals who are separate and unique.) Further, individuals dramatically affect systems: It is impossible to know when the actions of one individual will shift a whole system into a new pattern for either good or ill. (As chaos theory is showing, through the influence of very small actions order is continually arising from what had seemed like chaos.)

We, as individuals, can neither predict nor control what will happen because of our actions and choices. All we can do is be as conscious as possible of the systems in which we are embedded and the pressures they are applying. Through this action, we can then make more meaningful choices as to what to support and what to oppose. Ideally, having made our choices, we will then act with a fierce commitment toward those things that represent health, well-being, and fulfillment for ourselves, the people we care about, and the systems within which we are embedded.

> **Thought Experiment—Getting to Know Your Worldviews**
>
> Spend a few moments and become as clear as you can about two or three of the main stories within which you live. As you do, realize that those stories are not true; neither are they false—they are simply your stories. You do not need to get rid of them (probably couldn't if you wanted to), but you can recognize that they are your stories, not you.
>
> Which means you can work with them, understand them in new ways, reinterpret them. (Your stories are simply an interpretation of past events among many possible interpretations, built through selecting some facts and excluding others.) As an advance assignment, you can even develop a new story or that is more useful or more in harmony with the broader currents of life that you are living in now. (If you can do this with a playful attitude, it will be especially helpful.)

Catching this glimpse, gaining a perspective from which to understand and evaluate various worldviews, we will become more accomplished at escaping their imprisonment while using them more skillfully in pursuit of a fulfilled and meaningful life. In short, we will engage in the exhilarating and sometimes scary journey of participating fully in the creation of our own lives and of the world in which we exist.

Skeptico: How do we accomplish such a monumental undertaking?
Wisdom Seeker: To a great extent, we do so through three central aspects of being human: imagination, intention, and attention (the subjects of the next chapter).

CHAPTER 10

Imagination, Intention, Attention

One day, when walking in the mountains, I had an image of writing a book, of sharing the ideas presented in workshops through the years. Where did this image come from?

Whatever its source, this image has absorbed thousands of hours of my life, pushing aside countless other things; much of my life energy for several years has been shaped and molded by this image. Of course, I had to make many decisions along the way about what to do with each particular moment. Still, that one image has been a primary organizing framework for several years.

There is a deep paradox here. We are only alive in the present moment, yet we live in relation to patterns and currents. Our lives have meaning only in relation to the patterns we choose, or the ones that choose us. How do we interact with, and partially create, these patterns? What is this human capacity that allows us to make choices about aligning with, or trying to change, the currents within which we exist? The starting point of it all seems to be imagination. Can you imagine a human life without it?

Imagination

As we move though life, there are three tools at the heart of what it means to be a human being, and each is essential if we are to play an active role in our own lives: imagination, intention, and attention.

To understand the central role imagination plays in human life, simply catalog the things we do that rely on it. For instance, reading a novel requires imagination. Only if our imagination comes alive does a story hold our attention or affect us in a significant way. When reading a novel, it is the imagination that fills in the scenes and engages the emotions so that we come to care about the events portrayed.

In the same way, becoming involved in a movie requires imagination (for most movies, anyway). Only if your imagination pulls you into the scenes, helping you envision what it would be like to be participating in the events, does the movie take on life and interest for you. Only when this happens do you feel fear, passion, arousal, anxiety, tenderness, an adrenaline rush, and more.

All art, in fact, requires imagination, both to create it as well as experience it. Art begins with a vision; an artist imagines something that does not exist and begins the process of manifesting it into the world. Sometimes the initial vision occurs in a dramatic way, as when Mozart saw a score that was "almost complete and finished" in his mind. He goes on to say he did not "hear in my imagination the parts successively, but…all at once."[66] But how could a whole piece of music come into being all at once? Mozart tells us: Imagination.

The power and importance of imagination do not stop in the artistic realm, however—not by a long shot. Any life venture starts with imagination, necessity, or both. To create plans for a new building requires imagination, as does planning a vacation, a picnic, or a party. Or consider creating a business. Every entrepreneur must have imagination; a person wishing to start a business must envision something needed and then imagine ways to fulfill that need. Perhaps the task is to create a better product, or it might be to find a way to build interest in a new product or service. As the process unfolds, the entrepreneur must play out various scenarios in his or her imagination, considering various ways the project might go forward (including production, sales strategies, personnel, and on and on). At every step, imagination is required.

Reason also comes into play in evaluating possible strategies, but it is imagination that provides the possibilities with which the reason of the entrepreneur works. Then, after a new service or product is launched, imagination is again essential in the sales process. Those who are selling must be able to imagine what potential buyers are interested in, must be able to put themselves into the mind or heart of the potential purchaser so as to know what to say that will appeal to their interests. The creation of any sales or marketing presentation depends upon imagination.

Skeptico: What about science? It doesn't have much to do with imagination, does it?

Wisdom Seeker: What would science be without imagination? Basically, it wouldn't exist. The great scientists did not build up theories out of facts but wrestled with a problem that no one understood and imagined a picture of how things might fit together that solved the problem. As Karl Popper, one of the greatest philosophers of science in the twentieth century, put it: "Scientific discovery is akin to explanatory story telling, to myth making, and to the poetic imagination."[67]

His words certainly hold true with regard to Newton, Copernicus, Galileo, Kepler, Einstein, Niels Bohr, Max Planck, and many others. Thought experiments created much of modern science, as these geniuses imaginatively solved a problem and then began to look for facts to support or refute their new theories. (Often it was many years before the facts could confirm their imaginative insights.) Einstein saw this clearly: "I believe in intuitions and inspirations.... I am enough of the artist to draw freely upon my imagination. Imagination is more important than knowledge. Knowledge is limited. Imagination encircles the world."[68]

Another example of the power of imagination concerns the placebo effect. In thousands of studies, a high percentage of those not receiving a medication show significant signs of improvement. How can this be? The power of imagination. The person being given a dummy pill imagines that it will help, and so it does. This effect is so powerful that a new drug must only best the placebo by five percent to be approved by the regulatory authorities. Consider what this means: There is an assumption in research trials that the placebo will likely be almost as effective as the drug itself.

The dramatic nature of the placebo effect has led some medical researchers to suggest that much of the healing that occurs in every medical modality relies on the power of imagination. Insofar as this is the case (and it is certainly at least partly so), when we go to a doctor, a significant portion of the healing that follows involves the imaginative belief that the visit has begun a healing process. (Recognizing this helps explain why so many remedies through the ages—although lacking a direct physical mechanism—have worked, sometimes for a lot of people, over long periods of time.)

Then there is psychotherapy, which frequently involves imagination. A good therapist imaginatively enters into the world of the client, gets a sense of where the client is coming from, and begins to help that person understand his or her situation more clearly. Psychoanalyst Donald Winnicott goes so far as to assert that our ability to relate to others begins with imagination; that when a young child senses that his or her actions are harming the mother, that child develops the capacity to imagine the mother's feelings (he calls this the "capacity for concern").[69] In Winnicott's view, this is how the possibility of mutuality in relationship arises.

Skeptico: Is it imagination, then, that leads to love?
Wisdom Seeker: Absolutely. As psychologist Rollo May put it, "Imagination is the life-blood of Eros."[70] This is true for love at all its levels. For those who think of love as lust, it is imagination that creates desire for a specific person by creating an image of a fulfilling engagement with that person. A purely biological urge might arise that is hormonal, but to direct that desire toward a particular person, the imagination must create an image of fulfillment with a specific other. (Not that only one person can be imagined as fulfillment, but the imagination must focus on a specific person to fire the possibility of satisfaction. If one possibility is thwarted, then the imagination might turn to another, and then another.) To recognize the

importance of imagination here, simply notice that even those completely caught in sexual desire do not feel it toward every person they meet or think about; they feel it only toward those whom their imaginations can envision as fulfilling the desire (the stronger the hormonal urge, though, the wider the net is usually cast).

At the level of more complex, ongoing relationships, it is imagination that creates a picture of how spending time with someone, or forming a committed union, will provide the satisfaction one seeks. Even in the dimension of selfless or unconditional love, it is the ability to imagine what another person needs that allows us to respond in a way that speaks to that person's true situation. In other words, love at all of its levels is intimately entwined with imagination.

Another realm that relies upon imagination is religion. All religions are carried by stories that inspire followers to imagine ways to act and live that will bring them into alignment with the teachings; it is by entering imaginatively into the stories and their meanings that adherents are carried toward a personal vision of how best to live. Further, creative images are used for meditation and instruction: By meditating on sacred symbols, sacred persons, and sacred art, followers of various traditions open to experiences that will enhance and strengthen their engagement. Religions also use rituals, initiations, and ceremonies to evoke the imagination and engage it with the deepest questions of life. And perhaps the ultimate spiritual experience is to imaginatively enter into a direct knowing of the ground of being.

> **Thought Experiment—Creating and Pursuing Projects and Plans**
>
> Can you think of a way to go forward with any plan or project without your imagination: creating a business or planning a vacation, a creative project, a political campaign, a scientific experiment, a recreational outing, or a program of study?

Skeptico: That's a problem, then, because I don't think I have a very good imagination.

Wisdom Seeker: Everyone has an imagination, and most people have a strong one. The differences between people usually have to do with how they use it. I think you have a very good imagination.

Skeptico: How can you say that? What's the evidence?

Wisdom Seeker: I can demonstrate it in just a few seconds. Do you ever worry?

Skeptico: Well, yes.

Wisdom Seeker: Are you ever afraid? Do you ever have anxiety?

Skeptico: Unfortunately, yes.

Wisdom Seeker: Then you have a good imagination.

Skeptico: How so?

Wisdom Seeker: Your imagination must be strong, for these things are products of negative imagination. All involve creating images of potential problems and dangers.

Skeptico: But I have to look out for problems and try to avoid dangers.

Wisdom Seeker: Certainly, but using your imagination to envision what could go wrong does not necessitate fear, worry, or anxiety. These three poisons involve imagining bad things that *have not happened* and then getting caught up in imagining what the consequences *might be* if they did happen. Have you ever noticed that the great majority of things you worry about never happen? Most never will, so why worry about them? As Shakespeare has it, "Cowards die many times before their deaths; the valiant never taste of death but once." In other words, if you start imagining all the ways you might die, you experience the fear of death many times over.[71]

As you go about your life, plan wisely, but do not use your imagination to create worries. Envision what might go wrong in your plans, and adjust accordingly by creating positive solutions. This is a valuable and productive use of imagination.

Imagination and Reason in Conflict

Imagination and reason have, at times, been seen as opposed, but when they are viewed this way, and one becomes dominant, the other then stages a resurgence, attacking its "opponent" when it seems to have tipped the balance too much in its favor. The Romantic poets of the late eighteenth and early nineteenth centuries (such as Wordsworth, Shelley, Keats, and Coleridge) were rebelling against what they perceived as an overly rational tendency in the preceding Age of Reason. Yet the Age of Reason grew up in opposition to what its proponents perceived as the irrational and superstitious views of the medieval period.

There are so many examples of this tug of war: Immanuel Kant tried to show why life must be governed by reason, but to his credit, he said that the starting point of things human lay with the imagination. The way I would summarize his view in *The Critique of Practical Reason*: Imagination is the power or energy that drives our being. All of our knowing arises from the power of imagination.[72] Kant clearly saw that the human ability to affect the course of one's life, and that of others, begins with imagining alternatives and possibilities. Unfortunately, his understanding of the importance of imagination diminished with some of those who followed him (due partly to his Teutonic insistence that, despite the importance of imagination, the goal was to live a dutiful, orderly, and rational life).

Georg Wilhelm Friedrich Hegel took up some of Kant's ideas and went on to posit that the world could be understood fully by reason (and that his system of thought encompassed the broadest rational truth). This view was quickly attacked by such figures as Kierkegaard and Nietzsche, who pointed to the folly of thinking that all of human life was orderly and rational. Kierkegaard insisted that he did not even understand the most basic teachings of his own tradition and that he himself and the people he knew had motives that were not rational and did not fit into Hegel's grand scheme. Nietzsche pictured a madman[73] who broke into a seemingly orderly world (but one that had been rotting from within for a long time) to declare a new vision of what human life was about.º In a similar vein, the novelist Fyodor Dostoyevsky portrayed people who knew they were acting from irrational motives, even self-destructive ones, but chose to do so anyway. (In *Notes from Underground,* the central character states that he often acts from spite, even though he knows such actions will be harmful to him.)

Imagination and Reason in Harmony

Having recounted some of the conflicts, let me rush to assert that reason and imagination do not need to quarrel; many wise figures have understood that they can and should work together, and various attempts have been made to envision their proper relationship. The Romantic poets started with the primacy of the imagination but tried to bring reason into the picture as part and parcel of it. Wordsworth said in the *Prelude:*

> Imagination, which, in truth
> Is but another name for absolute power
> And clearest insight, amplitude of mind
> And Reason in her most exalted mood.[74]

In other words, when reason is at its best, it is united with (perhaps even the same as), imagination. Ralph Waldo Emerson captured another way to view how the two relate: "The animal eye sees, with wonderful accuracy, sharp outlines and colored surfaces." Then, when reason is brought to bear, "grace and expression" is added, which arise from "imagination and affection." Taking another step, if "Reason be stimulated to more earnest vision, outlines and surfaces become transparent, and...causes and spirits are seen through them." "These delicious awakenings" lead to "the best moments of life."[75]

º In the section titled "The Madman" in *The Gay Science,* a man enters the town market and cries out loudly, "I seek God! I seek God!" He encounters a group of mocking atheists who laugh at him. The "madman" proclaims: "God is dead. God remains dead. And we have killed him. How shall we comfort ourselves, the murderers of all murderers?"

Shakespeare was another great soul who understood the importance of imagination. Several currents are brought together in his brief line: "The lunatic, the lover and the poet are of imagination all compact." With the aid of Helen Luke, I understand this to mean that if the imagination overwhelms reason, there is insufficient groundedness to allow a person to live effectively in the world—resulting in the lunatic. In the lover, imagination (as discussed above) allows us to "create an image of fulfillment with a specific other." As for the poet, Shakespeare sums up his view in *Midsummer Night's Dream:*

> The poet's eye, in a fine frenzy rolling,
> Doth glance from heaven to earth, from earth to heaven;
> And as imagination bodies forth
> The form of things unknown, the poet's pen
> Turns them to shapes, and gives to airy nothing
> A local habitation and a name.[76]

Which I take to mean that an inspired artist can glance toward the mystery of existence and catch a glimpse of something most of us are too busy or too self-centered to notice. (That which is truly important seems an "airy nothing" when one's gaze is focused on the mundane.) Great artists, on the other hand, find a way to bring that which they have glimpsed in the "heavens" down to "earth," to find a way to manifest here on this plane the vision they have seen—in a form that the rest of us can experience and understand. Through creative imagination, artists give a "local habitation and a name" to their visions; they bring their glimpses into expression in the world of form in a specific time and place.

Skeptico: As we have talked, I've been wondering about the difference between intuition and imagination.

Wisdom Seeker: Very good question. As with so many issues, a lot depends on definitions. Some of those quoted above probably used these words interchangeably; others thought of them as differing. For me, the difference is this: Intuition is knowing something suddenly; it provides an understanding of something that has already happened or fills in gaps with regard to things you did not fully know before. Sometimes it provides a glimpse into an aspect of yourself that you had not yet understood. Intuition is information that shows up in the mind that explains, that helps to make sense of a situation or a person. Sometimes it provides a sense of how currents are flowing, what they are leading toward, how things will play out in the natural course of events without any action on your part. Intuition tends to have a passive quality about it that involves flashes of insight and understanding.

In contrast, imagination has more to do with how one engages with the world; it is more active. I form pictures of possibilities, of events that might be achieved, of things I could create through my actions. When using the imagination, actions often must be taken to bring what is imagined to fruition; in fact, actions to be taken are often part of the imaginative experience. So intuition is about understanding the flow that is already in motion, while imagination has more to do with images of possibilities, about how we might affect the flow as it moves forward, things we can create or make happen in life. In the end, though, intuition and imagination are closely related and frequently overlap.

Skeptico: How can I use imagination in my life?
Wisdom Seeker: This is the best use of imagination I know: Create yourself! By forming images of who you would like to be, of projects and plans to undertake, you begin to create your own life imaginatively. By committing to images you deem worthy—the way you will be with others, the values by which you will live—your life is shaped and molded.

Images are seldom fulfilled exactly as we have envisioned them; nevertheless, they function as does the trajectory set by a ship navigating a stormy sea. Winds and waves blow the ship around, and there is always the danger of shipwreck, but if we, like the captain of a successful ship, hold firm to the wheel of our images (adjusting as forces buffet us to and fro), then frequently the ship of our lives will sail into a port significantly related to the images to which we have held firm.

The analogy of guiding a ship through a storm suggests another central aspect of being human: consciously choosing actions. Sailing a ship involves decisions about which I know little, but some people have developed the skill to make wise decisions in turbulent seas. Some of their decisions might be reflexive, based on long years of training, but others inevitably require a thoughtful, conscious response. It is the same with life: The more we have consciously developed the ability to navigate the waters in which we sail, the more likely we will be able to make good decisions and have a successful voyage.

It is here that we meet creation at its most profound, for by consciously participating in the creation of our own lives, we participate in the creation of the world. At this creative edge, the individual imagination interacts in some mysterious way with the collective imagination and with the pattern in which we exist. No one person can control the pattern, and there are forces beyond our control we do not understand, but the great stories of the world say that by our choices we can affect our own lives, the lives of others, and even the unfolding of the larger pattern itself. Is there proof of this? No. But it is one of the strongest legacies we inherit from the wisdom traditions of humankind.

There is great danger as well. When a person or a group comes to believe that they understand the pattern fully and know where it should go, insisting that others conform to their views, great harm is usually done. Healthy co-creation happens with humility and self-awareness—each person making their individual decisions, as best they can, in harmony with what is right and good. Some will inevitably be mistaken or only partially right, so the process will be messy and imperfect, but the danger of a mass movement heading over a cliff of destruction is avoided. In the end, each of us is simply tasked to do what we can. Mother Teresa said it well: "We cannot do great things. We can only do small things with great love." As the pattern then unfolds, some might be seen as great, and others not, but this is not for the individual to judge concerning his or her own actions. We each simply do what seems to be our task, in harmony with what is good and right.

Imagination Gives Rise to Intention

Skeptico: You seem to be talking only about humans. Do other species have imagination?

Wisdom Seeker: There is no way for me to know whether members of the animal kingdom use imagination. In watching their behavior, it does not seem they form and act on long-term goals the way we humans do. This appears to be one of the main distinguishing characteristics of human beings: the capacity to choose among urges, desires, and goals, then set intentions that are pursued over time, sometimes long periods of time. In the animal kingdom, goals seem to happen more instinctively, rather than through a conscious process of choosing, at least in most cases.

I do not wish to assert that our co-inhabitants of this planet never act from conscious intentions, however, for I do not know whether this is the case or not. We don't tend to think of them acting this way, but that could be human prejudice or lack of understanding. What does seem to be true is that human beings are far more likely to form and act from conscious intentions over long periods of time in a way that most studies indicate is not the case in the animal kingdom. If acts from conscious intention do exist in other species, it seems we humans have carried it further, both for good and ill.

It also seems that most animal behavior comes in response to urges and impulses, restrained and guided by conditioning given during their upbringing (either by their own kind or by we humans). Of course, many human actions are motivated by impulse and restrained and guided by cultural conditioning. At times, however, something else comes into play: We interrupt urges and impulses and override conditioning, often taking actions that are hard to explain by those factors alone. For instance, someone forgoes food and comfort to climb a mountain; another gives away all possessions and becomes a monk; a third leaves an easy life to help the poor. Other examples: Someone dedicates her life to creating a political revolution; another endures great hardship to become an artist; a third gives countless hours to building an organization; another spends years in school to develop skills that will provide reward only in the distant future. What all these and so many more examples have in common is that an *image* has led to a path of intentional, sustained action over time.

Furthermore, because we often have many different images of things we might do, from the very large (win an Olympic medal, build a great corporation, become a famous artist, run for president), to the very small (take a walk this afternoon, get a haircut next week, try a new restaurant, get a new phone), at each level we are constantly dealing with images of actions we might take. These images stream forth, but then something extraordinary occurs: We choose one action over another; we put together a coherent pattern of actions over time that leads to outcomes different from those of others.

Skeptico: I thought you said that much of what we do springs from unconscious motives.

Wisdom Seeker: That is so. Much of the initial motivation for human action pours forth from the unconscious; many of our initial impulses are not consciously chosen. At some point, though, a decision between impulses is made, and in this decision-making process, there is often a conscious weighing and choosing, both about the goals to pursue and the means by which to pursue them. In other words, we make choices—choices that cannot be predicted, choices that are experienced as involving conscious volition.

Skeptico: That sounds like an argument for free will. You don't believe in that, do you?

Wisdom Seeker: There is a current of thought that denies the human ability to choose, which from time to time has become fashionable (with such free-will deniers as Thomas Hobbes in the seventeenth century and Steven Pinker in the current one). No evidence has ever been found to support their theory, though. Rather, it is a metaphysical conjecture growing out of a mechanistic theory of existence, and I have never seen any evidence for it—only assertions that free will does not exist by those who have chosen to assume this to be the case.

Perhaps Thomas Hobbes was the first to take the view that humans are strictly mechanical beings and that if we knew all the prior factors, we would be able to predict with 100 percent accuracy what actions will follow. This, of course, denies any role for conscious choice. As far as I can tell, nothing much has been added to the argument since Hobbes.[p] On the contrary, quantum theory is in the process of delivering what is likely to be a fatal blow to determinism, for it is becoming increasingly clear that the actions of particles cannot be predicted; at any given instant what a particle will do is not fixed, is not determined.

Further, the most frequent modern "proof" given for determinism has a fallacy at its core. The argument is to concede that we humans might sometimes perform random or chance acts, but that random acts are not what anyone really means by free will, so therefore free will does not exist—even if we sometimes act randomly. This, however, is but a word game that tries to trick listeners into believing that all the alternatives have been considered, which is **not** the case. Another alternative is that some values really do exist beyond the individual, with which we can choose to align ourselves (discussed more fully in the next chapter). Another is that there is a *telos*, a meaning to a particular life, toward which a person can turn, or from which one can turn away. Still another alternative is that a person can create a conscious intention toward something that feels worthwhile, and by that choice (and with persistence), affect the outcome of life in a meaningful way.

Skeptico: All that is pretty abstract. Give me an example of what you mean.

Wisdom Seeker: For me, it involves times when a feeling comes up—maybe anger—and instead of acting immediately from that anger, I pause and try to understand why I am angry. Or when someone

---

[p] Chapters 8 and 10 present a number of reasons why this is not the best assumption to make.

hurts my feelings and I want to cut them out of my life, but I reflect a little and realize that I care for that person, and I have probably hurt their feelings before, and they did not go away. Another major occasion is when I am deciding what to do, and after considering several alternatives, I pick the one that is difficult or not in my immediate self-interest. In these and many other moments, there is a clear sense that several pre-programmed factors are influencing me but that I can pause, reflect, and make a choice that is not programmed, that involves a certain degree of freedom.

Skeptico: Do any worldviews support the idea that I really can make choices that matter?

Wisdom Seeker: Actually, denying free will runs counter to the almost universal belief that we have the ability to make meaningful choices, and it is in conflict with most systems of thought we humans have used to guide our lives for thousands of years. Both Plato and Aristotle said we have the ability to make meaningful choices. All religions say we can choose to live by values that arise from a source beyond desires and conditioning (well, a few religious groups do hold to predestination, but most of those say we can still make meaningful choices concerning how we will respond to our predetermined lot).

Hinduism says that consciousness preceded the material world and that by making a conscious effort to recognize our identity with the ultimate reality, the outcome of our lives will be affected substantially.[q] Several modern physicists (Eugene Wigner, David Bohm, Arthur Eddington, Henry Stapp, Roger Penrose, to name a few) say that quantum mechanics requires consciousness. Some, following the thought of mathematician John von Neumann, say that consciousness

---

[q] Hinduism cannot be put into a short summary statement, of course. Although many in the tradition hold that we have a choice, some Advaita Vedantists do not. Their view is that there is no "doer," no individual self exists who can do anything—there is only one great cosmic dance in which we are each fulfilling a part. The only task of life, then, is to recognize this fact. Yet even in this view, it does seem we have a choice as to how we will go about arriving at this fundamental recognition.

is necessary to collapse the wave function so that the probabilities that underlie existence can take on actual form. Interestingly, this view allows for a mechanistic understanding of how the universe works while providing a way for human choice to enter.

Skeptico: Well, which of those is right?

Wisdom Seeker: As with so many things, I do not know. But what is certain is that most of humanity has believed we have a degree of free will, and there are many possible ways to understand how that might be so. In fact, there is no reason to reject the possibility that it is decisive in how a life unfolds. The most dramatic statement I know of the power of conscious choice is attributed to Goethe (but seems to have originated with Haim G. Ginott):

> I have come to the frightening conclusion that I am the decisive element. It is my personal approach that creates the climate. It is my daily mood that makes the weather. I possess tremendous power to make life miserable or joyous. I can be a tool of torture or an instrument of inspiration, I can humiliate or humor, hurt or heal. In all situations, it is my response that decides whether a crisis is escalated or de-escalated, and a person is humanized or de-humanized.[77]

Skeptico: Do you think that's true?

Wisdom Seeker: That statement is certainly on the opposite end of the spectrum from believing there is no free will. My personal sense is that it is closer to the truth than determinism. There have been times in my life when it seems likely I acted from conditioning, but there have been other times it seems clear that I made meaningful choices. The crucial thing to understand is that the denial of free will is not empirical or scientific. Neither free will nor its denial can be proven, so I can decide which possibility to organize around, and for me, the best assumption is that my choices make a difference. That seems more likely to lead to a fulfilled life than denying the almost universal feeling that we humans have a certain amount of freedom to choose.

> **Thought Experiment—Do You Have Free Will?**
>
> Do you believe you have a choice about the books you will read, the friends you will spend time with, the hobbies you will undertake, the effort you will put into work, the food you will eat, or the thousands of other things that feel like choices? Those who deny free will say this is not the case, that all your actions were previously determined by factors of which you are unaware. Since this is a speculative theory, can you think of any reason to believe it, rather than trusting your own sense that you make choices that affect your life?

Intention and Will

Conscious choices, intention, will: these are all ways to speak of capacities that overlap and intertwine. The way we bring images into reality is through intention; by creating conscious intentions toward outcomes, we affect our own lives and sometimes the lives of others. This is not to say that our intentions control things, for there are many forces at play: the intentions of others, the natural processes of the physical world, unconscious forces inside of us, and more. But our intentions affect what happens, sometimes dramatically. There is interplay between the world and us that affects the course of events, put dramatically by William Murray in his book *The Scottish Himalayan Expedition*:[r]

> Until one is committed, there is hesitancy, the chance to draw back. Concerning all acts of initiative (and creation), there is

---

[r] This quote is sometimes attributed to Johann Wolfgang von Goethe because William Hutchinson Murray attributed the inspiration for these lines to Goethe and attributed the last two lines to Goethe himself. There is considerable question about the translation of even those two lines from Goethe's original German, but this does not take away the power and meaning of the paragraph, nor the fact that Murray was inspired by Goethe. Murray, and perhaps Goethe, is telling us that by forming and acting on a clear intention, our lives, as well as the world, will be changed.

one elementary truth, the ignorance of which kills countless ideas and splendid plans: that the moment one definitely commits oneself, then Providence moves too. All sorts of things occur to help one that would never otherwise have occurred. A whole stream of events issues from the decision, raising in one's favor all manner of unforeseen incidents and meetings and material assistance, which no man could have dreamed would have come his way. Whatever you can do, or dream you can do, begin it. Boldness has genius, power, and magic in it. Begin it now.[78]

Yet another way to think of this extraordinary human capacity of intention concerns finding a purpose for life. William Cowper suggests that this is the pathway to happiness: "Existence is a strange bargain. Life owes us little; we owe it everything. The only true happiness comes from squandering ourselves for a purpose." Those committed to a purpose will, at times, push all kinds of barriers aside to achieve that purpose—sometimes barriers in the world, sometimes barriers within themselves. A fierce purpose can override fear, hunger, pain, sexual drives, degradation, humiliation, and most everything else, to reach the intended goal.

To get a sense of this, just think of history's heroes and heroines: Didn't they all have a strong sense of purpose? They imagined possibilities, then directed their will, their intentionality toward those images. Human history is filled with the stories of those who changed the course of events through a mighty commitment to a purpose: Jesus, Buddha, Joan of Arc, Gandhi, Nelson Mandela, Lincoln, Teresa of Avila, Martin Luther King, Jr., Mohammed, Confucius, Marie Curie, Einstein, Alexander the Great, and many more.

This commitment to a purpose among the illustrious is easy to recognize, but its importance among the rest of us is no less significant. Libraries, as well as family histories, are filled with accounts of people who did special things by finding and committing to a purpose. Sometimes ordinary people became extraordinary (and sometimes famous), and many have discovered what George Bernard Shaw found for himself: "This is the true joy in life, the being used for a purpose recognized by yourself as a mighty one."[79]

One example is Italian psychiatrist Roberto Assagioli, an early follower of Freud who broke from Freudian thought in part to emphasize his understanding of the importance of will. For Assagioli, it is the will, guided by imagination, that allows humans to take control of their lives and move toward fulfillment. His view of will, though, was not simplistic, but many-faceted. In addition to the asserting will, he recognized a will that could accept, or could choose to yield. It was even the role of will to surrender the ego position at appropriate times.[80]

Assagioli's beliefs were put to the test when, as a Jew in fascist Italy, he was jailed and put in solitary confinement, not knowing if he would ever be released. In this extreme circumstance, his imagination rose to the challenge, and he used his will to develop "inner freedom," saying, "We should of course realize the freedoms from fear, want, etc., but the right emphasis should be given to that inner freedom, without which all others are not sufficient. My dedication is to the task of helping men and women free themselves from inner prisons."[81]

Most impressive of all, he found that he could use his imagination to create an attitude for living and use his will to implement that decision, no matter the circumstances. "I realized that I was free to take one or another attitude toward my situation, to give one or another value to it, to utilize it or not in one or another way." Thus in prison, Assagioli used much of his time to develop "a sense of universal love." He worked to be able to "focus the love" and "to specialize its quality: a compassionate love towards the inmates of my prison and towards all prisoners and inmates of hospitals; tender love to the members of my family; brotherly love towards my friends; a love of admiration, gratitude, veneration towards the Great Souls…."[82] That is an impressive use of one's will.

The Power of Attention

Assagioli's experience makes clear that consciously directing one's attention can have a dramatic effect in the unfolding of life. How does this work? At any given moment, there are thousands of things I could be focusing on. I could be thinking about past experiences: good moments, bad moments, successes, failures, losses, joys, movies I have seen, songs I have liked, world events that affected me, personal events that troubled me, and on and on. I could be thinking about the future: planning a trip, envisioning a meeting, imagining a romance, worrying about money, fretting about a relationship, organizing a project, thinking about my work, and on and on. I could be focusing on one of the people I know and then specifically on any one of hundreds or thousands of moments, good or bad, I have experienced with that person. I could be focused on a thousand sensory inputs available right now—sights, sounds, smells, tastes, and tactile sensations of every kind. How, then, do I decide, amongst all these possibilities, where my attention will be?

For most of us, most of the time, where our attention is placed seems ***to just happen to us***—it is not something over which we exert control. It is mostly an unconscious process; we simply follow habits of mind into which we were conditioned when young. It's as if the patterns of those we grew up with seeped into us by osmosis; either that, or we rebelled against early influences by creating opposing patterns that then became our habits. Within this unconscious pattern, though, most of us have experienced—at least a few times—making a conscious choice about where to place our attention. Have you?

Thought Experiment—Directing Your Attention

Just for a moment, pick an object in your environment. Do it right now, and place your full attention on that object, keeping it there for a few seconds. Try, as best you can, to let go of other thoughts, and focus on that one thing.

If you do this exercise for just a few seconds, or have done it in the past, you discover the tendency of the mind to jump around from one thought to another, with one thought triggering the next, a smell or a sound setting the mind off in yet another direction. Keeping your mind where you "intend" is very difficult. And yet, learning to put the mind where you choose, and to keep it there through conscious choice, is perhaps the most powerful tool in one's toolbox of life.

> **Thought Experiment—Directing Your Attention Two**
>
> Think about someone you know. Let that person fill your thoughts as fully as you can, concentrating fully and completely.

Now consider: By picking that particular person, hundreds of other people you could have chosen were pushed aside. Did you pick someone who elevated your experience of yourself, or your life, or did you pick someone who drained your energy without any benefit? (I might choose to focus on a difficult person, but if I do so, hopefully it will be in a way that is useful for insight and understanding.)

Now, consider the particular aspect of the person you put at the center of your attention. Why did you focus on that aspect, versus the many other things you could have chosen? As a matter of fact, *how* did you choose the aspect of the person on which to focus? Did it just "happen"? When we think about the people in our lives, we do not have to let our thoughts happen by chance. Instead, by making conscious choices about what to focus on in regard to others, our relationships will be dramatically impacted. (I might consciously choose to focus on what is wrong with a person, or with myself in a relationship, but hopefully I will do so in a way that helps me understand how best to relate to that person—or that I no longer wish to do so.)

> **Thought Experiment—Directing Your Attention Three**
>
> Think about someone you know, consciously choosing to think about that person with respect, tenderness, or love.

You have the power to make this choice. You can consciously decide whom you will think about, how you will think about them, and what aspect you will focus your attention on (at least part of the time). By doing so, you claim the power to change your relationship to the people and things in your life. As Henry David Thoreau put it: "By a conscious effort of the mind we can stand aloof from actions and their consequences; and all things, good or bad, go by us like a torrent. I may be either the driftwood in the stream, or Indra in the sky looking down on it. I may be greatly affected by a theatrical exhibition; on the other hand, I may not be affected by an actual event, which appears to concern me much more."[83]

This power of attention is one of the great tools we have at our disposal as human beings. The Danish philosopher Søren Kierkegaard once said that a genius is someone who can focus on just one thing. To me this means that if I wish to create something, or affect the world in some way, or even change myself, a primary method is to practice directing my attention.

> A student asked a great Zen teacher:
> What is the essence of Buddhism?
> The teacher replied: Attention
> The student said: But I have practiced that. What else is there?
> The teacher paused, and said: Attention! Attention!
> The student, a bit perplexed, replied: But how do I do that?
> The teacher, with great emphasis, reiterated: Attention! Attention! Attention!

If we begin to grasp the importance of placing our attention, if we see that we can consciously participate in this process, we are by that act actively engaged in the creation of our world, and ourselves. As Thoreau captured it: "The universe constantly and obediently answers to our conceptions. Let us spend our lives in conceiving then."[84]

This is not easy, of course. It takes a great deal of practice to be able to place one's attention where one chooses, rather than being led around by old habits and whims. Nor is it easy, even if you have the ability, to decide *where* to place your attention. Yet there is nothing that will have a greater impact on your experience of life. A saying I once heard: By your attention, you create your world!

Skeptico: What is the difference between intention and attention?

Wisdom Seeker: I think of intention as involving choice, selecting between images, choosing the goals I will set. Attention, on the other hand, has to do with where I will place my focus right now. To operate effectively, I consciously choose intentions and then place my attention, moment to moment, on things that I feel will further the intended plan.

Skeptico: How do attention and imagination relate?

Wisdom Seeker: I think of imagination as providing the possibilities and attention as the way we allocate time and energy to specific actions—actions that will fulfill the intentions we have chosen from among the possibilities. We cannot do everything we imagine, so by forming intentions and then directing our attention to some things and not to others, we participate in the creation of our lives.

Skeptico: Are there any limits to what we can (or should) imagine and intend?

Wisdom Seeker: There are few limits to what we can imagine, but there are definitely limits to what it is healthy to intend, the most important being the values by which we will choose to live. That is the focus of the next chapter.

CHAPTER 11

Whose Values—Yours, Mine, or Ours?

I met a bear on the trail today; no one else was around. We stared at each other for a long time before I broke the communion, shouting and waving my arms in the air (and feeling a little foolish in the process). Through my actions, I assumed the world was a jungle and that aggression was the best answer to the anxiety I felt.

After my eruption, the bear looked at me for what seemed like several minutes, then turned and slowly lumbered away. (Was she afraid, or did she think my antics were too ridiculous to be around?)

Acting aggressively is the response I learned when encountering bears on a trail, and in that moment I did not consider the alternatives. As I continued walking, however, I remembered many stories of those who had entered a space of ease with animals in the wild. Would quiet wonder have been a better response in this situation? (As it turns out, only two people have ever been killed by a bear in a southeastern national park, and one of those cases is somewhat unclear as to the bear's culpability.)

We are continually deciding, consciously or unconsciously, how we will approach the world. Will we think of it as a jungle in which we fight or flee with each feeling of fear or anxiety? What if many fears and anxieties are unfounded? Will we view everything and everyone as if they were objects to satisfy personal needs and desires? What if other people resist being viewed this way—what then?

What Is a Human Being?

What makes a human being "human": the use of complex language, the ability to build sophisticated tools, the creation of art, the capacity to reason? Each of these has been proposed. Another candidate would have to be the existence of values: values that cause us (at times) to put the good of others before our own; to stay our hand from acting on immediate impulse; to choose the difficult rather than the easy path in service of a higher cause.

I have struggled for years to clarify the values by which I will live. In doing so, I have wrestled with the ideas of Nietzsche, who believed that power should be the ultimate arbiter of values. In his vision, the "Will to Power" is to be a central feature of the "Übermensch," the superior being to come. (Although Nietzsche's sister distorted his ideas in the book *Will to Power*,[85] published after his death, Nietzsche definitely put forward the view that the strong should take what they wanted, should have the courage to do what they wanted without being dissuaded by moral values, which in his view were nothing but the creation of the weak to manipulate the strong.)

When I encountered the bear on the trail, I acted from Nietzsche's point of view, hoping my aggression would convince the bear to cede the trail to me. Yet I do not believe this is the best way to live in relation to my fellow human beings (at least most of the time). However, if there are values beyond raw power by which to live, what are they? Where did they come from? More, is there any reason to believe that my values are shared with you?

There is no doubt that people raised in the same culture have some values in common, and in this way some conflicts are eliminated within each culture. But not all, not by a long shot. Even in a shared culture, the desires and urges of individuals often run counter to cultural rules; that is why the rules are necessary—to restrain whims and urges, to avoid the disruptions that widespread expression of unruly whims would cause.

Skeptico: Such as?

Wisdom Seeker: Oh, things like the drive for power, wealth, sex, control over others, relishing war, and adventures that risk the safety of others.

> **Thought Experiment—Value Questions**
>
> If you could take by force whatever you wanted, with no fear of reprisal, is there any reason you wouldn't do so?
>
> Are there limits to how you will express your sexual urges? If so, where did those limits come from? Who set them? Why?
>
> When will you use discipline to do what you "need to do" versus being gentle with yourself? When will you push yourself to get things done versus giving yourself a needed break?
>
> Will you do what you think is right even if it might cost you something you badly want? Why would you do that? What if it were to cost the love of someone you hold dear? What if it were to cost you a million dollars?

As I began to sort out the values by which I would live, it became increasingly clear that there are many different rules and values in my culture that are in conflict. For instance, I often heard these opposing admonitions while growing up:

> If you don't stand up for yourself, others will take advantage of you! Be tough, be strong, don't be a patsy, don't be a wimp.

But:
If you don't serve others, what good are you? Be loving. Take care of others! Turn the other cheek. Go the extra mile.

Be somebody, make your mark, achieve, win, succeed!

But also:
Be a good person! Be modest. Don't have a big head.

Love is the thing. Sacrifice everything for the love of your dreams.

But:
Be faithful. Do your duty. Be loyal to your parents/children/spouse. Don't abandon your responsibilities for a passing fancy.

Don't let fear of what people think stand in your way. Stand up for what is right! Be brave.

But also:
Don't make waves, don't cause trouble, don't fight city hall. Fit in. Be a loyal citizen.

You only live once. Go for it. Take the risk. Don't let fear hold you back.

But:
Be careful. Don't be foolish. Don't take too many chances.

Many Different Motivations

There are many different messages in every culture, often conflicting, and there are many different motivations inside each of us as well. The first motivations are usually getting enough to eat, having a comfortable place to sleep, and finding a safe place for the activities of the day. When these are reasonably satisfied, attention turns to other things, such as finding sexual fulfillment. If offspring follow, most of us are motivated to care and provide for the young.

If a certain amount of satiety is reached in these areas, attention often shifts to acquiring power. At a minimum, most of us want enough power to feel secure (the ability, through personal strength or alliance with others, to protect ourselves, our belongings, and our loved ones from attack and harm). But the genie of power is difficult to put back in the bottle; once present, it can easily become a lifelong drive for more and more and more, conflicting with and overriding other desires.

Yet power is only one among many motivations, such as the craving for fame and wealth, or the longing for excitement, entertainment, and adventure. Then there is the desire to increase the prestige of one's primary identity group, be it family, clan, tribe, sect, or country. Still another urge is to be is creative—to bring into existence something that did not exist before, including music, poetry, literature, businesses, organizations, movements, and on and on. The urge to create is one of the strongest forces in human life.

Another strong current in most of us is the quest for knowledge—the desire to learn, to know. Sometimes this urge has to do with skills that help in fulfilling other goals, but it also can be a pure desire for knowledge; we find pleasure, even delight, in learning.

Beyond even these motivations, there are others, perhaps not felt by everyone, but when activated, are no less powerful, such as the urge to develop deeply bonded relationships, to be of service, or to develop a meaningful connection to the spiritual realm (called such names as finding Enlightenment, knowing God, living in harmony with all that is, submission to Allah, accepting Jesus, merging with the Divine, and so on).

Among all these motivations, how do we decide which are the most important, which will take precedence? For me, drawing up this list brings to mind the many times various currents have vied for my time, energy, and attention. In a sense, all these motivations are the raw material with which we work throughout our lives; they arise as givens from enculturation, or from our genes, or from somewhere beyond both. When they arise, they are in competition with each other for our time and energy—and this continuing competition is one of the great issues of life.

Of course, many of us have been enculturated to push aside some of these motivations, to push them down into the unconscious. (Perhaps we were taught that wanting power or being ambitious is wrong, or that we should not feel certain sexual urges.) Sometimes family or culture have insisted that one motivation is of primary importance, and we have refused to let others into consciousness. The problem is, just because a drive is unconscious does not mean it is absent or that it isn't powerfully affecting our lives. The strongest enculturation can fall away in an instant with an intense urge, leading to a totally "out-of-character" action.

Being human, then, means being constantly bombarded by many conflicting urges and desires that need to be balanced and reconciled, yet nothing within the urges and desires provides any guidance about how to decide between them. Each pushes to be fulfilled, so they are constantly in conflict, and this is precisely the reason we need values: We must have some means by which to give weight to one motivation over another, some way to decide between alternatives.

Isn't this where reason comes in, to help us make this kind of decision? Reason is a marvelous tool for sorting things out—once key starting assumptions are in place. But reason (at least as most people use that word today) does not give us those starting assumptions. For instance, reason does not give guidance as to whether we should use our resources for ourselves or for the good of others: this depends on our values. Reason does not instruct whether we should work hard, or alternatively, try to have a good time; that judgment depends on the goals we have set. Nor does reason, in the way many people use that word today, tell us whether we should break a law. For instance, if someone decides to steal or rape or kill, reason as used in common parlance can just as easily be employed in plotting to accomplish these acts as to dissuade a person from undertaking them. As for the most important things in life, reason by itself cannot determine whom we will love, the nature of our creative expression, the careers we will pursue, what we will enjoy, the deep friendships we will develop, or the nature and degree of spiritual experience.

For reason to do its work, a few core values must be present. An example: Once, while traveling, I met an attractive woman who was married. She was alone on the trip, however, and clearly interested in pursuing an "in-the-moment" relationship. My question was: Should I follow my natural urges or restrain them in deference to the "idea" of marriage, even though I was single? Reason did not give an answer, for this was a question of values.

> **Thought Experiment—What Would You Do?**
>
> A friend calls and needs help, but you are very busy on an important project. Will you help your friend or finish your project?
>
> Being of service to the needy feels very important, but getting ahead in life requires a great deal of time. Which will get the majority of your energy and attention? How will you decide how much time for each?
>
> You like spending time with one person, but someone else needs your attention more. With whom will you choose to spend the most time?
>
> A person you know says something very hurtful. Do you defend yourself, counter-attack, keep quiet but stay away from that person, or absorb the blow and stay in the relationship, perhaps even giving kindness in return? How will you decide between these various approaches?

Living with Others

Besides struggling with conflicting motivations within, we also have conflicts with those around us—all those "others" who have urges and desires that are not (alas) the same as our own.

> What happens when I want something you want, and it is not possible for both of us to have it?
> What happens if I take something from you?
> Is speeding in my car normal, or is it reckless endangerment of everyone in the path?
> A war is approaching—is it justified? What is my obligation toward a war I do not believe in?
> How will murder be defined? How will it be punished? Is capital punishment justified, or is that murder? What about the assassination of terrorists—is that murder or prudence?
> What is theft, and how is it different from being a sharp businessperson? Is it OK to praise something you are selling to the point of exaggeration? Is leaving a little personal income off your income tax return "what everyone does," or is it stealing from everyone?

I have wrestled with each of these questions and many more. I have searched for a broad, overarching answer.

One strategy: To put aside all personal urges and desires and commit to living only from "higher motivations." Through this act maybe everything will work out perfectly; if I give up all ego-centered drives and act exclusively for the highest good, perhaps there will be no conflicts. After all, don't all religions teach that following one's personal urges is not the right path?

If only it were so simple. Having tried this a few times, and having watched a number of friends do the same, I have come to respect the testimony of psychology when it says that "putting aside" one's urges and desires is easier said than done. In fact, modern psychology grew from the work of Freud, who was dealing with mental illnesses that arose from people ignoring and pushing into the unconscious feelings that a puritanical and rigid society suggested they shouldn't have.

Freud's thesis has now been researched extensively so that today a library could be filled with books documenting the wreckage (unhelpful aggression, fear, anxiety, rage, drug abuse, depression) caused by pushing inner currents into the "shadow." Carl Jung coined this term, about which he says in his *Collected Works*, "Everyone carries a shadow, and the less it is embodied in the individual's conscious life, the bleaker and denser it is.... If it is repressed and isolated from consciousness, it never gets corrected and is liable to burst forth suddenly in a moment of unawareness."[86] In other words, when we rigidly keep ourselves from core motivations, the pent-up energy eventually explodes into our lives, often in destructive ways.

Unfortunately, there is no easy escape from the difficulty presented by conflicting urges and desires; it a lifelong struggle. Even a commitment to follow "higher motivations" starts with a dilemma—which higher motivations?—for there are many different and competing candidates vying for our loyalty.

> **Thought Experiment—The Time of Your Life**
>
> Will you commit your time and energy to a cause you believe in, even if it takes you away from spending time with your family?
>
> Will you give time and attention to the spiritual dimension of life—at the expense of your career?
>
> How much time will you allocate to being creative in ways that do not bring monetary reward? If you are artistic, will you use your creativity to pursue fame and fortune, or will you follow your creative vision no matter where it leads? Is the creative urge about something more than success in the world? If so, what, and where does that belief come from?
>
> If you enjoy learning, what kinds of knowledge will you pursue? How much time will you give to the pursuit of knowledge for its own sake versus knowledge that will be useful in a career?

These questions, and many others, are at the center of being human—and our answers define who we become as well as the nature of the lives we lead. Our responses, whether made consciously or unconsciously, determine how we understand ourselves and whether we will be able to discover meaning and/or fulfillment in life. And crucially, our motivations, even the higher ones, will not provide the answers. All motivations want to be fulfilled, and they do not provide a means to choose between them; only values can serve as a compass in negotiating the difficult terrain between competing motivations.

Where Do Values Come From?

Nietzsche admonished us to have the courage to follow our desires and urges; that is the point of life, said he. If trying to fulfill every desire is the only force at play, however, then power is the sole arbiter of our actions toward others. Nietzsche affirmed this conclusion, glorified it, even. Yet accepting this has been difficult for many who have followed Nietzsche part of the way. They shy away from the obvious conclusion to which his trail leads: Unless there is a transcendent ground upon which values are based, the only option that remains is power. Nietzsche had the courage to face this directly, acknowledging that if each and all try to get as much of the good stuff in life as possible for themselves, we will be in constant competition. We might disguise our motives—from others, and even from ourselves—but this is only a game we are playing as we each try to get what we want.
Skeptico: Is there an alternative?
Wisdom Seeker: Yes, absolutely: to organize around the age-old belief that some values exist beyond the individual, beyond wishes and rationalizations, even beyond enculturation. We might access these values by following the rules of a culture that is based upon them, or we might get in touch with them directly ourselves. Both these routes, though, assume the existence of transcendent values.

As discussed earlier, we first encounter values through enculturation; every culture has a set of teaching stories that suggest how we should live, and these stories carry the culture's guidance concerning the values that are crucial for a fulfilled life. It is upon these stories that human cultures have been built and on which the functioning of every community depends; each individual is dependent on one of these cultural systems as well (either the one in which we were raised or a new one we have adopted).

Skeptico: I am not dependent on those old stories. I just know within myself what is right and wrong. I just know the "right" answer to value questions!

Wisdom Seeker: Many people feel as you do, but consider this: From what source do your answers spring? With a little exploration, you will discover that these "internal" answers mostly come from things you were taught as a child, blended with points of view you picked up from influential people along the way. And behind the teachings of these early caregivers and influential people will always be found one or more of the great wisdom traditions of human history.

Skeptico: And where do you think these came from?

Wisdom Seeker: All began with founders who asserted that the values they offered came from a transcendent realm;[s] all those who created the successful value systems by which human beings have lived for thousands of years believed there were transcendent values to serve as the basis for successful human thought and action. This is not proof that such values exist, of course—every one of the founders of the world's wisdom traditions could have been deluded. But to make that risky bet means to cut oneself off from the sense of harmony that many have suggested to be the result of aligning with transcendent values. In a modern version of Pascal's wager, the Dalai Lama told Arlo Guthrie in an interview: "Well, there might be an afterlife and there might not be. So when I meditate, I put myself in that afterlife right now so that if I ever have to die, I won't even notice it. If there is no afterlife, OK....

---

[s] One definition of how to think about the transcendent is by Dr. Leonard Swidler, professor of Catholic thought and interreligious studies at Temple University: "That which goes beyond the everyday, the ordinary surface experience of reality. It can mean spirits, gods, a Personal God, an Impersonal God, Emptiness, etc., etc."

It wasn't such a bad discipline anyway."[87] This is the same wager we all have to make with regard to values.

Let Your Conscience Be Your Guide

Besides cultural teachings, the main way we access our values is through conscience, the inner moral compass where values seem to reside. In Chapter 5, we explored how conscience is at least partly created by culture, but do we also have a sense of right and wrong, good and bad, that is not created by others? In other words, are there some values that are inherently a part of what it means to be a healthy human being? Most thinkers throughout history have believed this to be the case, and all legal systems are based on the assumption that there is a moral sense in everyone (except the severely mentally impaired). No major legal system, now or throughout history, has begun with the assumption that all laws are arbitrary. Some minor ones are viewed as arbitrary, like the speed limit for cars (or chariots). But all systems of justice have held that some laws are fundamental; that there are certain things any sane person should know to be wrong.

For instance, it is not a valid defense in any system of justice for a murderer to assert that it was OK to kill someone in cold blood simply because he or she wanted to kill another. Neither is it a defense to say you were unaware that murder was wrong, for the law is based on the assumption that all of us know that killing in cold blood is wrong; it is not a rule made up out of thin air.

In a recent book, *What Children's Minds Tell Us About Truth, Love, and the Meaning of Life,* Alison Gopnik makes a compelling case that very young children have a moral sense, although it is often overridden by their immediate impulses. If she is right, what cultures really do is cultivate this innate moral sense rather than arbitrarily writing values on the blank slate of a child's consciousness. This suggests also that the soil from which reformers spring up from time to time in every culture, calling on members of a society to correct practices that seem unconscionable (even practices that have been sanctioned by the culture), is a deep inner sense that some things are simply "right" and "just," while others are "wrong." The appeal is to a "higher law" that exists beyond the culture (but which any person can access). In other words, this is an appeal to conscience.

Immanent versus Transcendent Values

Skeptico: Because most everyone seems to have a conscience, perhaps values come from inside; they are simply inside everyone.

Wisdom Seeker: That is a good definition for what some call immanent values: they simply arise in each person. There might well be something inside each of us—something immanent in everyone—that guides the formation of values. But if each person's immanent guidance is different, if each conscience is different, we are back to the dilemma of having no basis upon which to create laws or organize relations with each other except power.

Skeptico: How so?

Wisdom Seeker: If one person immanently believes that rape and murder are wrong but the next person does not, on what basis will we determine who is right? If my conscience and your conscience do not share common ground, what is left but power?

Skeptico: Maybe the same values are immanent in everyone.

Wisdom Seeker: If so, how did they get to be the same, and how do we know they will stay the same? It does not suffice to say that they simply appeared in everyone simultaneously. For this to have happened, there would have to have been a source that synchronized the implantation in all at the same moment. Further, after this was done, how would the synchronization be maintained?

Think about this in a slightly different way: If values are strictly immanent, in which person are the correct ones stored, for we have had countless disagreements about values through the eons? If we have a disagreement, which person or group is the reference point— which person or group's view is the valid one? There is also the issue of change: If values change in cultures over time, which they seem to do, which person or group has the currently valid set? Do they change simultaneously in all living persons? How on earth would they do that? If they don't change simultaneously, however, we are back to the question of which person or group is the repository of the correct set of values at any given moment.

The only explanation I can find for how the same values could be immanent in everyone is that they reside in a transcendent ground to which all have access. Disagreements arise because we have a tendency to distort what we perceive from that ground to suit our own purposes. In other words, we each have access to a shared set of values, but we often override what we find there in favor of an interpretation that supports an immediate impulse, as we did when we were children. This would explain the role of wisdom figures in human history. They are the ones who have reached a place, beyond personal preferences, which allows them to see more clearly the values everyone could access but are hidden from most of us by our personal agendas.

In the end, the idea of "immanent in everyone" must fall on one side or the other of the divide between power and transcendence. Either values have a reality outside of any one person or group and everyone can access them, or power is the only means by which we can resolve disputes and differences. If values are immanent but different in each person, we can try persuasion and reason, but if we don't agree, there is nothing left but power.

Alternatives to a Transcendent View

According to Aldous Huxley, "The thin and precarious crust of decency is all that separates any civilization, however impressive, from the hells of anarchy or systemic tyranny which lie in wait beneath the surface."[88] This is dramatic, highlighting how dependent we are on a few common principles, such as decency. But where do these principles come from? The answer given by every lasting human culture has been that values such as justice, decency, and fairness come from the transcendent dimension. This is true of the teachings of Confucius,

Moses, Buddha, Socrates, Lao Tzu, Hindu sages, Jewish prophets, Jesus, Mohammed, and many other foundational figures. Were they all deluded?

Anyone who chooses this answer has another question to face: If all the great wisdom figures were mistaken, and no values transcend personal wishes and desires, what right does anyone have to assert that another should live by a standard he or she does not wish to live by? If there are no transcendent values to which we can jointly refer, and I have enough force to make you do what I want, why should I not do it? If I want your money, and I am strong enough, why shouldn't I take it? If I want to have sex with you, or to kill you, and I am strong enough, why would I choose not to do so? If my group wants to do away with science, or burn a church and wipe out all its members, and we have enough force, what is there to restrain us?

Through the ages, several possibilities besides transcendent values have been proposed to solve this dilemma, but all are problematic:

Self-interest: It has been suggested that abiding by some values is in one's self-interest. The problem is, which values? My highest value might be to get as much money and power as I can. You might try to convince me that it is in my self-interest not to steal, or rape, or kill to do so, but if I don't agree, on what basis can you assert that I should do as you say? You can try to persuade me, but if I am not persuaded, what right do you have to tell me what to do? If values are not grounded in something larger than personal opinion, then your opinion does not override mine, so there is nothing but someone else's power versus mine to keep me from killing, stealing, and raping if that is what I choose.

Instinct: Perhaps values are instincts that developed to help us survive as a species. If so, we are immediately thrust back into the dog-eat-dog world[t] of pure power. Why? If values are but instincts to help a species survive, any individual can refuse to abide by them at any moment with no negative consequences to his or her life. In fact, in such a

---
[t] Dogs get a bum rap with this expression—most dogs I have known have been fairly considerate toward me.

world, the greatest advantage would accrue to those who could persuade everyone else to abide by values, while not doing so themselves. Each person would find advantage in trying to manipulate others with high-sounding ideals, so values would become useful tricks to persuade others to act in ways that benefited the trickster (Nietzsche's view in a nutshell). If the only argument for a value is that an action opposed to it might hurt the "species" in the long run, it will have no effect on someone motivated by a personal desire right now. (Imagine trying to dissuade someone contemplating rape, theft, or murder with the argument: "Don't do it! It's not in the interest of the survival of the species!")

Here is the heart of the matter: If values are simply among the many instincts that developed to help us survive, there is no reason I should not override the instinct to be fair or just any time I decide there is something I want with which that instinct interferes. We override instincts all the time. (I am hungry but want to finish this project; I need to find shelter from this storm, but my loved one is in need; I have an urge for sex with that person, but she is married to my friend; my body is tired, but I want to finish the race.) There is a strong instinct to preserve one's own life, but many people override that instinct with values they hold dear, risking their lives in the process. Through the years, a number of people in Japan have even chosen to kill themselves when they felt they had infringed an important value. Whether this is a value you hold or not, it is a clear sign that values are different from even the most basic instincts.

We don't always override instincts with values, but many humans actually do so quite often. This seems to be tied to the development of consciousness: The more consciousness, the more one is likely to choose values over instincts. Values seem to be at a higher level than instincts. If this were not the case, the instinct to take what I want or to kill would be of the same order and have the same weight as the instinct to be kind or compassionate. If the two were of the same order, chosen values would not override instinctual urges with any regularity. (Today I am feeling a little tired, so maybe I will be compassionate, but tomorrow, I will go out there and enjoy raping and pillaging to my heart's content.) Yet the lives of kind and compassionate people through the ages demonstrate that it is quite possible to make this choice with regularity.

Values, of course, are enculturated, but all cultures assert that their values originally came from a shared ground. A significant mark of difference between the two is that I can change my values, but I cannot change my instincts. I can override instincts, but this does not get rid of them. On the other hand, I can put aside an enculturated value and decide to hold a different one, then use that new value to override an instinct, or even use it to replace an old value. Values can be built up over time and incorporated into one's life in a conscious way. As Charles Reade put it, "Sow an act, and you reap a habit. Sow a habit, and you reap a character."[89] This involves a conscious process at a very different level of my being, whereas instincts arise unbidden and are just there, the raw material I must mold and shape with values. The ability to consciously mold one's values provides a clear divide with instincts.

Perhaps We Can Vote: What about the vote of the majority? Can this create workable values? It might help, but on what basis will we cast our votes? Will I vote on the basis of whether my vote will help me or my preferred group to get what we want? If so, we are back to raw power. On the other hand, all democracies in human history have had values embedded in their beliefs, values attributed to the transcendent dimension; it is to these values that appeals are made as a vote approaches. If such values exist, and enough of us vote in the service of shared values, then a functioning society can be fashioned through democracy.

Without transcendent values, however, a democracy is immediately thrust into the domain of power, the power of one group over another. If the majority in a society wants to use others as slaves, and they have the power to do so, what is the argument against it? If a majority wants to create gas chambers to kill people they don't like, what argument does one use to stop them? If the majority of people in a nation want to go to war to take another nation's land or wealth, on what basis can they be persuaded otherwise?

My Group Only: Perhaps there are values that apply only within one's tribe, religious group, or culture and do not extend to those outside the group. This is a complex issue, for many people throughout history have lived and acted from such a belief. The thing to notice here, however, is that most all those who have held this view have believed that their values came from a transcendent source and thus have rejected Nietzsche's view. (Whether values can be both "my group only" and still come from a transcendent source is a thorny issue, to be dealt with later.)

Can Biology Help?

Is it possible that we will find the origin of our values in our cells, our genes, our DNA? There are some interesting thrusts in this direction, such as the suggestion by sociobiologists like E. O. Wilson that people act altruistically to protect their gene pools. However, at this point, there is only the observation that people act altruistically and the possible explanation that they do so to protect their gene pools; there is no evidence for this explanation that I can find, just the metaphysical speculation. For this theory to hold up, several issues must be addressed:

1. **Which "gene pool" are we talking about?** Using myself as an example, would my gene pool consist of my personal offspring, my close family, my extended family, my tribe, my race, my species, or all living beings? Which gene pool am I motivated to protect? If the theory involves a "narrow pool," how does it account for the many examples of humans who have risked their lives to save someone they did not know? How does it deal with the amazing stories of people who have risked their lives to save animals or to protect the environment?

2. **Is it more than just protecting the young?** There is a clear inclination in many living things to protect and defend the young living in their immediate environment. Not just their own kind, either, for it has been shown repeatedly that this phenomenon often extends to newborns that are not from the same gene pool: Animals adopt and raise the young of another species; some birds even lay their eggs in the nests of other bird species, knowing that if the eggs hatch there, the "adopting" parents will care for the interlopers as if they were their own. This seems to be even more true with humans: We often adopt and care for young ones far removed from our gene pools, frequently even caring for newly born pets as tenderly as our own offspring. This inclination to take care of the young is a strong force, providing counter-evidence to the idea that we act to protect a narrow "gene pool."

3. **What if "gene pool" were defined more broadly, to include extended family or tribe?** More problems. If my genes are making decisions, how exactly do they deal with the idea of "family" or "tribe"? As I make a decision about how to act, how does my DNA know that someone is my direct offspring? Let's say I have a son I do not know I have. If I come upon a fight between a friend and a total stranger (but the stranger is my unrecognized son), whom would I defend? Wouldn't I defend my friend and not my son? How would my DNA know that it was supposed to jump into the fray and "protect my gene pool" by siding with the stranger? The difficulty is this: "Family," "extended family," and "tribe" are concepts, ideas, and my DNA doesn't function by using concepts and ideas, at least as far as I can tell.

4. **Going a step further, how do my genes take control of my actions and decisions?** When I am faced with a decision, one that means life or death for another, or myself, how exactly does my "gene pool" take control of me and make a decision? Let's say I am in a war and deciding whether to risk my life to save a wounded buddy; how do my genes get involved in the decision? Or perhaps I am asked to undertake a risky assignment, to go on a mission to save the life

of someone I have never met and who is of a different race? Do I undertake the assignment? To make this decision, I consider what I believe, the kind of person I want to be, how much fear I have, what it would mean to all those I love and those who love me. In this process, how exactly do my genes get involved? How do I consult them? I have trillions of cells in my body, all made up of many strips of DNA. Which ones do I consult? How do I find out if they all agree? Do I take a vote of the trillions of DNA strips within me?

Attempted levity aside, how could genes, or DNA, take control of my decisions and actions? There is no workable theory I can find that explains how this might happen. On the other hand, there is significant evidence pointing in a different direction. A number of those who have risked life and limb for another have been asked why they did such an extraordinary thing. The answers have to do with values, often revolving around empathy and compassion, of feeling another's plight as being one's own. Other reports involve values such as duty and responsibility, with such statements as, "It was simply the right thing to do" or "I couldn't have lived with myself if I hadn't done what I did." In all these accounts, I have never found anyone who mentions "protecting the gene pool" as a motivation. Of course, people do not always consciously know why they act as they do, but all reports by those who actually risked their lives for another suggest that values are the motivation, not protecting a hypothetical "gene pool." Moreover, to contradict so many firsthand reports with an unproven hypothesis that has little evidence behind it is flimsy ground upon which to construct a theory of human behavior.

The "gene pool" theory of motivation seems to have grown out of a metaphysical belief that everything has to have a biological explanation. Straitjacketed by this belief, its proponents argue that because altruism and other values seem to exist, and the only possible source for them is biological, then some biological theory must explain them. This is a wonderful example of circular reasoning—you start with an assumption and then use the observations that grow out of the assumption as evidence for the assumption. In exactly the same way, those who start with the assumption that space beings landed on earth and began human civilization always find a great deal of evidence for this theory lying about (as a number of popular books demonstrate). Many religious people start with the assumption that there must to be a God like the one they posit, and their theories use that assumption to "prove" the belief. In essence, "gene pool" theorists are using the same kind of argument to counter the religious theories they reject.[u]

Beyond Biology

The proposal that genes can organize and operate around ideas, that trillions of cells made up of trillions of DNA strips (as well as trillions of guest mitochondria) somehow get together and agree on values requires a magical leap of faith. Further, there is no agreement among those who propose biological theories as to which values are crucial, so this view is of no help in trying to organize our lives nor in organizing our societies. Biological arguments provide no basis upon which to agree with our fellow beings on how to act in relation to one another. (Would you be moved by the argument that you should refrain from doing what you wanted because of someone's theory about what your DNA wanted?)

There is a confusion of levels here. Some motivations, as opposed to values, do arise at the genetic level. Our cells crave food or water and send signals to the brain to that effect, which results in actions. But some actions and decisions happen at another level, a level that requires concepts and ideas (such as risking death for a cause, forgiving someone who has wronged us, deciding to sacrifice for another, working to build a friendship over time). How do genes know what the issues are at this level? How do they weigh in with their opinions or take part in decisions? There is no reason to conclude that values such as justice, kindness, compassion, courage, honor, patience, and

---

[u] I wonder at times if those making the "gene pool" argument shouldn't be charged with practicing theology without a license.

fairness come from the genetic realm. Moreover, history is filled with examples of those who have overridden the strongest biological urges, such as hunger and cold, in service of a higher value.

We do sometimes follow genetic motivations, but when they clash with values, why should we choose to obey the genetic signals rather than what we feel to be "good" or "right"? What point of view do genetic motivations serve, anyway? What if some strips of my DNA have different purposes than my conscious self, or if some of my individual cells have different aims from my ego? What if my liver is at variance with the yearnings of my higher self? Perhaps the trillions of mitochondria that inhabit my cells have taken over and are trying to motivate me in ways that serve their interests rather than my own. Maybe a few pesky genes have organized a rebellion and have set off on a course to fulfill their own agenda, which is not the same as "mine" (cancer, perhaps?).

In other words, why should we follow the motivations that arise from genes or mitochondria rather than the values that we have decided are important at the ego level or at the spiritual level of our existence? Why should I make a conscious effort to live by something that came about by natural selection if I don't like it? Perhaps a new urge is an improvement for me, or for the species. If the motivations in my genes arose through trial and error over the eons, maybe a new thought today about how I should live is an advanced development.

Given all these difficulties, biology is not the best place to turn in trying to understand values, especially because there are many other sources to consider. Even the father of evolutionary biology, Charles Darwin, was deeply interested in the role of morality in human life, spending much more time laying out its importance in his second book, *The Descent of Man*, than focusing on the idea of "the survival of the fittest." In his first book, *The Origin of the Species*, he was primarily focused on the forces that affect the animal kingdom, but when dealing more extensively with humans in *Descent*, he continually focused on the importance of love and stayed open to the mysterious source of its arising. (He mentions "survival of the fittest" only twice in *Descent* but speaks of love ninety-five times.)[90]

Skeptico: What is the best alternative to a biological view?
Wisdom Seeker: No one model has been firmly established.
Skeptico: Well, what are the alternatives?
Wisdom Seeker: There are several possibilities, but keep in mind that they are not mutually exclusive; they might all be ways of expressing something that is ineffable. Within the framework of that thought, the Hindus say that consciousness preceded biological development and that at the deepest level there is only one consciousness, of which we are each a part. Perhaps shared values flow from that connected place.

Rupert Sheldrake has amassed a wealth of interesting evidence to demonstrate that there is a morphogenetic field, a field of information outside any one member of a species, in which each member of the species shares. This information can change over time, but the field is transcendent to the individual yet continually affecting the perceptions and actions of each member in real time. This idea helps solve the mystery of how some animals are able to do things they were never taught or how a flock of birds can respond to each other faster than any method of communication we know. Perhaps values, then, are stored in a morphogenetic field.

Carl Jung proposed another kind of shared field called the "*collective unconscious*," and Buddhists say that we all share in the one Buddha-nature. In fact, all spiritual traditions have held that some values arise from a transcendent domain. Capturing many of these currents, Joseph Campbell said in *The Inner Reaches of Outer Space*: "The universally distinguishing characteristic of mythological thought is…a sense of identity of some kind, transcendent of appearances,"[91] by which he means that we are all united in some mysterious way behind our surface experience of being separate.

Given all these possibilities, and more, we are not sentenced to a biological prison in understanding the source of values. It is also worthy of note that many individuals throughout history have refrained from having a family so that they could pursue spiritual paths; others have given their lives to a cause in which they believed rather than perpetuate their family interests—sacrificing themselves to help those of other races and forsaking their own group to protect and care for the downtrodden of another. There are countless examples from all periods of history, such as those who risked and sometimes lost their lives in protecting people they did not know from the Nazi death camps or those who organized the underground railway to help slaves escape from the American South. Many of these individuals have been regarded as the best in their cultures, and a few have come to be considered among the greatest figures in all of human history. Their lives stand in direct opposition to theories about "protecting the gene pool," and the respect they have received makes such theories seem insubstantial.

The Case for Transcendent Values

We all have a drive within us to get what we want, to get the good things in life for ourselves. Starting from that point, we will either (1) use whatever means are available to fulfill these urges and drives, limited only by the power others have to prevent us, or (2) organize our lives, and the lives of our communities, around values that are shared with other human beings, values we believe to be grounded in a transcendent source. Along the first path we will live by Nietzsche's "Will to Power"; along the second, values will become the mechanisms by which we sort through our drives and sometimes subjugate them to a higher good. In a world that includes transcendent values, we will have guideposts to help us prioritize the conflicting motivations within, as well as to help us organize our relations with others in the world outside.

Psychologist Lawrence Kohlberg, a professor of psychology at the University of Chicago and Harvard conducted a series of influential studies with regard to values and moral development. His conclusion: There are six stages of moral development in human beings, and the order of development is neither random nor reversible. In other words, the development of values moves up through six stages in the same order in each person. Every person does not move into the highest stages, but when movement does occur in a human life, it is always up the same ladder.[92]

One can adjust and refine how the stages are defined and even postulate a different number of stages. Carol Gilligan, a groundbreaking professor at New York University, has shown how the stages are different in men and women.[93] But the underlying idea—that we move through stages of moral development—seems solid. The relevant part of his work for our purposes is that Kohlberg's highest stage of moral development corresponds strongly with the teachings of the world's great wisdom traditions. The essence: When we arrive at the highest reaches of moral development, we decide how to act toward others by putting ourselves in the shoes of the other, by getting in touch with how we would like others to act toward us and those we care about.[94] Another way to say this is that at the highest stage of moral development, we try to see (and act) toward others with eyes of compassion, love, kindness, and consideration. Further, although different cultures interpret this highest stage in different ways, some version of it exists in all. It therefore transcends culture. What this means is that the highest stage of moral development, as all the great wisdom teachers have said, springs from an underlying ground that is universal.

If this is true—if at least a few values are shared and enduring (and we can jointly refer to them in working out our relationships with each other)—then we live in a different world from that of pure power. In this kind of world, attempting to live by values does not mean, as Nietzsche proposed, being duped by those who invented them. In a world where values are transcendent to the individual as well as to any one cultural group, the crucial task is to discern those values that are universal and apply them to real-life situations as best we can. In this kind of world, individuals and movements can successfully inspire us to return to, or practice more faithfully, values we share. In such a world, disputing parties can consult their consciences to find common ground, greater confidence can be placed in juries to decide what is "fair" and "just," and laws and customs can be developed that carry moral weight because they are not arbitrary—do not serve only one person's or one group's agenda.

If transcendent values exist, then reason and persuasion can be used to help others discover them, and some of us might even conclude that it is wise rather than foolish to sacrifice personal wishes and desires in favor of a higher good. For values to function in this way, however, we must believe that they exist as a reality outside of one person's view or interpretation. The most common way to experience them might be as a voice from within (as immanent), but if we feel that our inner compass is attuned to a field that is shared, then our immanent sense is grounded in something transcendent.

In geometry, the concept of a circle, and in mathematics, constants such as pi, present analogies for transcendent values. These seem to exist beyond any one person's or one group's view or definition of them. When we speak of or draw a circle for one another, we are using words and images to describe something that has an independent existence. When we measure the proportion between certain things, we discover that that proportion is always the number "pi," independent of our wishes and opinions. (Pi is the ratio of the circumference of a circle to its diameter.) In the same way, shared values have a standing beyond any one person's or one group's view.

For me, perhaps the best analogy for and the best way to get at the existence of transcendent values involves consciousness itself. Consciousness seems to exist in me, but also in you. There is something shared, so we can talk about it with each other, study it, reflect on it together, and find commonalities in our understandings. Something about consciousness seems transcendent to the individual, as is the case with values. What it finally comes down to is this: We have many conflicting motivations within us and many conflicts in our relations with each other. In dealing with these conflicts, is there something universal to which we can attune, and in so doing receive guidance for our lives and for settling our differences? For those who point to conscience, we must ask whether it has a foundation beyond the individual. If not, we are thrust back into the Nietzschean camp of power.

If, on the other hand, conscience has a reference point that is shared, then something immanent in all of us leads to transcendent ground.

All the world's wisdom traditions assert that such values do exist, yet it is a bit disconcerting to discover there are disagreements about what these values are and how they should be applied. One reason for the disagreements, though, might be that among these precious gems, the ones emphasized by different teachers will vary according to the needs of a particular time and with individual circumstance. In a famous Confucian dialogue, the sage tells a student to wait before he acts, to seek the advice of his father and elder brother before taking action. A short time later, he tells another student, "He who hesitates is lost." A third student hears both conversations and is puzzled, "Why do you give contradictory advice to these two men?" Confucius replies, "One drags his feet, so I tried to speed him up a little. The other is hyperactive, so I tried to slow him down."[95]

In a specific time and place, a wisdom figure might emphasize what is needed at that time, but that emphasis, after being handed down for generations and becoming institutionalized, could easily be out of balance in a new era, which would mean that all interpretations by the traditions would need to be refreshed from time to time to remain healthy. (Thomas Jefferson made exactly this argument after the founding of the United States, saying a new revolution would probably be required every fifty years.) This, however, is not an argument that core values change, but that every interpretation is partial, or based on the needs of a particular time and place.

Another reason for the variance could be that each tradition has, at times, touched transcendent values and brought them into human life, but also each has had moments in which individuals inserted their non-transcendent prejudices and opinions.

Whatever the reasons for the differences, our task is to find the core principles that apply to all. To do this, we will have to put aside dogmatism and arrogance and undertake the hard work of sorting through conflicting views to discover the vein of gold running through the base ore. We will never be perfect in this, but (switching metaphors) if we can catch a glimpse of the pole star of true values, that light will guide us as we sail the treacherous waters of life. Then, no matter where our ship might be on life's ocean, that light will direct us toward the harbor of meaning, peace, and fulfillment and provide help for finding harmony with all those "others" we meet along the way.

Either our values arise from this transcendent place, or we live within Nietzsche's curse, in a world of pure power. There is no final proof as to which is true. Which will you choose?

Skeptico: Let's say I do choose to try to live from the deepest values. Where do I find out what they are?

Wisdom Seeker: The best place to look is to the lives and teachings of the wisest who have lived among us, those men and women who represent the epitome of fulfillment and meaning.

Skeptico: But which ones, for there are many? And you admit that their messages are not the same.

Wisdom Seeker: Look to those who inspire you, touch your heart; those who move you deep inside to join them in living toward things that seem to be of the greatest importance right now. Whatever comes up for you as most important, whether it be peace, love, freedom, service to others, wisdom, creativity, joy—or something else entirely. Trust yourself, realizing that this deep feeling will provide motivation for you to make the effort that will be required to live the values you have chosen. In the next chapter, I will try to share how this works for me.

CHAPTER 12

Wisdom from the Past

Over the course of my life, there have been a handful of people who, when they spoke, made me feel I was in the presence of wisdom beyond that of others—sometimes far beyond. What made the difference? What set them apart?

The conclusion that forces itself upon my mind is that they were in touch with a larger view than the rest of us, saw things from a perspective most of us rarely reach. Those who possess this ability have a firm grasp of the big picture, tend to avoid dogmatism, and accept things as they actually are, while conveying a vision of how they could be better. They often possess a number of additional traits: an honest understanding of themselves (both their failings and their strengths), the ability to inspire others to rise to their highest potential, sincere consideration of others, and frequent expressions of joy or compassion.

Through my life, if I had a decision to make, I would turn to these wise ones for guidance. Is it not true for you? It seems so for most members of the human tribe. There seem to have always been a few wise ones to whom we have turned for guidance about our lives and our values, and their words constitute a precious heritage (in a few cases constituting the foundations upon which our civilizations have been built). Few, if any, of these wise ones were perfect, but their wisdom and understanding provide the best guidance we have for living.

The Testimony of the Best and Brightest

Through history, there have been stories of those who seem to have found fulfillment, meaning, contentment; a sense of purpose, joy, and/or peace. Of those lucky few, books have been written, movies made, and many stories told. However, in most cases, their lives seem beyond our capacity to emulate. It feels like these "special" ones were born with a gift, had help we do not have, or followed a path that is too difficult to duplicate. For the vast majority of us, Søren Kierkegaard was probably right in saying that there are but two kinds of people: those who are suffering and know that they suffer and those who are suffering but do not know it. His conclusion about the two types is especially instructive: The ones who know they are in despair and are suffering are further along, for they can at least begin to do something about their difficulties.

This is where the wise ones come in, those who have been viewed as the exemplars of wisdom in human history; perhaps we can't fully emulate them, but we can profitably turn to them for guidance.

Skeptico: Is there any guidance they all share?

Wisdom Seeker: Yes: To live by some set of values is crucial for a fulfilled life.

Skeptico: Maybe, but I can think of many examples in which people followed someone's idea of "values" and came to a bad end or did terrible things.

Wisdom Seeker: Unfortunately, that is too true. Any value can be twisted, misused, or abused by greed and ambition, or it can be applied in the wrong way or at the wrong time. Someone said that one of the cruelest things a person can do is to say the truth with malice, or anger, or at the wrong time.

Skeptico: I'm glad you are finally seeing things more clearly.

Wisdom Seeker: But this does not suggest we can do without values. The second piece of advice the wise ones give is that we must use our own reason and intuition in choosing, understanding, and then applying the appropriate values in our lives.

Skeptico: That sounds good, but I don't have any idea where to begin. With so much disagreement about values, even among wisdom figures, to whom do I listen?

Wisdom Seeker: Another good point. Yet perhaps a lot of the disagreement has to do with the fact that people are different from each other and thus need different guidance when facing their unique problems. What's more, the times in which people live can be radically different, so the values needed to give direction or correct imbalances can vary from situation to situation. Your point is still valid, though. There are significant differences of opinion, even among the wisest figures, about which values are central. This is frustrating and makes it very hard to know what to do. Yet there is an equal or even greater danger on the other side of the ledger: The danger of ignoring or dismissing the wisdom of human history, and thereby failing to find values that will carry your life toward fulfillment.

Skeptico: So what should I do?

Wisdom Seeker: My best thought would be that, in spite of the disagreements that have raged through history, and in spite of the difficulty of knowing which ones to follow, you are more likely to find a full and fulfilled life for yourself if you honor some of the values passed down to us through history.

Skeptico: Such as?

Wisdom Seeker: Love, Justice, Friendship, Kindness, Gratitude, Courage, Responsibility, Temperance, Integrity, Discipline, Forgiveness, Compassion, Trust, Faith, Patience, Humility, Service, Peacefulness, Hope, Moderation, the pursuit of Wisdom, and Authenticity—to name several main candidates.

Skeptico: But I have heard some of these words used as justifications for great wrongs!

Wisdom Seeker: True again, but this does not mean values are unimportant, only that our minds are capable of twisting definitions to self-centered purposes, or even evil ends. The work, then, is to develop a sincere understanding within oneself as to the deeper meanings of the values that are important and then to apply the discipline and courage necessary to bring them into manifestation in one's own life.

Skeptico: My other problem is that all those words don't seem to fit into the same category; some are feelings, some emotions, some virtues, and some actions.

Wisdom Seeker: Good point. First there is the problem of language and definitions. All these words have many different meanings, in different languages, in different ages—and even for the same person at different times. Second, what is considered as a virtue by one person might be considered a goal or even a natural way of being by another. For myself, to try to separate them into boxes of categories is of little help, and besides, all the categories constantly overlap. As philosopher Dr. Martha Nussbaum put it, "Emotions at their core contain judgments of value—about fairness, rights, priority, reciprocity—the core ideas of moral or ethical living." Thus, for me, the only important thing is to find a few words that inspire me to live toward them, however I understand them right now.

Skeptico: OK, I am willing to give it a try, but your list is too long. I can't work on all of those at once!

Wisdom Seeker: Right again! That list is much too long to work with. No one can give attention to all at once. Yet this list is the core of the collective guidance we have been given. Perhaps all values eventually merge, but until you discover how they do so for yourself, my suggestion is that you find a few of them that resonate at a deep level within you and then work toward those with determination. Moving with discipline and integrity toward a chosen set is all that is asked, and this will bring you as close to fulfillment as your current possibility allows.

Heeding the Wisdom

Skeptico: Before I make my choices, is there any further guidance you can give?

Wisdom Seeker: Perhaps some of my favorite quotes will be of help to you:

Lao Tzu:
Do you have the patience to wait
till your mud settles and the water is clear?
Can you remain unmoving
till the right action arises by itself?[96]

I have always thought I had to make things happen; this belief is part of my heritage, and operating from it has been enormously valuable. Yet now it is also a hindrance, so more and more I try to pay attention to the Tao Te Ching and, as the years go by, have the patience to settle into clarity as often as I can.

※※※

Lao Tzu:
I have just three things to teach:
simplicity, patience, compassion.
These three are your greatest treasures.
Simple in actions and in thoughts,
you return to the source of being.
Patient with both friends and enemies, you accord with the way things are. Compassionate toward yourself, you reconcile all beings in the world.[97]

It is often much easier to be compassionate toward others than toward myself, but more and more I see that I cannot truly be compassionate toward others unless I am compassionate toward myself. Again, Lao Tzu was on to something.

※※※

Alice Walker:
In blocking off what hurts us, we think we are walling ourselves off from pain. But in the long run, the wall, which prevents growth, hurts us more than the pain, which, if we will only bear it, soon passes over us. Washes over us and is gone. Long will we remember pain, but the pain itself, as it was at the point of intensity that made us feel as if we must die of it, soon vanishes. Our memory of it becomes its only trace. Walls remain. They grow moss. They are difficult barriers to cross, to get to others, to get to closed down parts of ourselves.[98]

In hearing about Alice Walker's life, and reading these words in *The Temple Of My Familiar,* the sense is strong that she understands exactly what it means to confront pain, so her words capture a truth for me. It is only in becoming conscious of the dark currents in myself, currents I have hidden away because they bring pain, that I will ever be able to connect with others or with my own authentic self.

Hans Reichenbach:
If error is corrected whenever it is recognized, the path of error is the path of truth.

Like it or not, I have made many mistakes and will likely make many more. Perhaps, if I can see them aright, I can use those mistakes to grow and learn, can let them become the grist for the mill of my unfolding toward fulfillment.

Paul, in his letter to the Corinthians:
Though I speak with the tongues of men and of angels, and have not love, I am become as sounding brass, or a tinkling cymbal.

And though I have the gift of prophecy, and understand all mysteries, and all knowledge, and though I have all faith, so that I could remove mountains, and have not love, I am nothing. And though I bestow all my goods to feed the poor, and though I give my body to be burned, and have not love, it profiteth me nothing.[99]

Is Paul really saying that acquiring all knowledge, being able to do miracles, giving everything you have to the poor, and even sacrificing your life—that all these are meaningless without love? I think he is, and because these words have been taken as meaningful by so many of us throughout human history, I am doing my best to discover what love really is and how best to live it.

Søren Kierkegaard:
Where am I? Who am I? How did I come to be here? What is this thing called the world?…. How did I come into the world? Why was I not consulted?…. And if I am compelled to take part in it, where is the manager? I would like to see him.

Skeptico: Wait a minute! I was following you up to that point. But where on earth does that quote fit in?
Wisdom Seeker: Well, it seems to me that if the struggle is not leavened with humor, it will be too heavy to bear. I think Kierkegaard understood this fully, for even though his life was difficult, humor shines through in his writing.

D. H. Lawrence:
We are not free when we are doing just what we like…. We are only free when we are doing what the deepest self likes. And there is getting down to the deepest self! It takes some diving.

There are so many motivations within us. Which shall we follow? To try to follow them all is a fool's errand, doomed to failure. The trick of a fulfilled life must be, as Lawrence says, to find the motivations that will actually bring fulfillment. But that takes some "diving," some serious exploration of the sometimes-muddy waters of our own natures.

Abraham Maslow:
Without the transcendent and the transpersonal we get sick, violent and nihilistic or else hopeless and apathetic. We need something "bigger than we are" to be awed by and to commit ourselves to.[100]

Maslow was the father of the modern psychological movement that began to take a more penetrating look at the positive side of human nature and human possibility. In *Toward a Psychology of Being*, he points to something he found necessary for fulfillment—a connection to something "larger" than personal goals and desires. He is echoed by Theodore Roszak in *Where the Wasteland Ends:* "Until we find our way once more to the experience of transcendence, until we feel the life within us and the nature about us as sacred, there will seem to us no 'realistic' future other than more of the same."[101] (And the "same" he envisioned was not pretty.)

Barry Lopez:
No culture has yet solved the dilemma each has faced with the growth of a conscious mind: How to live a moral and compassionate existence when one is fully aware of the blood, the horror inherent in all life, when one finds darkness not only in one's own culture, but within oneself. If there is a stage at which an

individual life becomes truly adult, it must be when one…accepts responsibility for a life lived in the midst of such paradox. One must live in the middle of contradiction, because if all contradiction were eliminated at once—life would collapse. There are simply no answers to some of the great pressing questions. You continue to live them out, making your life a worthy expression of leaning into the light.[102]

These words in *Arctic Dreams* are deeply inspiring, for he captures the essence of what I can be certain of, in spite of all difficulties. I cannot force the results I wish for, cannot avoid pain and loss, and cannot control events. But this I can do: I can lean toward the light. As clearly as I can discern it, I can choose, in my thoughts and actions, to support what seems to be "the Good." I do not have to be perfect in this, but as life unfolds, I can make a commitment to lean toward the Light, whatever my conception of it might be.

T. S. Eliot:
And all shall be well and
All manner of thing shall be well
By the purification of the motive
In the ground of our beseeching.[103]

Inspired by the words of Julian of Norwich, Eliot conveys that all *can* be well in the end, no matter what has happened in one's life; even in spite of whatever difficulties now exist. Eliot lived in a very difficult time and went through many personal struggles, but in finding a place within from which to write these words, he must have found the possibility they suggest, at least for a moment. His words inspire me to feel that if I can purify my own motives and focus on the ground of my being, all can truly be well.

Making It Personal

The crucial thing is to find the stories and images that touch you and then unearth the values at work within them so you can more consciously and consistently make them your own. This will require commitment and effort, as well as a goodly portion of time and energy, but the starting point is simple: Select the values that seem important for you—right here, right now—and begin. They can change (almost certainly will change) over time. (Both the values chosen, as well as your understanding of them, will change; in fact, if your understanding of them does not change, you are almost certainly not growing.)

In my journey, growing up in a small town, neither poetry, philosophy, nor metaphysical thought was high on the list of subjects discussed in school or at the dinner table—at least not the way these topics exploded into my awareness during my early years of college. When these radiant, radical *ideas* first burst in, I was intrigued, enthralled. A few professors were actually talking about things I had begun to grapple with inside myself. Their words, and the readings they assigned, provided a way to begin the journey in earnest.

For several years, I read and studied, but upon leaving college and jumping headfirst into the "real world" of politics and business, I discovered that what had seemed important in the classroom had little had to do with living in the modern world. (Or so it seemed at the time.)

Occasionally, however, I would recall things I had read, especially by those who had themselves been deeply engaged in life, those who had actively grappled with social issues, politics, and power—and reflected on what they had learned. I began to read such writers again, and to reflect.

In time, I began to connect a set of dots, realizing that some of the discussions around the dinner table and at family gatherings *were, indeed, related* to what I was reading and experiencing now. Gradually these three streams began to merge: ideas from college days, pieces of wisdom from my childhood, and the reflections of thinkers through the ages who seemed to be speaking about what was truly important and how one should live.

Thus for me, thinking about and feeling my way into questions about how best to live seems like entering an ancient stream, a dialogue that has been going on for several thousand years. In this unending conversation about life and living, I am joining all those who have gone before, all those who have grappled with the question of what it means to be a human being. Many now feel like friends and confidants in the conversation about life.

Toward which I Aim

In ancient Greece, the name given to those who wrestled with life's ultimate questions was *Philosopher* (*Philos*: Loving; *Sophia*: Wisdom; *Philosophy*: Loving Wisdom).

To love wisdom is to enter the ultimate conversation to which we are each continually invited. It has many entryways: theology, metaphysics, religion, epistemology—many others as well: art, science, psychology—the list is very long. Whatever name you wish to use, it is the quest for wisdom, for meaning, for truth—the human search to answer the fundamental questions: What am I doing here on this earth? How did the world come to be? Does it, do I, have a purpose? Is there a right and a wrong way to live? Who decides? What is the good life? And crucially, what will I do with the rest of my life, with the remaining minutes of my days?

For me, to engage in this conversation is to be a philosopher. And what better way to engage in philosophy than through poetry, as did many of the wisest ones of old. So here is poem for you, to summarize the many themes of this book. (Emphasizing that this is not who I am but where I choose to aim.)

Being a philosopher is to immerse oneself in the wisdom of others—
all those who have gone before to show the way.
It is to realize that what is to be discovered is not new

but forever present, waiting to shine forth from each life
that will recognize the pattern
and then undertake the difficult work of incorporating what is learned
into the moment-by-moment living of daily life.

Being a philosopher is to focus on the whole—not just the parts.
It is the attempt to live a whole, complete, integrated life—
with an inner harmony twixt and between all the different facets of
    oneself.
It is to find the harmony within the chaos of human relationships,
of the human community.
It is to live in harmony with the earth, with nature, with others,
with life itself.

Being a philosopher is to discover, in the words of T. S. Eliot,[v]
that "all shall be well, and all manner of thing shall be well,
By the purification of the motive, in the ground of our beseeching,"[104]
    which is to say
that you become so clear about who you are, your deepest motives,
    what is truly important,
that when you move, or speak, or act,
all of you says and does and means the same thing.
All the different parts of yourself are integrated, unified, clear,
and what you believe, what you say, and what you do, are one.

Being a philosopher is to learn to surrender,
so that the harmony of life can move through your very being.
For, somewhere inside, I sense that there is a harmony with which
we can learn to blend our song,
a current so deep that it becomes the flow of life itself
and in which we can, finally, learn to "live, and move, and have our
    being."[105]

---

[v] Eliot took the first line here, and his inspiration for the thought, from Julian of Norwich.

So, as the many instruments of an orchestra
gradually align themselves into one great symphony,
the multitudinous instruments of our lives
begin to align themselves with each other,
and then, finally, with the symphony of life itself.

Perhaps it's important to notice that
Being a philosopher begins with **being**
    which is to be fully present in each moment;
    to live this moment fully, completely, unconditionally;
    not to live in the jumbled soup of past memories
    or the fevered imaginings of a future carnival ride,
    but to be here, now, fully alive and awake to this moment;
    now, here,
    with all one's attention, energy, vitality, and meaning focused
    now.

Being is to be who you are
    with acceptance,
    with humility,
    with pride;
To claim in your soul
the happy and the sad,
the good and the bad.
To claim the weakness and strength,
the victories and defeats,
and to say: YES!
YES, that is me. YES.
Being is the direction in which you are leaning,
in which you are moving.
It is the goal toward which you aim.
It is the sighting of your intention
toward a vision which is greater
than your heart or your mind can contain.

Being is to find Inner Peace—
not wrestling with the past,
nor calculating the future,
but to rest in a serenity of spirit,
which (in the words of Karl Durkheim)
"comes from sensing a meaning
that embraces unmeaning."
It is to live so that you can
suffer "the slings and arrows of outrageous fortune,"[106]
while somewhere inside, the suffering is transfigured
and you come to rest in that place
"where you do not suffer."
You live, "knowing you are safe,
no matter what the world sends your way."[107]

Being is to somehow unite all the paradoxes of life within yourself
    in some incomprehensible way,
a way not understood, but simply lived each moment.
It is to take in all the conflicting, discordant, competing streams of
    your life,
        of life itself,
and resolve them anew in each moment—
lightly, naturally, simply, spontaneously.
A fulfilled life is to follow the wisdom of Max Ehrmann
and "Take kindly the counsel of the years,
Gracefully surrendering the things of youth."
Affirming that "you have a right to be here,"
And learning to "be at peace with God, whatever you conceive God
    to be."[108]

Being a philosopher is, in Shakespeare's words,
    "to take upon us the mystery of things,
        as if we were God's spys."[109]
Then, as Helen Luke reminds,

"the most trivial of happenings is touched by wonder,
and there may come, by grace,
a moment of unclouded vision."[110]

A fulfilled life means to become transparent to the transcendent—
It is to gradually remove the veil that hides
the love, the truth, the wisdom, and the joy
that reside at the heart of things.
It is to make oneself a vessel through which these jewels can shine;
to provide a pathway through which love, truth, wisdom, and joy
can manifest themselves in the human dimension.
Love: that spontaneous energy that radiates out to the other,
or to others; or to Nature, Life, or the Divine:
> with no thought of oneself,
> with no thought of result or reward.

That blissful moment of resting outside the anxieties and cares of the world—
> free of fear, free of desire, free of longing, free of hope,
> free of time, free of oneself.

Truth: the recognition of all that is:
> seeing and absorbing every fact about yourself, about others,
> about the world.

It is the rock upon which is built all true communication—
> and it is more—

it is to find that way of expression of *what is*
> that finally serves
> > to lift up, to enlighten, to inspire—
> > not only others, but also yourself.

Wisdom: to see the harmony that lies behind the chaos—
> to sense the current which flows under, around, and through
> > all of life,

>   "to apprehend the point of intersection of the timeless with time."[111]
>   Wisdom is: "Life become conscious of itself."[112]

And **Joy**: that spontaneous laughter that bursts from the depths,
>   pushing aside all the trials and tribulations of life—
>   gloriously affirming that "whether or not it is clear to you,
>   the universe is unfolding as it should."[113]
>   It is being bathed and immersed in the fullness of life,
>   swimming freely for an instant in the energy of the universe itself.

To Be Is To Serve:
Yet to know that there can be no final help for another
>   till one has healed oneself.

It is to follow the ages-old admonition, ***"Know Thyself,"***
>   so completely—

That one's private ill cannot become righteousness
>   directed toward others,
>   or the world.

It is to Know Oneself so carefully that ambition
>   cannot be disguised as virtue.

It is to Know Oneself so fully that you do not serve
from your need to serve, nor to escape your pain.
You do not serve for recognition, or for credit, or for gain.
You simply kneel to help those
>   who cross your pathway,

for they are there, and you came this way.
And do not serve just those who seem needy,
lest to judge their need
be your unseen need to feel greater than they.
Simply serve those encountered along your pathway—
>   give yourself to each "other" you meet.

Give—that person there, right beside you—

your time, your attention, your care.
Give to each all the love and compassion
you once thought to be your share.
Give with a generosity of spirit,
all the wisdom and truth you can find,
and watch how your store is not depleted
    but mounts ever nearer the sublime.

In the end, you serve with no thought of service;
Every act and every pause—simply in tune.
Yet, if this harmony is lived deep within you,
as you walk past, barren trees spring to bloom.
For if you live from the deep ground of being,
your life flows outward as unintended service.
And the spontaneous act of your living
is a new expression of the oldest truth on earth.
And then, the *example* of your life is the ultimate service
in a world full of hunger for some glimpse of this truth.

Finally, in Thoreau's words,
    "All that a man has to say or to do
    that can possibly concern mankind,
    is in some shape or other
    to tell the story of his love, to sing."[114]
Which I take to mean that somehow your song
can embrace all the pain and suffering,
the defeat and loss,
the horror, the evil, the despair;
take it in, and somehow remingle all those discordant currents—
    never denying—
    but accepting, transforming, transcending;
till the song of love re-emerges from deep within
in the unique tenor of your own voice,
re-emerges as an inspiration and a hope.

And your song, new, yet old as life itself,
inspires each and all to sing their song,
to transform and transcend themselves, so that they might
lend their voice to the glorious harmony, which is life itself.

This is my intention, my vision of what I seek.
Yet I am so very far from living, from **being** these things,
I am filled with humility.
Yet to have such an image, an intention, is the beginning.

※※※

Skeptico: I feel some of these things but don't know how to go about living them. How do I do that?
Wisdom Seeker: Turn to the Epilogue, and I will say what I can.

EPILOGUE

Skeptico: I have waited long enough. How do I make decisions on the important issues of life? How do I decide how to live?
Wisdom Seeker: All right. Let me summarize my sense of how you got here and what you can do.

1. One morning you woke up, and here you were—you were aware of being alive. It seemed natural enough when it happened, but it is actually an amazing thing when you think about it. Where did you come from, and how did you come to be aware that you exist? Both are great mysteries. However, by the time you became aware of your existence, your urges, desires, whims, feelings, needs, and emotions were also there, continually rising up, mostly without any conscious intent on your part.
2. As you gradually developed awareness, adults were around (who can seem like giants when you are small) responding to your impulses and feelings (sometimes well, sometimes poorly). They took care of your needs (some of them, anyway), and they told you what to do and what not to do (sometimes gently, sometimes harshly). They told you stories about who you were and what you were doing here. They guided you toward behaviors they considered acceptable and away from those they considered not.
3. Gradually, as you grew, you became aware that you had the power to make decisions, that at any moment you could do one thing and not another. Pretty soon you felt as if you were making lots of decisions, although you were mostly following the instructions you had been given. By this time, you had molded the raw material of your urges and feelings into a pattern for living, using the messages and stories of your youth for guidance.

4. Then a radical thing happened: You began to notice that many of those messages conflicted with each other and that many others did not fit with what you actually wanted. Paying close attention, you found that the people conveying the messages didn't always live by them, either. It got pretty confusing (for some of us, it got very confusing). You also noticed that many people were living by frameworks different from yours, and some of them were doing quite well; some even seemed to be doing better than you, so you started questioning your worldview. Dramatic moment: The thrill of realizing freedom and the anxiety of recognizing that you now must make decisions in a more conscious way.

Skeptico: That is a big part of my question. How do I make decisions if I have abandoned the framework and rules of my youth?
Wisdom Seeker: You can't abandon the old framework entirely, but you can see it for what it is and begin to work with it more consciously. If you have also realized that following whims and feelings one after another does not work very well, you are ready for the next step.

5. You are ready to fully engage the marvelous gift of human reason, the ability to step back from your urges and desires, as well as from cultural training, and consider for yourself how to act and how to live. When you become free from the rush of whims and feelings for a moment, and from your enculturation, you discover you can take into account numerous facts, ideas, feelings, rules, and motivations, and think about what seems right *to you*. You can consider for yourself the best way to pursue the motivations that seem important.
6. Hopefully, you will simultaneously have discovered intuition, for only intuition can provide a feel for the broader picture in which you are living; only intuition can help you see how the various currents relate to each other; and in its highest reaches, only intuition can provide a sense of "knowing," a clarity and confidence about the world, others, and yourself. Here is the place where reason and intuition come together in a harmonious way, and here

you have the possibility of a deep "felt sense" of what is important, worthwhile, and right for you and your life.

7. As this "felt sense" develops, another current will come into play: values. Of course you can simply follow the values you were given. But if you begin to see the arbitrary nature of, and even the distortions in, some of those values, you have a crucial question to answer: Are values simply societal rules created for the good of the collective that you can break with impunity if you can get away with it, or are some values necessary for a fulfilled life, maybe even an essential tool for finding and living such a life? In other words, are some values embedded within the overall pattern in which you exist, and thus only by living in harmony with those values will you find fulfillment, meaning, or happiness?

Skeptico: You sure are taking a long time to get to how to make decisions.
Wisdom Seeker: I know. I apologize, but unless you develop and hold a clear sense of how decisions arise, you will never be able to make good choices. Now, however, we are ready.

8. Moving through the preceding steps, you will gradually come to the realization that you have a certain amount of freedom: freedom to choose, freedom to participate consciously in the important decisions of your life. Urges, desires, feelings, and emotions will continue to stream forth (from who knows where), influencing everything you do, but there will now be a space in which you can weigh everything that is arising and decide which currents to follow. You will be able to consciously consider the intentions you will set, as well as the appropriate methods to fulfill them.

9. Recognizing and savoring this freedom, focus on the people who seem to you to have had worthwhile and meaningful lives; study how they lived and the wisdom they passed along, and then engage your reason and intuition in considering how their words and examples for living apply to you and your life.

10. As hints and guesses emerge, invite that incredible human ability, imagination, to do its work. Fueled by your urges and feelings and recognizing the boundaries provided by the cultural teachings you accept and the values you choose to live by, invite your imagination to offer up images of how your life can most meaningfully move forward. Work with it to create images of the things you might do, the projects that seem worthwhile, the ways in which you can relate to others fruitfully.
11. Consider those images carefully, and then commit to a plan of action. Set a clear intention, engage your will toward the path that you have chosen, and practice over and over, returning your attention to the things that facilitate movement along the chosen path. (Considering too long and committing too quickly are both dangers, but finding the right balance is learned only through practice—and mistakes.)
12. Therefore, accept that you will make mistakes. Adjust as best you can and proceed—again, and again, and again. As T. S. Eliot said, we are "undefeated" as long as we "go on trying." This does not mean continuing on a path that intuition and reason suggest is in need of correction. Occasionally take stock of where you are, the progress you have made, and regroup, reimagine, and refocus. Then, once again proceed with as much courage and determination as you can muster. This is the path to fulfillment.

Skeptico: After thinking about these things all this time, what have you chosen as the intentions toward which you will live?
Wisdom Seeker: This is what I choose:
    Attempt to align with the greatest Harmony;
    Seek Wisdom and follow it the best I can;
    Try to do what is Good;
    Discover and live fully what feels like mine to do in this life, my work, my *telos*;
    Find, live, and share the highest form of Love I can discover;
    In the openings, in the gaps where there is the slightest possibility, choose Joy.

ACKNOWLEDGMENTS

I want to express my deep gratitude to Ralph Gonzalez, Ronda Redden Reitz, and Sandra Sundari Smith for their long-running encouragement and invaluable help in creating this book.

I am also indebted to Phillip Moffitt, Sue Painter, Birney Hand, and Bob Adams for valuable suggestions and feedback during the process of creation.

My heartfelt thanks to all.

SUGGESTED READINGS

Bucke, Richard Maurice, MD. *Cosmic Consciousness*. New York: E. P. Dutton, 1969.

Campbell, Joseph. *Creative Mythology*. London: Penguin, 1968.

—. *The Hero with a Thousand Faces*. New York: First Princeton/Bollingen Paperback Press, 1972.

—. *The Inner Reaches of Outer Space: Metaphor as Myth and as Religion*. New York: Alfred Van Der Mark Editions, 1986.

Coffey, Maria. *Explorers of the Infinite*. New York: Tarcher/Penguin, 2008.

Coxhead, Nona. *The Relevance of Bliss*. New York: St. Martin's Press, 1985.

Deikman, Arthur J., MD. *The Observing Self*. Boston: Beacon Press, 1982.

Jahn, Robert G. and Brenda J. Dunne. *Margins of Reality: The Role of Consciousness in the Physical World*. Orlando, Florida: Harcourt Brace Jovanovich Publishers, 1987.

Durkheim, Karlfried Graf. *Zen and Us*. New York: E. P. Dutton, 1961.

Eliot, T. S. *Four Quartets*. New York: Harcourt, Brace and Worls/Harvest, 1971.

Emerson, Ralph Waldo. *The Spiritual Emerson: Essential Writings by Ralph Waldo Emerson*. Edited by David M. Robinson. Boston: Beacon Press, 2004.

Frankl, Viktor E. *Man's Search for Meaning: An Introduction to Logotherapy*. 3rd ed. New York: Touchstone/Simon & Schuster, 1984.

Harman, Willis, and Howard Rheingold. *Higher Creativity*. New York: Tarcher/Penguin, 1984.

Huxley, Aldous. *The Perennial Philosophy.* New York: Harper and Row Publishers, 1945.

James, William. *The Varieties of Religious Experience.* New York: Penguin, 1985.

Jung, C. G., Aniela Jaffe, Richard Winston, and Clara Winston. *Memories, Dreams, Reflections.* NY: Vintage, division of Random House, 1965.

—. *Psychology and Religion: West ad East.* Vol. 11. In *The Collected Works of C. G. Jung.* New Jersy: Princeton University Press, 1975.

Kohlberg, Lawrence. *The Philosophy of Moral Development: Moral Stages and the Idea of Justice, Essays on Moral Development.* Vols. 1–2. New York: Harper and Row, 1981.

Laszlo, Ervin. *Science and the Akashic Field.* Rochester, Vermont: Inner Traditions, 2007.

Lebeaux, Richard. *Thoreau's Seasons.* Vol. 8. Amherst : University of Massachusetts Press, 1984.

Lincoln, Abraham. *Meditation on the Divine Will.* Vol. 5. In *Collected Works of Abraham Lincoln.* Edited by Roy P. Basier. Newark: Rutgers University Press, 1953.

Loye, David. *Darwin on Love.* Boston: Benjamin Franklin Press, 2007.

Luke, Helen M. *Dark Wood to White Rose.* New York: Parabola Books, 1989.

—. *Old Age, Journey into Simplicity.* New York: Parabola, 1987.

Nietzsche, Friedrich Wilhelm. *Ecce Homo.* Translated by R. J. Hollingdale. NY and London: Penguin, 1979.

—. *The Gay Science.* New York: Vintage Books, 1974.

—. *Will To Power.* New York: Vintage, 1968.

Pearce, Joseph Chilton. *The Crack in the Cosmic Egg.* New York: The Julian Press, 1988.

Radin, Dean, PhD. *The Conscious Universe.* New York: HarperCollins Publishers, 1997.

Schumacher, E. F. *A Guide for the Perplexed.* New York: Harper and Row Publishers, 1977.

Sheldrake, Rupert. *A New Science of Life: The Hypothesis of Morphic Resonance.* Rochester, Vermont: Park Street Press, 1981.

Smith, Huston. *The World's Religions.* New York: HarperCollins, 1985.

—. *Why Religion Matters: The Fate of the Human Spirit in an Age of Disbelief.* New York: HarperCollins Publishers, 2001.

Thoreau, Henry David. *Walden.* New York: North American Library, 1962.

Underhill, Evelyn. *Mysticism.* Oxford, London: Oneworld Publications, 1999.

Whitehead, Alfred North. *Science and the Modern World: Lowell Lectures 1925.* New York: The Free Press, 1967.

Wilbur, Ken. *A Brief History of Everything.* Boston and London: Shambhala, 1996.

—. *Sex, Ecology, and Spirituality: The Spirit of Evolution.* Boston, Mass.: Shambhala, 1995.

—. *The Atman Project.* Wheaton, Illinois: The Theosphical Publishing House, 1980.

Wittgenstein, Ludwig. *Tractatus Logico-Philosophicus.* Translated by C. K. Ogden. London: Oxford University Press, 1921.

Wolff, Robert. *Original Wisdom: Stories of an Ancient Way of Knowing.* Rochester, New York: Inner Traditions, 2001.

ENDNOTES

Introduction

[1] Erwin Schrödinger, *What Is Life?* (Cambridge, United Kingdom: Cambridge University Press, 1944), Epilogue.

[2] William James, *A Pluralistic Universe*, Lecture VII: The Continuity of Experience (Nebraska, University of Nebraska Press, 1996), 288.

Chapter 1: It Starts with Questions

[3] T. S. Eliot, *Four Quartets* (New York: Harcourt, Brace & World/Harvest, 1971), 31.

Chapter 3: 10,000 Decisions Create a Life

[4] T. S. Eliot, *Poem: The Love Song of J. Alfred Prufrock* (New York: Mariner Books, 1967).

[5] Ken Wilbur, *Sex, Ecology, Spirituality* (Boston: Shambhala, 1995), 78.

[6] The first part of this quote is from a letter: Albert Einstein, "Letter of February 12, 1950, to Robert S. Marcus." The last two sentences are not in that letter but are very widely attributed to him, such as here: http://www.simpletoremember.com/articles/a/einstein/ (accessed November 9, 2012), number 15.

[7] T. S. Eliot, *Four Quartets* (New York: Harcourt, Brace & World/Harvest, 1971), 31.

Chapter 4: Whim

[8] A. H. Chapman and M. Chapman-Santana, "The Influence of Nietzsche on Freud's Ideas," *The British Journal of Psychiatry* 166 (1995), 251–253.

[9] Ernest Jones, *The Life and Work of Sigmund Freud, II*, (New York: Basic Books, 1955), 344.

[10]Solomon, Song of Songs, Verses 1:2, 13; 3:1, 4; 7:6,10 (King James version of the Bible).
[11]Joseph Campbell, *Creative Mythology* (London: Penguin, 1968), 246.
[12]Coleman Barks, *The Essential Rumi* (New York: HarperCollins, 2004), 54.
[13]Barks, *The Essential Rumi*, 54.
[14]Bede Griffiths's quote was copied long ago, and the book is not referenced.
[15]Barks, *The Essential Rumi* (New York: HarperCollins, 1995), 10.
[16]Karlfried Graf Durckheim, *Zen and Us* (London: Penguin, 1991), 71.
[17]Durckheim, *Zen and Us*, 71.
[18]Ibid.

Chapter 5: Cultures and Community

[19]I am indebted to Howard Bloom for reinforcing and further clarifying my own thoughts and ideas about this topic in his article, "The Ghosts of Millions in the Lonely Mind," *What Is Enlightenment*, August–October 2008.
[20]Proverbs 22:6. (King James version of the Bible).
[21]Naomi Eisenberger and Matt Lieberman, "Why It Hurts to Be Left Out: The Neurocognitive Overlap between Physical and Social Pain," in *The Social Outcast: Ostracism, Social Exclusion, Rejection and Bullying*, eds. Kipling D. Williams, Joseph P. Forgas, and William Von Hippel, (Massachusetts: Cambridge University Press, 2005), 109–130.
[22]David Brooks, "Demography Is King," *The New York Times*, April 29, 2008, sec. Opinion.

Chapter 6: Are You Rational?

[23]William Shakespeare, *First Folio Edition of Shakespeare: The Norton Facsimile*, ed. Charlton Hinman Hamlet, "Prince of Denmark, Act II, Scene 2" (New York: W. W. Norton & Co, 1996).
[24]Francois-Marie Arouet, AKA Voltaire, *A Philosophical Dictionary*, 2, sec. 1, (London: W. Dugdale, 1843), 473.
[25]Ludwig Wittgenstein, *Tractatus Logico-Philosophicus*, trans. C. K. Ogden, (Germany: Wittgenstein, 1921).
[26]James Burke, *The Day the Universe Changed* (New York: Little, Brown and Company, 1986), 334–336.

[27] Richard Cytowic, *The Man Who Tasted Shapes* (New York: Tarcher/Putnam, 1993), 161.
[28] Christian de Quincy, "Radical Nature: Rediscovering the Soul of Matter," *Noetic Sciences Review*, Spring 1994, 42.
[29] Dean Shibata, "Personal Decisions Exercise the Emotional Part of the Brain," lecture for The Radiological Society of North America 87th Scientific Assembly and Annual Meeting, November 26, 2001, Chicago.
[30] William James, *Varieties of Religious Experience* (New York: Penguin, 1985), 388.

Chapter 7: The Place of Intuition

[31] Henry David Thoreau, *Walden* (New York: North American Library, 1962), 147.
[32] Jean Jacques Rousseau, *Oeuvres Completes* vol. V (Paris: Poincot, 1873), 103.
[33] John Stuart Mill, *A System of Logic, Ratiocinative and Inductive* (South Carolina: Forgotten Books, 2012), 3.
[34] Willis Harmon and Howard Rheingold, *Higher Creativity* (New York: Tarcher/Penguin, 1984).
[35] William I. B. Benneridge, *The Art of Scientific Investigation* (New York: Vintage, 1957).
[36] Pitirim A. Sorokin, *The Crisis of Our Age* (New York: Dutton, 1943).
[37] Megan Rauscher, "Big Decision Time? Best to Sleep on It," *Science*, February 17, 2006.
[38] Dr. Ap Dijksterhuis, Think Different: The Merits of Unconscious Thought in Preference Development and Decision Making. *Journal of Personality and Social Psychology*, 87, 586–598.
[39] Ralph Waldo Emerson, *"Divinity School Address,"* Divinity College, Cambridge, July 15, 1838.
[40] Drew Westen, *The Political Brain* (New York: PublicAffairs, 2008).
[41] Sir Francis Bacon, *The New Organon* XLVI (Cambridge, UK: Cambridge University Press, 2000).
[42] First Epistle of John, 4:1 (King James version of the *Bible*).
[43] Rebecca Goldstein, *Incompleteness: The Proof and Paradox of Kurt Gödel* (New York: W. W. Norton & Co, 2005).
[44] Friedrich Nietzsche, *Ecce Homo*, trans. R. J. Hollingdale (New York and London: Penguin, 1979), 72–73.

Chapter 8: What Is Reality?

[45] Jane Wagner, *The Search for Signs of Intelligent Life in the Universe* (New York: Penguin, 1991).

[46] Colin Blakemore and Grahame F. Cooper, "Development of the Brain Depends on the Visual Environment," *Nature*, 228, (31 October 1970), 477 quoting H. V. B. Hirsch and D. N. Spinelli, *Science*, 168, (1970), 869.

[47] Charles Tart, *Waking Up* (Cambridge, Mass: Shambhala, 1987), 76.

[48] Tart, *Waking Up*, 77.

[49] A. S. Eddington, *Science and the Unseen World* (New York: Macmillan, 1937), 34.

[50] William Tiller's quote was copied many years ago into my collection of quotations, and I do not remember the source. However, this idea fits within the overall frame of understanding he has presented.

[51] Ivo Kohler, "The Formation and Transformation of the Perceptual World," *Psychological Issues* (Madison, Conn: International Universities Press, 1964), 174.

[52] Werner Heisenberg, *Across the Frontiers* (New York: Harper, 1974).

[53] Werner Heisenberg, *Physics and Philosophy* (New York: Harper, 1971).

[54] *Spirituality and Health*, January-February 2011, 14

[55] This quote is widely attributed to the Talmud, but I have never seen a specific reference. It seems to have first been attributed to the Talmud in a 1961 Anaïs Nin novel, *The Seduction of the Minotaur*, which reads, "Lillian was reminded of the Talmudic words: 'We do not see things as they are, we see them as we are.'" I do not know if the idea originated in or was inspired by the Talmud, but the belief is widespread, so I follow that assumption here.

[56] Niels Bohr, *His Life and Work*, ed. S. Rozenthal (Amsterdam: North-Holland Publishing Company, 1967), 328.

[57] Leonard Feinberg, PhD, "Firewalking in Ceylon," *Atlantic Monthly* 203, no 5, (May 1959), 73–76.

[58] Gilbert Grosvenor, "Ceylon," *National Geographic* 129, no. 4 (Apr 1966), 479–486.

[59] Herbert Benson, *Timeless Healing* (New York: Scribner, 1996), 163.

Chapter 9: Worldviews—Path or Prison?

[60]Thank you, Lou Thacker.

[61]Leo Tolstoy, *The Death of Ivan Ilyich* (New York: Bantam, 1981).

[62]John Tierney, "Go Ahead, Rationalize. Monkeys Do It Too," *The New York Times*, sec. Science, November 6, 2007.

[63]David Richio, *The Five Things We Cannot Change: And the Happiness We Find by Embracing Them* (Cambridge: Shambhala, 2005), 140.

[64]Abraham Lincoln, "Meditation on the Divine Will," *Collected Works of Abraham Lincoln*, vol. 5, ed. Roy P. Basier (Newark, NJ: Rutgers University Press, 1953), 403–404.

[65]Ibn-Al-Arabi, *Ibn-Al-Arabi: The Bezels of Wisdom* (New Jersey: Paulist Press, 1980).

Chapter 10: Imagination, Intention, Attention

[66]P. E. Vernon, *Creativity: Selected Readings* (New York: Penguin Books, 1970). This quote is taken from a letter by Mozart to publisher Friedrich Rochlitz, which was published in the *Allgemeine Musikalische Zeitung*, vol. 17 (New York: Konrad, 1815), 561–566. Some researchers now consider the letter inauthentic, but Mozart's first biographer, in collaboration with Mozart's wife, also gave an account of how Mozart composed that has a similar flavor. See Franz Niemtschek, *Leben des K. K. Kapellmeisters Wolfgang Gottlieb Mozart, nach Originalquellen beschrieben, (Prague, In Der Herrlischen Buchhandlung, 1798)* 54–55.

[67]Karl Popper, "The Rationality of Scientific Revolution." In Harré, R. (ed.), *Problems of Scientific Revolution: Progress and Obstacles to Progress in the Sciences* (Oxford: Clarendon Press, 1975).

[68]George Sylvester Viereck, "What Life Means to Einstein," *Saturday Evening Post*, October 26, 1929.

[69]Donald W. Winnicott, *Winnicott on the Child* (Cambridge, Mass: Da Capo Press, 2002).

[70]Rollo May, *Love and Will* (New York: W. W. Norton & Co., 2007), 43.

[71]William Shakespeare, *Julius Caesar* (Mineola, New York: Dover Publications, 1991), Act II, Scene 2.

[72] See Bernard Freydberg for a good discussion of this aspect of Kant: *Imagination in Kant's Critique of Practical Reason (Studies of Continental Thought)*. (Bloomington: Indiana University Press, 2005).
[73] Friedrich Nietzsche, *The Gay Science* (New York: Vintage Books, 1974), 181.
[74] William Wordsworth and Jonathon Wordsworth, The *Prelude: A Parallel Text* (New York: Penguin Classics, 1996).
[75] Ralph Waldo Emerson and Edward Waldo Emerson, *The Complete Works of Ralph Waldo Emerson*, Nature: Idealism (New York: Wm. H. Wise and Company, 1923), Chapter VI.
[76] William Shakespeare, *Midsummer Night's Dream* (Arden Shakespeare; 2nd revised edition, September 6, 1979), Act V, Scene 1.
[77] Although this quote is often attributed to Goethe, it comes from a book by Dr. Haim G. Ginott, *Teacher and Child: A Book for Parents and Teachers* (New York: Avon Books, 1972), 15–16.
[78] William Murray, *The Scottish Himalayan Expedition* (London: J. M. Dent Publishers, 1951).
[79] George Bernard Shaw, *Man and Superman* (New York: Quill Penguin Classics, 2008), Epistle Dedicatory.
[80] Roberto Assagioli, *The Act of Will* (Amherst, Mass.: The Synthesis Center, Inc., 2010).
[81] From Roberto Assagioli's notes of his time in prison, which he titled "*Freedom in Jail.*" The notes are housed at the Institute of Psychosynthesis, Assagioli Archives, Florence, Italy.
[82] Assagioli, "*Freedom in Jail.*"
[83] Henry David Thoreau, *Walden* (New York: A Signet Classic from New American Library, 1960), 94.
[84] Thoreau, *Walden*, 70.

Chapter 11: Whose Values—Yours, Mine, or Ours?

[85] Friedrich Nietzsche, *Will to Power* (New York: Vintage, 1968).
[86] Carl G. Jung, *Psychology and Religion: West and East, The Collected Works of C. G. Jung*, Vol. 11, (New Jersey: Princeton University Press, 1975), 131.
[87] Studs Terkel, *Hope Dies Last: Keeping the Faith in Troubled Times* (New York: The New Press, 2004), 84.

[88] Aldous Leonard Huxley, *Quotes.net*. STANDS4 LLC, 2012 http://www.quotes.net/quote/5885 (accessed November 17, 2012).

[89] Charles Reade, http://en.wikiquote.org/wiki/Charles_Reade (accessed November 17, 2012).

[90] David Loye, *Darwin on Love* (Boston: Benjamin Franklin Press, 2007).

[91] Joseph Campbell, *The Inner Reaches of Outer Space: Metaphor as Myth and as Religion* (Novato, California: New World Library, 2002), 81.

[92] Lawrence Kohlberg, *The Philosophy of Moral Development: Moral Stages and the Idea of Justice, Essays on Moral Development*, Vols. 1–2 (New York: Harper and Row, 1981).

[93] Lawrence A. Blum, "Gilligan and Kohlberg: Implications for Moral Theory," *Ethics* 98, no. 3 (April 1988), 472–491.

[94] Kohlberg, *The Philosophy of Moral Development*.

[95] Confucius, *Confucian Analects, The Chinese Classics: Translated into English with Preliminary Essays and Explanatory Notes, The Life and Teachings of Confucius* XI, ed. James Legge. (London: N. Trübner, 1869), 21.

Chapter 12: Wisdom from the Past

[96] Stephen Mitchell, *Tao Te Ching* (New York: Harper Perennial, 1988), verse 15.

[97] Mitchell, verse 67.

[98] Alice Walker, *The Temple of My Familiar* (New York: Harcourt Brace Jonovich, 1989).

[99] 1 Corinthians, 13:1 (King James version of the Bible).

[100] Abraham Maslow, *Toward a Psychology of Being* (Princeton, New Jersey: D. Van Nostrand Company, 1968), iv.

[101] Theodore Roszak, *Where the Wasteland Ends* (New York: Bantam Doubleday Dell, 1973).

[102] Barry Lopez, *Arctic Dreams* (New York: Charles Scribner Sons, 1986).

[103] T. S. Eliot, *Four Quartets* (New York: Harcourt, Brace & World/Harvest, 1971).

[104] Eliot, *Four Quartets*.

[105] Acts 17:28 (King James version of the Bible).

[106] William Shakespeare, *Hamlet*, Act 3, Scene I.

[107] Karlfried Graf Durkheim, *Zen and Us* (New York: Penguin Books, 1991).

[108] Max Ehrmann, *The Desiderata of Happiness: A Collection of Philosophical Poems* (New York: Crown, 1995).

[109] William Shakespeare, *Shakespeare's Works* 15 (New York: Harper and Brothers, 1884), 34.

[110] Helen Luke, "Old Age," *Parabola*, 197, 30.

[111] Eliot, *Four Quartets*.

[112] Richard Wagner, *Richard Wagner's Prose Works Vol. 8, Posthumous, et*: (Whitefish, Montana, Kessinger Publishing, 2010), 354.

[113] Max Ehrmann, *The Desiderata of Happiness: A Collection of Philosophical Poems* (New York: Crown, 1995).

[114] Richard Lebeaux, *Thoreau's Seasons* (Amherst: University of Massachusetts Press, 1984), 234.

www.ingramcontent.com/pod-product-compliance
Lightning Source LLC
Chambersburg PA
CBHW051750040426
42446CB00007B/296